HEINRICH HEINE AND THE OCCIDENT

Heinrich Heine

AND THE OCCIDENT

MULTIPLE IDENTITIES,

MULTIPLE RECEPTIONS

Edited by
Peter Uwe Hohendahl
and Sander L. Gilman

UNIVERSITY OF NEBRASKA PRESS
Lincoln and London

LIBRARY OF CONGRESS CATALOGING IN PUBLICATION DATA
Heinrich Heine and the occident : multiple identities, multiple receptions / edited
by Peter Uwe Hohendahl and Sander L. Gilman.
p.   cm.
Includes index.
ISBN 0-8032-7251-0
1. Heine, Heinrich, 1797–1856—Appreciation—Europe,
Western.   2. Heine, Heinrich, 1797–1856—Appreciation—
Western Hemisphere.   3. Heine, Heinrich, 1797–1856—
Knowledge—Europe, Western.   4. Heine, Heinrich,
1797–1856—Knowledge—Western Hemisphere.
1. Hohendahl, Peter Uwe.   11. Gilman, Sander L.
PT2339.E85H45   1991
831'.7—dc20   90-25482
                                                                          CIP

CONTENTS

ILLUSTRATIONS

ACKNOWLEDGMENTS

The essays collected in this volume were originally presented at a symposium organized by the North American Heine Society and Cornell University at Cornell University September 29 to October 1, 1988. Without the generous support of the National Endowment for the Humanities and the New York Council for the Humanities, this conference and subsequent publication would not have been possible. We also want to thank the Goethe House, New York, and the Western Societies Program of Cornell University for providing travel support and administrative assistance. Finally, we want to express our appreciation for the editorial work of Andreas Gailus, Daniel Purdy, and Andreas Kriefall. Their efforts were invaluable for the preparation of the manuscript. The illustrations are reprinted by permission of the Heinrich-Heine-Institut, Düsseldorf.

HEINRICH HEINE AND
THE OCCIDENT

SANDER L. GILMAN AND
PETER UWE HOHENDAHL

Introduction

Heinrich Heine and the Occident—a title that invites at least two readings: first, Heine's way of looking at Western Europe and the Americas, the way he thematizes and conceptualizes the West in his writings; and second, the reception of Heine in the West, his impact, for instance, on French or Spanish poets and critics or his popular dissemination in Italy and the United States. Thus the ambiguity of the title is intentional, since the essays collected in this volume deal with both aspects: they focus either on Heine's perception of the West or on the reception of Heine's persona and oeuvre in the Western Hemisphere.

When we write about the "reception" of Heine and his works in the West, however, exactly which Heine are we writing about? Heine the bittersweet Romantic poet, the self-conscious modernist, or perhaps even the parodic prepostmodernist? Is he the author of texts set to music by Robert Schumann (1810–1856), Franz Schubert (1797–1828), Hugo Wolf (1860–1903), and Charles Ives (1874–1954), the words of which are quite often lost in the beauty of the music? "Die Wirklichkeit, nachdem sie das Tonreich durchwandert und auch die bedeutungsvollen Rampenlichter überschritten, steht auf dem Theater als Poesie verklärt uns gegenüber. Wie ein verhallendes Echo klingt noch in ihr der holde Wohllaut der Musik, und sie ist märchenhaft angestrahlt von den geheimnisvollen Lampen." ["Reality, after it has wandered through the world of sound and crossed beyond the aura of the stage lights, appears to us in the theater as perfect poetry. Like a bouncing echo, the pure sounds of music ring in it, and it is fabulously illuminated by mysterious lamps."][1] Or is he the poet of the political ballad, sung to the tune of the "Marseillaise," which glorified *the* emperor?

Or is he the poet on his sickbed, lamenting the frailties of the body while writing ironic masterpieces to reveal the flawed underside of

Romanzen und Balladen

für eine Singstimme mit Begleitung des Pianoforte

von

ROBERT SCHUMANN.

Op. 49.

Schumann's Werke.

Serie 13. Nº 14.

Die beiden Grenadiere.

(Ballade von H. Heine.)

Nº 1. Mässig.

Componirt 1840.

great sweeps of history? Is he the historian? (Popular, of course—even though he would have liked to, it is hard to imagine Heine, like Friedrich Schiller, actually teaching at a university.) Is he a historian of ideas who sees them as living forces in history?

Is he the German patriot, the reformer, the political visionary—the

"Moor's" [Karl Marx's] friend, the opponent of Ludwig Börne? Or is he the critic of the Communists, who feared that they would wrap their goods in his verses? "Et béni soit l'épicier qui un jour confectionnera avec mes poésies des cornets où il versera du café et du tabac pour les pauvres bonnes vieilles qui, dans notre monde actuel de l'injustice, ont peut-être dû se passer d'un pareil agrément—*fiat justitia, pereat mundus.*" ["Blessed be the greengrocer, who will prepare with my poems a wrapper in which to stuff his coffee and snuff for the poor old women, who in our present unjust world are denied such treats—*fiat justitia, pereat mundus.*"] Is he the liberal, the radical, or the conservative? "Die Chartisten verbergen unter legalen Formen ihren Terrorismus, während die Kommunisten ihn freimütig und unumwunden aussprechen." ["The Chartists hide their terrorism beneath legal forms; Communists reveal theirs freely and unapologetically."][3]

Is he the journalist? Indeed, for many *the* journalist, the creator of a new style of journalism that came to dominate German writing through the 1920s (from the "raging reporter" Egon Erwin Kisch [1885–1948] on the left to the "diarist" Joseph Goebbels on the far right]? This is the truly *new* journalism, personal, acidic, critical—the voice that identifies the forces of evil and then traps them in the *Inferno* of poetry for an eternity, forcing them to transcend their own times and become exempla for all of history.

> Kennst du die Hölle des Dante nicht,
> Die schrecklichen Terzetten?
> Wen da der Dichter hineingesperrt,
> Den kann kein Gott mehr retten.

> [Don't you know Dante's Inferno
> His frightening tercetts?
> He whom the poetry traps there
> no God can save.]

Or is he the journalist as contemporary critic, whose interest is the betterment of his world and whose journalistic claws are certainly not as vicious as those of the writers who attack him? "Und als den Allerselben und unverändert werden Sie ihn finden, wenn Sie wieder zusammentreffen mit diesen Menschen, der Harry Heine heißt, und schlicht und umgänglich wie ein Kind ist, und nur dann und wann höchst ernsthaft wird, und immer über die Narren in der Welt lacht, und täglich eine Bouteille Champagner trinken möchte auf das Wohlsein seiner Feinde." ["And you will find him the very same man, unchanged, when you meet again that man called Harry Heine, as simple and sociable as a child, and who only now and then becomes very serious, but always laughs about the fools of this world and would daily drink a bottle of champagne to the health of his enemies."][4]

Is he the Jew—the political Jew, assimilationist and convert; the self-hating Jew traveling through Poland; the Jewish Romantic seeking after his own ancestry in the Golden Age of Spain? Or is his "Jewishness" merely a label applied to him by his enemies, a label that he plays with but never takes seriously? "Der Taufzettel is das Entréebillett zur europäischen Kultur." ["The baptismal certificate is the entrance card into European culture."][5]

"Never takes seriously": maybe that is the mask, the mask of the frivolous poet, who is more French than German. "Real" German poets are "serious": Goethe is serious; Schiller is serious; Hölderlin is serious. "Ich weiß wohl, Doktor, Sie gehören zu den Dichtern, die einen eigensinnigen Kopf haben, und nicht einsehen, daß die Füße in der Dichtkunst die Hauptsache sind. Ein gebildetes Gemüt wird aber nur durch die gebildete Form angesprochen, diese können wir nur von den Griechen lernen und von neueren Dichtern, die griechisch streben, griechisch denken, griechisch fühlen und in solchen Weise ihre Gefühle an den Mann bringen." ["I know very well, Doctor, that you belong to the poets who have stubborn heads and so don't realize that the foot is the main thing in the art of poetry. An educated spirit can be addressed only by an educated form, which we can learn only from the Greeks and from those modern poets who strive to be Greek, strive to think Greek, strive to feel Greek, and thus bring their feelings to the reader."][6]

Yet Heine is playful, trifling, flippant, insouciant, airy, mercurial, capricious, whimsical—in other words, not serious:

> Auch die Schwarzen, die Eunuchen,
> Stimmten lachend ein, es lachen
> Selbst die Mumien, selbst die Sphinxe,
> Daß sie schier zu bersten dachten.

> [And the Blacks, the eunuchs
> also agreed laughing
> Even the mummies, even the sphinx
> thought they would almost burst with laughter.]

So he is not a real "German" author, even though he writes in German. He is "French," a German who has lost his roots (he is "really" a Jew, so he could never have had any German roots). Isn't he the sensualist who lives in Paris—for the upright middle-class Germans of the nineteenth and twentieth centuries, the city of decadence—writing art criticism and chronicles of the daily life and politics of this most degenerate city, not quite as an insider but also not really as an outsider either? For the French, meanwhile, he is the "German in France," a category of sycophant well known since before the revolution. Never really French, thinking French but speaking German. "Ich reise nämlich in einigen Tagen von hier ab, durchwandere einige Zeit Westfalen und Rheinland, und diesen Herbst hoffe ich in Paris zu sein. Ich gedenke viele Jahre dort zu bleiben . . . und nebenbei für Verbreitung der deutschen Literatur, die jetzt in Frankreich Wurzel faßt, tätig zu sein." ["I'm going to leave here in a few days, will wander through Westphalia and the Rheinland for a while, and in the autumn I hope to be in Paris. I intend to be there for a long time . . . and on the side, to be active in promoting German literature, which is now taking root in France."][7]

And to prove the whole thing, he's a syphilitic, and we know what that means. He is not like the best poets, healthy and creative. "Hauptzug der jetzigen Dichter: Gesundheit, westfälische, österreichische, ja ungarische Gesundheit." ["The primary characteristic of modern poets: health, Westphalian, Austrian, even Hungarian health."][8] He's a cripple because of his immorality. He is—in his very person—the "unclean" thing that he is in his writing. And all his readers know it. They know that he has been living with *that woman*, that ignorant shopgirl, and he has the nerve to comment on the sexual habits of Germans, Frenchmen, and Jews alike!

The first question to be addressed by any study of the reception of Heine in the West (or, indeed, anywhere else), then, is Heine's complex and seemingly mutable identity. It is not enough to say, as one could for a writer whose literary persona was more closely determined, that Heine is a "poet" (whether that is the best translation of *Dichter* or not could be debated). Goethe is a *Dichter*. Although he was also a politician, a civil servant, an art critic, a university administrator and innovator, a scientist (biologist, anatomist, geologist, physicist), in the main his reception has been that of a *Dichter*—even though the portion of his life (not his writing) devoted to poetry in all its forms was certainly smaller than that occupied by his other activities combined.

There is a consensus about Goethe's *poetische Sendung* [poetic vocation], partially constructed by the author in his autobiography, partially constructed by the critics who had already labeled him *the* poet of his day (and language) during his own lifetime.

Heine certainly worked as self-consciously and as hard on crafting his autobiography as did Goethe, perhaps even harder—especially if we take into account the fiction of his birth date, placed by him at the very opening of the new century, of the new age: Heine was to be born at the dawn of the new century, he was to be the poet of the future. In constructing calendars and clocks, we are always creating moments of opening and closure, of anticipation and gloom. We, at the end of another century, often stand looking toward the past, seeing our world as decaying, as collapsing; Heine, in creating his own literary persona, needed to see himself as the beginning of a new world, the brave new nineteenth century. And this instinct for self-creation continued during his entire life; he was constantly creating roles for himself, all of the aforementioned roles and more. But unlike the response to Goethe (who was Heine's model, as well as that of every other German poet of the nineteenth century), no consensus emerged as to what Heine was. His advocates saw him in a range of affirmative roles; his opponents, as the polar opposites of those roles. But polar opposite to what? Heine became the touchstone for defenses or attacks on a range of roles, all of which he seemed to exemplify and all of which he, quite self-consciously, incorporated into his fictive persona.

Heine's protean sense of self was not a quirky inability to decide who he was, nor a psychic weakness. Rather, like Nietzsche at the other end of that brave new century, he became aware that he was able to create various voices as well as various discourses, which appealed to (or repelled) various thought collectives of his own and subsequent times. He (and his early-nineteenth-century contemporaries) became aware of the multiplicity of discourses that exist in any society over time and was thus able to shift bases dynamically in response to personal and/or ideological pressures. It was not that Heine needed to create these various voices; he became aware that one created them whether one desired to or not. And as long as they were to be created, there was a need to control them, to use them to represent aspects of the self-consciously created fictive persona, the sense of the self as captured in the persona of the "writer." It is clear that the aspects Heine (or any other writer) stressed as constituting the self reflect inner fantasies of the self. And this fantasy shifts in its emphasis over time.

That is true about all writers, however, Goethe as well as Heine. Why is it that the rich complexity of Heine's sense of self never settled on one central definition for himself or for his contemporaries?

One can see Heine's sense of self (as well as the sense of him held by posterity) as having a single basic structure—not as clearly defined as *Goethe the Poet*, but differentiated clearly enough to offer a commonality of definition. For in all of the roles created by Heine for his various senses of himself there is a common thread: Heine as the outsider, the apostle of difference. Whether as politician, poet of whatever form, critic, journalist, German, Frenchman, or Jew, Heine stakes out for himself the role of the opposition. Now, for Heine, what is oppositional shifts over time. As the bittersweet Romantic poet gives way to the modernist, Heine responds to the poetry of his age (and not necessarily of his own language). Heine sees himself as a "European" when others see him as a "Jew"—two definitions of the "cosmopolitan" which haunt the nineteenth century. His Jewishness is in opposition to the synagogue and in alliance with the new "science of the Jews." But as the "science of the Jews" becomes more and more the "Protestantization of the Jews," Heine falls into seeing the Jew in terms of a Romantic (but still ironic) Jewish past. So, too, with all of the roles. As Heine himself becomes the hallmark of a "style"—that of the *feuilleton*—whether art critic or journalist, he responds, quite often parodying himself as he evolves in new, dialectically determined directions. But the constellation of definitions remains somewhat fixed.

New definitions are added throughout his life and into the long period of his decline. His final role, the invalid, is of course partially determined by the realities of his illness, but it is also a pose, a convention of the passive observer. The nature of his illness, its stigmatizing aspect, surfaces in this discourse of disease, which makes it very much his own: he becomes the exemplary syphilitic, with all of the implications of that label, in his own work—and then in the works of others, others who define themselves against Heine as "healthy," as well as those who, on the contrary, see themselves as "decadent," exploiting, as Heine had, the inherent relationship between the decay of the body and the truth of art. Indeed, this theme, anticipated in Heine's late work, becomes for his French contemporaries and followers, Charles Baudelaire, Stéphane Mallarmé, Jules Laforgue, and Comte de Lautréamont, the "true" definition of the poet.

Heine's creation of the ever-shifting world of oppositional images, his always being "other," makes him one of the most difficult of writers to categorize. And yet for much of the world, the "reading" of Heine—the focus on one aspect from the many sides engendered by Heine's sense of opposition—is so selective that only one or another of these images of difference appears. The contradictory images of difference become evident only when we examine the totality of those masks and names that Heinrich Heine created for himself.

In many ways, as Jürgen Habermas observes,[9] Heine anticipated the persona of the modern intellectual who depends on but also calls into question a highly differentiated social system whose various sectors are the domain of experts and specialists. The intellectual is faced with the task of bringing together again what have become separate spheres of knowledge. Heine harshly criticized the German Romantics for their supposed inability to cope with the modern world, but he continued, albeit in a more self-conscious and ironic way, their claim to relink the various aspects of modern culture.

It is not surprising, therefore, that Heine's image in Western Europe, after he had established himself as a major author, was both multifaceted and unstable. From the very beginning of his reception in the West, his critics were frequently at a loss how to describe and classify an author who appeared to continue the tradition of German Romantic poetry—possibly even as Goethe's heir—and at the same time was deeply involved in religious and political disputes; how to evaluate an author who also claimed to be informed about the history of German philosophy and music, who even dared to challenge the knowledge of foreign experts. It was clearly not easy to find a focus for an appropriate reception of such an author. On the other hand, it became obvious that this writer, precisely because he broke away from traditional German patterns, was more interesting and challenging than the typical Biedermeier poet like Karl Immermann (1796–1840) or Eduard Mörike (1804–1875). The only exception might have been Ludwig Börne, but his range as author was much more limited. As formidable literary critic and witty cultural commentator, he was almost Heine's equal, but he could not offer the dazzling display of poems and narrative prose that captivated Heine's French, Italian, and English readers.

Heine was very conscious of this problem when he tried to establish himself in Paris after 1830. He planned to bring out his early writings in French translation. Yet as Michael Werner shows in this volume, Heine wanted not only to be recognized as a German poet and literary commentator, but also to be taken seriously as a critic of German philosophy as well as an expert on general cultural questions. He fully realized that he was not entering a vacuum of knowledge. Since the beginning of the nineteenth century, French literati and scholars had begun to observe the philosophical and literary scene *d'outre Rhin* more systematically. By 1830, when Heine arrived in Paris, two aspects of German culture in particular had found recognition as major European events: German Romanticism (with Goethe and Schiller as the dominating figures) and German Idealism (Kant, Schelling, Hegel). Any new author coming from Germany had to place himself within this context. Although Heine succeeded in finding acceptance as a literary figure (a second-generation German Romantic), he failed to make an impact as a critical commentator of German philosophy and historical scholarship. During the nineteenth century the French reception of Heine emphasized his literary achievements at the expense of his contributions to philosophy and intellectual history.

The initial response of English critics was not altogether different. The appreciation of Heine's wit and power as satirist did not extend to more serious topics such as religious and moral theory. Typical in this respect were the remarks of the *Athenaeum*, which had promised its readers a survey of German literature from Heine's pen. When Heine finally submitted his extensive treatment of German religion and philosophy (later *Zur Geschichte der Religion und Philosophie in Deutschland* [On the History of Religion and Philosophy in Germany]), the magazine politely declined to print the essays, arguing that the editors were prepared to trust Heine's judgment in literary matters but not necessarily when it came to philosophical and religious questions.[10] The initial hostility toward Heine in England, which also showed up in the early American reception, had to do precisely with Heine's reputation as a witty but immoral author who lacked the maturity and self-control expected from a major author (Goethe). Thomas Carlyle's vicious repudiation of Heine, for instance, was based on the Englishman's perception of the German literary tradition (represented by Schiller and Goethe) as morally and aesthetically sound.

It was only in the 1850s and 1860s that Heine's philosophical and social criticism was discovered in England by such major figures as

Matthew Arnold and George Eliot. Their essays significantly modified Heine's image in England (and North America) by bringing his importance for the definition of modern culture into the foreground. Heine became clearly a different author. This new profile has on the whole distinguished the English reception of Heine: the author comes across as a more serious critic and historian whose insightful analyses of modern Europe were received as helpful guidelines for the ongoing discussion in England. Thus Heine's influence, through Matthew Arnold's presence in English education, for instance, extended precisely to those areas that Heine failed to penetrate in France. But there was a price for this integration of Heine's work into mid-Victorian England: as Ilse-Maria Tesdorpf has argued in her study of Heine and Arnold,[11] the latter's cultural program tended to depoliticize Heine's texts, whose acute observations of social and political conditions in England and France before 1848 had lost a good deal of their relevance during the 1860s, particularly after the Second Reform Bill of 1867. Arnold's reading took the political punch out of Heine's writings so that they became serviceable for a more conservative program of *Bildung* that Heine would hardly have endorsed.

Heine's reception in the United States during the course of the nineteenth century also demonstrates the variations and confusions that changes in cultural climate and readership can produce.[12] Ralph Waldo Emerson, an intense admirer of Goethe, simply dismissed Heine in conversation as "a quack and a charlatan in literature." This comment was not too far from the pronouncement of Emerson's friend Carlyle (the British translator of some of Goethe's novels) that Heine was a "slimy and greasy Jew—fit only to eat sausages made of toads."[13] American literature of the first half of the nineteenth century was in thrall to Goethe. The publication of Madame de Staël's essay *The Influence of Literature upon Society* in Philadelphia in 1813 had set the tone: Germany was a serious culture. Heine was certainly not serious enough. Even Henry Wadsworth Longfellow, in a brief piece in *Graham's Magazine* in 1842, saw Heine as a "Young German," a school that was "seeking to establish a religion of sensuality and to build a palace of Pleasure on the ruins of the Church."[14] Pleasure and sensuality were not German enough for these American readers of Heine.

Heine was, however, read. The loose copyright laws that dominated American publishing during the nineteenth century (against which

Charles Dickens struggled and won) meant that editions and translations of the best-known German writers regularly appeared in the United States, where a huge German reading public existed. Germans had begun to settle in large numbers in German-speaking communities in North America in the early eighteenth century, and this presence was augmented by the economic and political emigration of even greater numbers of Germans from the 1830s to the 1860s. This audience meant that editions of Heine's works, such as the pirated edition brought out by the Philadelphia publisher John Weik beginning in 1855, had an extensive readership.[15]

Thus, German poetry was read and was admired. German was the language of poetry—not the language of science—for midcentury America. The great southern poet Sidney Lanier translated Heine while languishing in a Yankee prison camp in 1864. It was the early, "Romantic" Heine that attracted Lanier. In the 1850s, however, Charles Godfrey Leland began systematically to translate all of Heine into English. Leland was the famed author of the "Hans Breitmann" poems, which maintained their popularity in the United States until World War I. They were mildly ironic dialect poems in which a German-American commented on daily life in the United States. Unlike the political Irish dialect essays of Finley Peter Dunne, writing as "Mr. Dooley," the Hans Breitmann ballads were self-consciously poetry; indeed, of all texts written during the midnineteenth century in the United States, they are the closest to Heine's political verses.

The reception of Heine changed again with the times and with new developments in the reading public's taste. Russell Berman shows in this volume how extraordinarily parallel the world views of Walt Whitman and Heine were. Whitman's cry that "Heine was free—was one of the men who win by degrees"[16] is paralleled by quite another reading of Heine, one that, like Whitman's "free" poet, is also part of Heine's complex self-image. It is the image of Heine as the sick Jew, the double victim. Emerson's great protégée Emma Lazarus presented a view of Heine quite different from that of her mentor. A Sephardic Jew of great poetic strength, today known solely for her role as the author of the inscription on the Statue of Liberty, Lazarus saw Heine as her parallel. Like Heine, she was chronically ill. In her sonnet "The Venus of the Louvre" she depicts Heine's last walk through Paris, as he collapses beside a classical statue:

But at her feet a pale, deal-stricken Jew,
Her life-adorer, sobbed farewell to love,
Here Heine wept! Here still he weeps anew,
Nor ever shall his shadow lift or move
While mourns one ardent heart, one poet-brain
For vanished Hellas and Hebraic pain.[17]

The image of Heine has been softened, the edges rounded, at least in this "Jewish" reading of the poet. Heine becomes the poet's poet in this piece at the same time that his satiric voice has been transmogrified into the political voice of the Hans Breitmann ballads. All of these images—like the portrait of Heine on Ernst Herter's Loreley fountain in the Bronx Park, presented to the city of New York in 1893—are frozen in time with World War I. German poetry, German dialect comedy, indeed the very word *German* vanished, and the pejorative label *Hun* replaced it. Heine was no Hun. Heine the poet remained in American culture in settings by Charles Ives, but it is the Romantic Heine of Sidney Lanier. It was not until the 1970s, through the work of the California political radical Hal Draper, that all of Heine's poetry again appeared in American translation.[18] Draper had been deeply involved with American radical politics from the 1930s on, and at the end of his career (he died in January 1990), he turned to that poetic voice reflecting his own political perspective. Maybe "Hans Breitmann" really wasn't dead at all. Heine found a new voice in the 1980s. As the "Walker in the City," the New York Jewish critic Alfred Kazin noted, he is "still one of us."[19]

Incorporation and acceptance of an author imply adaptations, one of the empirical rules of cultural transfer. Arnold's use of Heine's critical prose for Victorian England, and Draper's translations of Heine's poetry for a politically liberal era in America, are but two examples of this process. Heine's multifaceted oeuvre was not only divided and reorganized when it crossed the border of another national culture, but it also had to fit the needs and interests of the host culture. Whenever these needs and interests changed during the course of the nineteenth century, the author Heine had to change with them or drop out of favor. Moreover, these needs frequently transcended the literary sphere. By and large the interest in Heine's texts was motivated and guided by broader cultural and political concerns—concerns for which the figure of the poet served as a convenient focus.

Both the Spanish and the Mexican receptions clearly illustrate this process. In Mexico, as Susanne Zantop argues in her essay in this volume, the increasing interest in Heine during the 1860s and the decline of this attention in the 1890s were closely linked to general trends in Mexican history that were seemingly far removed from the intentions of the author Heine and his cultural environment. Even his self-understanding as a cultural mediator between Germany and the West would not have covered the distance. Heine's poems, especially *Vitzliputzli*, became part of the Mexican struggle for a national identity in the shadow of the traditional colonial powers of Europe and the United States. The growing fascination with Heine coincided by and large with increasing interest in Germany and her culture in general. Ironically, German trade sought by the Mexicans also enhanced the standing of Heine's poetry. For a fairly brief span of time German culture became the cultural model for the Mexican elite. The enthusiasm for Heine, which peaked around 1884, was part of the preference for a European country that was not (yet) involved in colonial adventures. Yet even during this period the reasons for appreciating Heine were, as Zantop points out, dissimilar; they varied from the affirmation of a conservative Catholic nationalism to a liberal interest in creating a modern Mexican nation. Accordingly, Heine could be seen either as the embodiment of German Romantic profundity or as the radical and witty critic of the German state.

During the 1880s the Romantic image of Heine, which had defined most of the initial reception in Mexico, was replaced by the modernist image, stressing the "abysmal" qualities of the poet. The discovery of Heine's *Zerrissenheit* also reinforced his status as an oppositional writer among his Mexican critics and imitators. In other words, the shift from a reading praising Heine's poetry as a model of melodious simplicity to a reading that stressed its ambivalence and complexity had, in the Mexican case, a significant political connotation that is not evident in the English or Italian reception of the same time.

The Spanish interest in Heine, on the other hand, particularly the enthusiasm of the Generation of 1898, a group of Spanish intellectuals deeply concerned about the decline of Spanish power abroad and at home, is rather closely connected with a cultural configuration in which political elements played an important role. According to Egon Schwarz in this volume, the aim of the intellectuals to rekindle the great Spanish tradition not only informed their reading of Heine, as far as selection and emphasis were concerned, but also provided the lens for the reading process. By using Heine's commentaries on Cervantes' *Don Quijote* as a springboard, the incorporation of the German poet into the Spanish discourse became almost "natural." The voice of the outsider speaking about a great Spanish author was allowed to confirm the urgent need for a cultural renaissance, although the various writers and critics did not necessarily agree about the nature of Heine's advice.

The Spanish and the Mexican attempts to incorporate Heine's "modernism" were (either directly or indirectly) politically motivated, but the English and Italian transition to the modernist image was determined by different forces. By 1870 Heine's fame was firmly established in England. It was even legitimate to consider Heine the heir of Goethe —which was definitely not the case in Germany, where major critics (Wilhelm Dilthey among them) were determined to remove Heine from the German canon. The late Victorian writers and critics focused on the neopagan elements in Heine's texts, making use of his typology of Hellenic and Judeo-Christian cultures.[20] Heine's dichotomy allowed English critics such as Robert Buchanan and Walter Pater to articulate their own resistance to mainstream English culture. It is here that a common European trait comes into the foreground: Heine's highly ambivalent and ironic revival of ancient European myths found an echo not only in Germany (Wagner, Nietzsche) but in other Western European countries as well. Modern European culture grounded in the Christian tradition was felt to be stifling and limiting. Thus, during the last decades of the nineteenth century, critical commentators of modern civilization could easily accept Heine as their precursor. Obviously, it was a radical but also one-sided appropriation, which left as much out as it included. It especially narrowed Heine's liberal program of the 1830s by placing the emphasis exclusively on its hedonistic elements.

During the nineteenth century Heine remained a controversial author, not only in Germany but also in Western Europe and the Americas. The fact that he was more or less accepted as a major representative of the German literary tradition did not neutralize this controversial status. Heine's readers tended to be partisan. The various receptions reflected particular cultural and literary interests of the receiving groups and nations. To put it differently, Heine's texts were used to legitimize and strengthen highly divergent cultural programs and literary movements. Similar statements, of course, could be made about many authors. Still, Heine's ambivalent oeuvre, which supported not just different but even contradictory positions, invited "tendentious" and conflicting interpretations.

Several typical choices determined much of the reception in Western Europe and America: Heine the "German" poet; Heine the author of witty and satirical prose; Heine the political and social commentator; Heine the historian of religion and philosophy. From a more distant point of view, however, Heine's appropriation in the West appears to boil down to three configurations: Heine the poet, Heine the journalist and critic, and Heine the ideologue, that is, the herald of a new cultural program. Each of these configurations has room for aspects of the other two—as long as they remain in a supplementary role. Also, each of these choices brings out complementary characteristics. The emphasis on Heine's poetry, especially in the context of German Romanticism, tends to bring out the "German" quality in Heine: sweet simplicity. When later Heine's poetry was seen in the context of European modernism, a cosmopolitan European image of the author seems to prevail. Similarly, Heine's journalism—for instance, his struggle for political emancipation—carries cosmopolitan (French) rather than German connotations. Particularly for his French readers, it was obvious that during the 1830s Heine's position was rather close to that of the Saint-Simonians.

The political view of Heine—at least *grosso modo*—also included the acceptance of Heine's Jewish identity, which was rarely acknowledged in his role as "German poet." Heine's persona as herald of a new cultural program and myth maker again stresses the common European aspects and, by the same token, deemphasizes the national identity. In this context Heine becomes one of Nietzsche's *gute Europäer*, whose goal it was to transcend national boundaries. Readers from the political spectrum of the left have tended to deemphasize or even deny the German component in Heine's work, in spite of the fact that Heine himself felt rather strongly about this side of his identity. For European liberals and democrats, Heine's outspoken critique of Prussia and its authoritarian tradition occasionally served as a useful vehicle of criticism (the voice of the "insider" who knows), especially when the relationship between Germany and Western Europe was strained. World War I would be a case in point.

It is important to note that the rejection of Heine could invoke the same configurations. A conservative critic would underline the cosmopolitan, that is, inauthentic, character of Heine's poetry and denounce his political and social criticism as the expression of a rootless intellectual. A right-wing reader would add to this criticism the anti-Semitic slur, a possibility that is not entirely missing in the French and English discussion of Heine during the nineteenth century. Today, as Jost Hermand points out in this volume, Heine's Jewish identity as a cultural figure is relevant primarily in three Western countries: Germany (where the struggle for Heine's acceptance is still incomplete), Israel (where Heine's Christian baptism is still perceived as a stigma), and the United States (where various Jewish and non-Jewish groups make claims to present the true image of Heine).

After World War II these controversies, which had clearly enhanced but also marked Heine's reputation, lost much of their relevance. This new calm has not automatically increased Heine's fame in the West, however. On the contrary, it seems that by and large the acceptance of Heine's canonical status has not enlarged the number of his readers in Italy or France, South America or the United States. Rather, Heine has become the property of the academic critics, whose contributions, as Luciano Zagari shows in this volume for Italy, have substantially advanced and widened our understanding of Heine's oeuvre.

The loss of a popular readership outside academia was in part the result of recent German history. The appropriation of the German literary tradition by the National Socialists, who suppressed Heine's work, compromised this tradition in the eyes of Western readers. Paradoxically, in spite of his rejection by the Nazis, Heine's popular fame in the West has also been negatively affected by this problematic status of German culture. Furthermore, there is no denying the fact that the more recent images of Heine have not favored the popular dissemination of his work. The modernist image of the late nineteenth century, with its stress on Heine's aesthetic achievements and its celebration of tensions and dissonances in his texts, removed Heine from the realm of popular reception. The writings of academic critics after 1945 have only enlarged this gulf. The more the critics have insisted—and with good reasons—on the complexity of Heine's work, on the inscrutability of his poems, on the involution of his aesthetic theories as well as the complexity of his social and philosophical criticism, the more they took him out of the grasp of the general audience. There seems to be no road leading back to the image of Heine the writer of simple love poetry. On the other hand, there are fortunately also no indications that Heine's widespread acceptance (even in Germany) has turned him into the kind of classic whose Olympian posture has a narcotic effect on his readers. Finally, it should be noted that scholars have not been able to come up with the "definitive" synthesis of Heine's work, a deficiency we consider good news.

NOTES

1. Heinrich Heine, *Sämtliche Schriften*, ed. Klaus Briegleb, 6 vols. (Munich: Hanser, 1968–76), 3:316. Bracketed English translations are provided by the authors.
2. Robert Schumann, *Lieder* (Frankfurt am Main: Peters, n.d.), 1:163.
3. Heine, *Schriften*, 5:225, 5:422.
4. Ibid., 4:644, 1:768.
5. Ibid., 6:622.
6. Ibid., 2:422.
7. Ibid., 6:11, 3:844.
8. Ibid., 6:629.
9. Jürgen Habermas, "Geist und Macht—ein deutsches Thema: Heinrich Heine und die Rolle der Intellektuellen in Deutschland," in *Das Junge Deutschland: Kolloquium zum 150. Jahrestag des Verbots vom 10. Dezember 1835*, ed. Joseph A. Kruse and Bernd Kortländer (Hamburg: Hoffmann & Campe, 1987), pp. 15–38.
10. Sol Liptzin, *The English Legend of Heinrich Heine* (New York: Bloch, 1954), pp. 13–15.
11. Ilse-Maria Tesdorpf, *Die Auseinandersetzung Matthew Arnolds mit Heinrich Heine, des Kritikers mit dem Kritiker* (Frankfurt am Main: Athenäum, 1971).
12. On Heine and the United States, see especially Robert C. Holub, "Heine and the New World," *Colloquia Germanica* 22 (1989): 101–115; and Armin Arnold, *Heine in England and America* (London: Linden, 1959).
13. Cited by Clarence Gohdes, "Heine in America: A Cursory Survey," *Georgia Review* 11 (1957): 45.
14. Henry W. Longfellow, "German Writers: Heinrich Heine," *Graham's Magazine* 20 (1842): 134–137.
15. See the discussion in Holub, "Heine and the New World," pp. 110–112.
16. Cited by Horace Traubel, *With Walt Whitman in Camden* (New York: Rowman & Littlefield, 1961), 1:461.
17. Cited by Alfred Werner, "Heine in America," *American-German Review* 22 (1956): 5.
18. Heinrich Heine, *The Complete Poems of Heinrich Heine: A Modern English Version*, trans. and ed. Hal Draper (Boston: Suhrkamp/Insel, 1982).

19. Alfred Kazin, "Foreword," in *Heinrich Heine: Poetry and Prose*, ed. Jost Hermand and Robert C. Holub (New York: Continuum, 1982), p. xiii.
20. See Liptzin, *English Legend*, pp. 82–102; and Stanton Lawrence Wormley, *Heine in England* (Chapel Hill: University of North Carolina Press, 1943).

WORKS CITED

Arnold, Armin. *Heine in England and America*. London: Linden, 1959.

Gohdes, Clarence. "Heine in America: A Cursory Survey." *Georgia Review* 11 (1957): 44–49.

Habermas, Jürgen. "Geist und Macht—ein deutsches Thema: Heinrich Heine und die Rolle der Intellektuellen in Deutschland." In *Das Junge Deutschland: Kolloquium zum 150. Jahrestag des Verbots vom 10. Dezember 1835*, ed. Joseph A. Kruse and Bernd Kortländer. Hamburg: Hoffmann & Campe, 1987.

Heine, Heinrich. *The Complete Poems of Heinrich Heine: A Modern English Version*. Trans. and ed. Hal Draper. Boston:Suhrkamp/Insel, 1982.

———. *Sämtliche Schriften*. Ed. Klaus Briegleb. 6 vols. Munich: Hanser, 1968–76.

Hermand, Jost, and Robert C. Holub, eds. *Heinrich Heine: Poetry and Prose*. New York: Continuum, 1982.

Holub, Robert C. "Heine and the New World." *Colloquia Germanica* 22 (1989): 101–115.

Liptzin, Sol. *The English Legend of Heinrich Heine*. New York: Bloch, 1954.

Longfellow, Henry W. "German Writers: Heinrich Heine." *Graham's Magazine* 20 (1842): 134–136.

Schumann, Robert. *Lieder*. Frankfurt am Main: Peters, n.d.

Tesdorpf, Ilse-Maria. *Die Auseinandersetzung Matthew Arnolds mit Heinrich Heine, des Kritikers mit dem Kritiker*. Frankfurt am Main: Athenäum, 1971.

Traubel, Horace. *With Walt Whitman in Camden*. New York: Rowman & Littlefield, 1961.

Werner, Alfred. "Heine in America." *American-German Review* 22 (1956): 4–6.

Wormley, Stanton Lawrence. *Heine in England*. Chapel Hill: University of North Carolina Press, 1943.

J O S T   H E R M A N D

One Identity Is Not Enough:
Heine's Legacy to Germans, Jews, and Liberals

*I*n many Western nations Heine remains more controversial than any other German writer of the
nineteenth century. Through the various roles he assumed (among
others a baptized German Jew, a journalist well versed in the philosophical mysteries of Hegelianism, an occasional friend of Marx, an
irrepressible wag, a follower of Saint-Simon striving for erotic emancipation, an aesthete enamored of his own stylistic elegance, a sin-
ner penitent and contrite, a critic, and last representative of German
Romanticism), he has managed to irritate all those intellectuals who
have attempted to define themselves solely in terms of one political,
ideological, religious, or secular identity. Because such intellectuals
tend to see such one-sidedness as the highest form of a life in balance
with itself, they often view Heine in all his diversity with some hostility. And yet it could be said that Heine, a German Jew living in the
early nineteenth century and viewed with the greatest skepticism, was
forced into a precarious double role that denied him from the start the
possibility of leading a one-sided, narrow, and faultless existence.

The figure of Heine has been met with the least resistance in those
Western democracies in which a successful bourgeois revolution had
prepared the way for the toleration and then acceptance of various minority groups—in other words, countries such as Holland, England,
France, Italy, and the United States. And yet it is also true that, during the nineteenth century, progressive movements in the Spanish- and
Slavic-speaking countries had also accepted Heine (more or less) as a
model bourgeois liberal. In all of these countries even Heine's status as
a Jew did not work against his reception. His work was quickly made
available in translation, achieved a certain popularity, and in the end

was accepted as part of the canon reserved for those authors considered to be "good liberals." Nevertheless, it is true even today that the
assimilated Jewish intellectuals of these countries are more likely to
acknowledge Heine enthusiastically as one of their own than are the
"natives." In fact, such acknowledgment by assimilated Jewish intellectuals often takes the form of a highly personal sense of identification,
especially with respect to Heine's liberal cosmopolitanism and his so-
called Jewish sense of humor.

Two countries form exceptions to this general trend: West Germany
and Israel. In almost all other Western democracies the Jews make up
at worst a merely tolerated, at best a respected, minority group. In the
cases of West Germany and Israel, we are dealing on the one hand with
a country where there are almost no Jews and on the other hand with
a country where, except for the Palestinians, there are only Jews. Con-
sidering Heine's status as both German and Jewish, such a situation
serves as a less-than-favorable starting point for a fair assessment of his
achievements. It is clear that in West Germany, in the wake of the expulsion or extermination of the Jews between 1933 and 1945, the problem
of Jewish assimilation and integration into the liberal camp has become
an issue of mere historical interest, which the younger generation can
know only from hearsay. In the case of Israel the whole question of
assimilation was rendered moot with the founding of the first Jewish
state. In other Western democracies, however, the problem of assimilation continues to be relevant, a fact that has kept interest in Heine alive
and has made him a far more relevant figure in such nations than could
ever be the case in West Germany or Israel.

With this perspective in mind, let us first turn to the West German
reception of Heine after 1945.[1] As was the case with many phenomena
that called up memories of the fascist past, Heine was for the most part
ignored in the Federal Republic during the first postwar years. Although
the German Democratic Republic celebrated Heine as early as 1956 as
one of Germany's greatest social critics and established his part of the
canon of required school reading, there was little interest in Heine in
the Federal Republic. When the figure of Heine as political poet was re-
discovered in the wake of the various political movements around 1968,
he was reintegrated into the intellectual context of the Federal Republic, but for the most part falsely or one-sidedly so. During these years
he was presented almost exclusively as an adroit liberal strategist, as
a German rather than a German-Jewish democrat. As a result, it has

been conveniently overlooked that Heine's liberal beliefs were deeply enmeshed with the fact of his own status as a Jew. In the end, Heine was officially rehabilitated but at the same time rather thoughtlessly stripped of his Judaism.

Right-of-center liberals such as Fritz J. Raddatz have made it especially easy for themselves by eliminating both the Jewish and the leftist elements from Heine's work, in effect turning Heine into a liberal of their own persuasion, a liberal who is quite content with sitting on the fence. In their eyes, Heine belongs in their camp along with all other uncommitted literati who are interested only in their own prestige and well-being.[2] Left-of-center liberals such as Jürgen Habermas and Hans Magnus Enzensberger acknowledged Heine in a substantially more committed fashion, seeing in him the prototype for an enlightened liberal intellectual, a type of intellectual that, unfortunately for Germany, has been much more common in France than in Heine's native country.[3] As Habermas has pointed out, echoing Heinrich Mann's Zola essay, it was because of this lack that, unlike the case in other Western democracies, a critical public sphere never arose in Germany, a public sphere that effectively spared most other Western democracies the fall into fascism.

Nonetheless, the Jewish question has also rarely been thematized by left-of-center liberals. This task has remained the province of those few Jewish liberals who, after 1945, continued to grapple with German-Jewish questions. In this group we can include Theodor W. Adorno, with his article "Die Wunde Heine" [The Wound That Is Heine]; Marcel Reich-Ranicki, with his public statements concerning the Heine festivities of 1972; Ludwig Rosenthal, a German Jew forced into Guatemalan exile, with his book *Heinrich Heine als Jude* [Heinrich Heine as Jew] (1974); and Hans Mayer, with the Heine sections of his book *Außenseiter* [Outsiders] (1975).[4] These authors no longer consider themselves to be simply German, but rather, using Mayer's formulation, "*Deutsche auf Widerruf,*" revocably German, Germans at will rather than Germans by birth. After the experiences of what has euphemistically been called *Kristallnacht* [Crystal Night] and Auschwitz, these authors no longer see in Heine merely a liberal outsider; they see in him above all a Jewish outsider, a figure as incapable of being smoothly integrated into the history of German liberalism as their own lives have proven incapable of being integrated into German history as a whole. For them there remains much in the case of Heine, and in their own lives, which remains unsolved, much that has remained a *Wunde*, a wound that perhaps never will close.

Heine has been subjected to even closer scrutiny by those intellectuals who feel committed to the state of Israel. Whereas Heine could be relatively smoothly integrated as a model German democrat into the intellectual context of the Federal Republic, in Israel integration of an assimilationist Jew such as Heine runs counter to the state's image of itself and has therefore yet to take place. In Israel, Heine is still considered a renegade, someone who let himself be baptized, thus turning his back on his own people. Many Israeli Jews do not even recognize Heine as a Jew; he is simply a German and thus not worthy of being accepted into the canon of exemplary Jewish figures. Even in the 1970s it still proved impossible to name a street in Tel Aviv after Heine.[5] As has been the case with Lion Feuchtwanger (1884–1958), Arnold Zweig (1887–1968), and other assimilated German Jews, many in Israel still see in Heine a westernized Jew who, in the course of adapting himself to conform with German and French cultural ideals, managed to discard so much of his own cultural heritage that little of his original Jewishness remained. At least that seems to be the opinion of the nationalistically minded, right-wing Zionists among Israeli intellectuals. Left-wing liberals such as Walter Grab, who argues in the name of a cosmopolitanism nurtured by the ideas of the French Revolution, may still acknowledge Heine's worth,[6] yet such voices belong to a relatively small minority.

There is one further exception among the Western nations, a country where, because of its large Jewish population and its relatively strong interest in German history and culture, the questions Heine poses as a German, a Jew, and a liberal have been kept alive: the United States. Here, too, Heine is far from antiquated. Many of the other Western democracies have been content to assign Heine to one of the more out-of-the-way niches in history's gallery of honor, a niche where one can marvel at Heine without, however, thinking through the consequences of such admiration. In the United States, Heine is not merely an object of respectable admiration; here he has managed to remain at the center of heated literary and political discussion.

After the 1930s and early 1940s, when he was the most cited German author next to Goethe among German exiles in the United States,[7] Heine was drawn into the ideological battles of the late 1940s. It was a time of political passions, rancor, and a strong reaction against all things German, once the Auschwitz atrocities became public knowledge and the witch hunts of the McCarthy era began to exercise their influence. After this period Heine could no longer be thought of in the United States as merely a good German-Jewish liberal. There were now competing versions of Heine, from the decidedly left-wing liberal who sympathized with (some might even say as a Left Hegelian anticipated) Marxist ideas, to the assimilated Jew who turned his back on his people, to the author who during the course of his life found his way back to Judaism, a position put forward by Israel Taback and Hugo Bieber, among others.[8] Such competition has brought with it a profusion of Heine representations that almost exceed in number those found in the Federal Republic or Israel. This abundance should come as no surprise, since the United States is home not only to so-called Americans, but also to established orthodox and liberal Jews, members of the German-Jewish emigration of the 1930s and their children, and many conservative and liberal postwar Germans—and each of these groups, because of its distinct background and educational tradition, either rejects Heine or tries, each in its own way, to integrate Heine into its view of the world. In this country the spectrum of possible reactions to Heine is, therefore, the broadest and most intense among German Americans, Germans, German Jews, American Jews, and Orthodox Jews, whereas the reaction of non-Jewish American liberals to Heine, if they are at all familiar with his work, tends to be muted or at best politely interested.

A non-Jewish German like myself who presents in lectures a sympathetic portrait of Heine can expect at least four different reactions on the part of Jewish intellectuals: (1) Approving nods from those liberal, cosmopolitan-minded Jews who see Heine as one of their own and are flattered when others express interest in him and hold him in high esteem. (2) Pleased astonishment from those Jews who are surprised that praise for a Jewish author like Heine could come from where it was least expected, that is, from a German. (3) A partly critical, partly sympathetic response from those who appreciate the interest in Heine and yet remain convinced that a German would be better advised to steer clear of Heine, since only a Jew who could call on two thousand years of trials and tribulations would be able to understand such an author. (4) Finally, a critically orthodox response bordering on the hostile which rejects any sympathetic treatment of that rogue Heine, still accusing him of turning his back on his people through assimilation. On top of that, such critics condemn Heine for abandoning himself not only to erotic libertinism, but also to a flirtation with Marxist ideas.

All such responses remain, after the German fascist atrocities, completely understandable examples of partisanship, strategies of legitimation and appropriation of Heine, responses that in no way should be dismissed as unjustified or even worse as laughable. The exact opposite is true. It is a mark of truly great authors that they divide their audiences, and Heine has managed to do that for all those who have been affected by the collapse of the now long-dead German-Jewish symbiotic relationship. One should therefore not brush aside such points of view as merely ideological, partisan, or even functionalistic. Whenever we are forced to deal with central questions concerning our own identity or world view, almost all of us come to decisions based on our own background, education, and nationality, as well as the reigning mood of the times. To a greater or lesser extent we project our own particular views and concerns onto the facts that have been handed down to us, no matter how hard we try to present ourselves as objective. Especially in the humanities there are no truths etched in stone, no strict regularities—that is to say, nothing already fossilized, cold, and dead; there is only that which stays in constant flux, remaining alive and vibrant, calling out constantly for more reflection, more reappraisals. That is especially true when, in a case like Heine's, we are dealing with continuing problems central to our understanding of the idea of personal identity.

We should not be surprised, then, that even all the so-called incontrovertible facts we possess about Heine tend to be colored by the perspective of each individual observer. Nevertheless, it is important to call to mind some of these facts to give the ever-burgeoning discussion concerning Heine's national and ideological affiliations some sort of historically grounded foundation, rather than consigning the discussion to the realm of ideology. It is perhaps appropriate to ascertain first how Heine saw himself as a German Jew and a combative liberal. We cannot deal with the topic exhaustively, since an abundance of both documentary material and secondary literature is involved,[9] and yet it could prove useful to recall at least a few details of Heine's biography. As we know, little here proves amenable to generalization. There do exist some definite ideological constants in terms of both Heine's Judaism and his liberalism, and yet such constants are often confronted with an equal number of changes and transmutations. In the case of a witty and ironic author such as Heine, one whose formulations often depend on a biting turn of phrase, much of what is said must be taken as being merely provocative or dependent on a particular situation, including in the area of ideology. And yet, even on the level of the most heartfelt convictions, we see in Heine some fundamental changes brought on by the vicissitudes of his personal biography, marked as it was by the Napoleonic occupation of the Rhine, the Wars of Liberation, the Restoration administered by Metternich, the Parisian July Revolution, the *juste milieu* of Louis Philippe, the 1848 Revolution, and Napoleon III's coup d'état.

As we know, Heine did not grow up in a Jewish ghetto, but rather was part of a relatively assimilated German-Jewish family in Düsseldorf. He attended a lycée in Düsseldorf that was marked by an enlightened French influence, and he experienced there both the Wars of Liberation and the rise of the German student associations (*Burschenschaften*). At first drawn to such associations because of their oppositional character, he soon found himself ruthlessly confronted by their anti-French and anti-Semitic tendencies.[10] "I am no German à la [Christian] Rühs or [Jakob] Fries," wrote Heine in 1823,[11] disgusted with the main spokesmen of xenophobia in Germany at that time. Given Heine's position, it is clear that his poetry of the early 1820s is the work of someone unpopular, even of someone rejected by society, someone who, despite his progressive convictions and his plans to go through with assimilation, felt very much that he had been left to fend for himself. He was able to find some sort of ideological refuge only in the Association for Jewish Culture and Sciences (Verein für Kultur und Wissenschaft des Judentums) in Berlin, which both gave back to him a sense of his own Judaism and inspired him to begin a novel entitled *Rabbi von Bacharach*, a work in which he planned to acknowledge his own interest in his people's long and troubled history. He broke off work on the novel shortly after its conception, however. Plans for the so-called Ganstown Project, in which members of the association would form a Jewish colony or perhaps even a Jewish state on the banks of the Missouri, also fell by the wayside. Despite all these good intentions, Heine decided in 1825 to go through with his baptism and at the same time to finish his legal studies at Göttingen with the hope that he would finally be able to establish himself, either as a lawyer or a notary, as an acceptable member of German bourgeois society. And yet, even with his baptismal certificate, this unavoidable "admission ticket to European culture," as Heine later characterized it,[12] almost all of his professional hopes were frustrated. He was left to ply his trade as a journalist and writer, professions that

in any event required little in the way of social status. To what extent
the blemish of his own baptism shamed Heine can best be seen in the
wicked sarcasm directed at Gumpelino, the baptized Jew in his *Bäder
von Lucca.*

To broaden his own horizons, Heine traveled extensively in countries such as England and northern Italy, although it must be said that
these two countries did not particularly appeal to him. Northern Italy
seemed to him to live shackled under the generally repressive rule of
the Austrians, and England seemed dominated by a false sense of emancipation, based as it was on the notion of free trade rather than that of
true freedom. Searching for a more hospitable atmosphere, he finally
decided in 1831—after the liberating tempest of the Parisian July Revolution—to move to France, a country that he had already envisioned
in the 1820s as fostering an atmosphere of tolerance and liberal ideals
which seemed to accept even minority groups as full-fledged members of society. The utopian socialism of Saint-Simon and his followers
seemed to offer Heine the ideological foundation for his own assimilation, one that could be expanded into a much broader liberation promising a more cheerful, more culinary, more sensual, more cosmopolitan
way of life, in effect a return to the days of a classically pagan Greece and
Rome. Despite his nostalgic attempts to hold his personal investment
in the German language, poetry, philosophy, and even mythology in re-
serve, Heine resolved to find his new ideological home in the forefront
of Saint-Simon's utopian socialism. After many years spent searching
for both a way out of his intellectual dilemma and a solution to his
own personal identity crisis, Heine felt that he had discovered in the
utopian socialism of Saint-Simon a world view that would cure him of
his German-Jewish schizophrenia. A sure sign of his new beliefs can be
seen in the closing section of a revised version of *Rabbi von Bacharach*,
completed during this time, which turns away from the troubled history of the Jewish people to concentrate on a Jewish free thinker who,
after rejecting religious orthodoxy, discovers that the only thing worth
saving from Jewish culture is the fine art of Jewish cooking.

It must be said, however, that this utopian euphoria did not last very
long. As the 1840s ran their course and Heine's health worsened to the
point where he was bedridden, his mood once again darkened, especially after 1848, when he saw that the longed-for revolution did not
take on the form he had envisioned for such a popular uprising. Whereas
in the mid-1830s he had spun out his paradisical dreams of a liber-

ated life, filled with "nectar and ambrosia, purple mantles, costly fragrances, voluptuousness and splendor, the dances of laughing nymphs, music and comedy,"[13] by the late 1840s he was more and more taken by ethical and/or religious impulses, impulses that led him once again to take an interest in the history of all peoples and classes still suffering from oppression. In support of this conclusion, we can call not only on Heine's *Geständnisse* [Confessions], his *Hebräische Melodien* [Hebrew Melodies], or the last poems from the so-called *Matratzengruft* [Mattress Grave], all of which speak of his renewed interest in his Jewish background; we also find Heine's quite moving comments regarding *Uncle Tom's Cabin*, a book that, after many years of liberal-atheistic hubris, finally made it clear to Heine that the oppressed with their backs whipped bloody by their oppressors understand more of the ways of this world than all the arrogant liberal intellectuals with their misguided knowledge and their excessive claims for what constitutes the good life.[14] In the wake of these insights Heine finally gave up his half Left Hegelian, half Saint-Simonian belief in the efficacy of a reformist avantgarde, an avant-garde that he had earlier regarded as the moving force behind all progressive change. Insights into ethical necessities and the happiness of the common man, rather than the earlier aesthetic pipe dreams, determined Heine's thinking during the last years of his life.[15] Although it would be wrong to describe this turning point solely in religious terms, or to say categorically that Heine had returned to the God of his fathers, he nevertheless energetically rejected any way of life that severed ties to the religious hopes and beliefs of the masses. For this reason alone, he seemed suspect to the Communist movement inspired by Marx, although Heine still followed the movement's growth with great interest.

This interest was not uncritical acceptance, however. Heine felt strongly that Marx's atheistic doctrine lacked a system of belief grounded in the trials and tribulations of the oppressed peoples of this world. For Heine, even Communism seemed marked by the arrogance of intellectuals striving for their own emancipation, in the process distancing themselves from the people. In the end, Heine died without the benefit of prayer, without the reading of Kaddish, without any religious blessings—and yet he died as a believing sympathizer, if not a partisan, of all oppressed peoples. He did not die as a well-meaning yet pleasure-seeking and parasitic liberal who set up his demands on life and his own egotistical desires for personal success as the measure of all things.

Thus as German, Jew, and liberal, Heine confronted the evils of his era by championing those tendencies he felt were the most progressive. That his life was more multifaceted than this brief summary might suggest goes without saying. A biography filled with as many contradictions and tensions as Heine's furnished enough fuel for dozens of polemical fires, both during his lifetime and long after his death in 1856, polemics that covered the spectrum from anti-Semitic defamations to panegyric effusions. As already mentioned, during the nineteenth century Heine's most enthusiastic admirers could be found first in those Western democracies where the bourgeois liberals set the tone, followed closely by those Spanish- and Slavic-speaking countries with viable bourgeois liberal movements.

In such places an image of Heine was established which, in line with the legitimation strategies of the various countries and movements, presented him as the great liberal, as a man who suffered under the political, social, and moral restrictions of a time still bound by feudalistic traditions, a man who saw the constraints on the free development of his own personality, who yearned for a greater depth of experience, who stood up for the open criticism of all reactionary ideologies and demanded that in all areas of human endeavor the individual had the right to move freely. In short, Heine was seen as a man who brought to bear against the powers of both the old aristocracy and the nouveau riche plutocrats a rhetoric based on a classically liberal conception of freedom, a rhetoric that, much to the delight of Heine's liberal admirers, envisaged a leading ideological role for intellectuals such as themselves in the new liberal society to come. In the face of an expanding capitalism, however, the bourgeois liberals of these countries and movements saw for the most part in Heine—and in themselves as well—a bourgeois outsider rather than an ideological leader of the bourgeoisie, an outsider whom they, yielding to their own utopian illusions, tended to envelop in the aura of avant-gardism or at least of modernism. Although many of these liberals, after scrutinizing more closely both their economic and political possibilities under capitalism, were subject to a wistful melancholy when forced to acknowledge that their pipe dream of a hedonistic, fully emancipated, and antiauthoritarian society probably never would be realized, they nevertheless continued to place their hopes in a liberal utopian vision of material abundance. In their eyes, such a utopia would allow no restrictions, offering instead nectar and ambrosia, music, comedy, and the dances of laughing nymphs, to use Heine's rhetoric. In a

time of ever-increasing material expectations, spurred by a rising standard of living, this new materialistic utopia replaced the former political utopias in the hearts and minds of most liberals.

With this change of utopian paradigms, the specifically Jewish component of Heine's liberalism—namely, that component dealing with all
forms of discrimination directed against the Jews—was for the most
part suppressed, along with all those leftist elements of Heine's liberalism which called for solidarity with the oppressed peoples and classes
of the world. In the eyes of most bourgeois liberals of the newly industrialized West, the order of the day lay in providing for their own
well-being, their own pleasure, their own freely developing personalities. As bourgeois liberalism became increasingly more parasitic, abandoning its ideals and its universalist ambitions for the sake of narrow
class interests, the notion of standing up for the rights of the oppressed
in other countries generated less and less interest.

On turning to the situation in Germany during the late nineteenth
century, we see a completely different pattern of Heine reception. This
contrast has much to do with the specific character of German liberalism, which suffered a major setback in the 1848 Revolution and was
able to get back on its feet during the 1850s and 1860s only by adopting a strongly nationalist program.[16] Such a strategy allowed these new
"national liberals" to trumpet the popular cause of German unification, but it also meant that all those who did not sympathize with German nationalism were more or less relegated to the status of outsiders.
As a result, those Jewish intellectuals who did not express unreserved
support for Bismarck's policies were labeled *Vaterlandslose Gesellen*
[rogues without a country], along with the unreconstructed left-wing
liberals of the 1848 Revolution and those aligned with the increasingly
oppositional Social Democrats. In the wake of such developments, the
attacks on Heine made by the German nationalists grew in intensity.[17]
Especially after the Franco-Prussian War and the founding of the Second
German Reich in 1871, when anti-French and anti-Semitic tendencies
grew tremendously, the nationalist camp did all in its power to expel a
"Frenchified Jew" such as Heine from the German cultural sphere.

It was not merely the small-time journalists who, filled with envy
and resentment, gleefully fell on Heine during this time; the osten-
sible greats of the nation also took Heine to task. Wilhelm Dilthey
stated simply that Heine as a Jew lacked any "positive, comfortable
relationship to both his country and his society," that Heine had con-

tributed to a "growing demoralization," to "nihilism," to "laxity," and
to a "dissolute glorification of the flesh and the senses."[18] Karl Goedeke
(1814–1887) referred to Heine's poetry as "flowers of poison" and pil-
loried Heine's "sharp, caustic wit" as an unfortunate manifestation of
his "Jewishness."[19] Heinrich von Treitschke (1834–1896) characterized
Heine as being "clever without being profound," "witty without convictions," "selfish, lascivious, mendacious and spineless," an "unpatriotic
German Jew" who lacked the "massive Aryan strength" necessary to
bring forth a truly great work. On top of that, Treitschke complained
that Heine, and in his opinion almost all other German Jews, felt only
indifference toward the "Greats of our Fatherland's history."[20] Franz
Sandvoß labeled the much-maligned Heine a "thorn in our flesh"[21] in
an 1888 pamphlet (Was dünket euch um Heine? [What Do You Think of
Heine?]) that was a veritable catalog of the aspersions cast against Heine
during this period.

The post-1871 German nationalists saw in Heine only an immoral
wag, a spineless scribbler without any sense of German nationalist
virtues, virtues easily summed up in terms such as the homeland, the
German temperament, depth of soul, inwardness, a sense of community, comradeship, solidarity. For them, Heine was merely an exponent
of Western liberalism, a doctrine that in their eyes was based on the
vices of egoism, sensualism, and gossip mongering. Characteristically,
many of these nationalists capped their arguments by asserting that the
best representatives of this Western liberalism were, of course, "rootless
Jews" such as Heine.

In view of the rising tide of chauvinism and the accompanying anti-
Semitism in post-1871 Germany, one question must have dominated
the thoughts of those Jewish and non-Jewish German liberals sympathetic to Heine: how could one counteract this abusive campaign directed against their hero? For many, the answer lay in distancing Heine
as far as possible from the more inflammatory movements of the early
nineteenth century, such as Young Germany, Left Hegelianism, or Utopian Socialism, and in their stead stressing Heine's ties to more respectable (because more "truly German") movements such as Weimar Classicism or the Heidelberg and Jena variants of German Romanticism. In
interpretations of this kind a bowdlerized version of Heine, cleansed of
the great historical-philosophical essays and his Wintermärchen [Win-
ter's Tale], could be presented as the sensitive poet who, especially in his
collection Buch der Lieder [Book of Songs] demonstrated as much feel-

ing and German temperament as the great Goethe. Instead of following
older liberals such as Karl Emil Franzos, who had laid special emphasis
on Heine's social criticism, his irony, and his biting political wit, these
new liberal defenders of Heine presented him as a sugared-over senti-
mentalist, destined to find his proper place between the gilded covers
of countless Wilhelminian poetry anthologies as a charming singer of
German virtues. Even a reputable Heine scholar such as Ernst Elster,
editor of the first critical edition of Heine's works, was not entirely free
from such tendencies. In the prefaces and commentaries included in
his Heine edition of the late 1880s, Elster stressed the poet's power of
feeling and his bonds with nature, at the same time distancing himself with as much vehemence as the anti-Heine nationalists from the
immoral, Frenchified dandy of "Verschiedene" and the positively scan-
dalous Platen affair.[22]

In such reactions we can see mirrored *in nuce* the decline of the
whole liberal movement in Wilhelminian Germany. Instead of continuing to steer an oppositional course, most of the liberals in this period
either limited themselves to a merely defensive strategy or withdrew
(in Thomas Mann's words) into the "power-protected inwardness" of
the various apolitical secessionist movements of the time, movements
in which they felt free to embrace an uncommitted aestheticism. As a
result, they abandoned their stake in the ideological discourse, ceding
it to the Wilhelminian ruling elite and to the representatives of the so-
called *völkische Opposition*, that is to say, the German Nationals, the
All-Germans, and other protofascist groups. This "opposition" was to
a large extent anti-Semitic and, not surprisingly, showered Heine with
abuse. Such invectives proved to be quite effective, especially between
1897 and 1906, when, respectively, the one hundredth anniversary of
Heine's birth and the fiftieth anniversary of his death neared. The few
liberals who headed efforts to erect Heine memorials met with considerable resistance. The "high point" (if one can use the term) of this
campaign against Heine was assuredly Adolf Bartels's 1906 book *Heinrich Heine: Auch ein Denkmal* [Yet Another Memorial], in which the
author set out to prove that Goedeke, Treitschke, and all the others
were quite right to reject Heine. In Bartels's study we can read that
Heine was in no way a poet, but rather a parasitic Jewish journalist who
made a living plagiarizing other poets.[23] Bartels characterized Heine's
political convictions as "a mixture of cheap opportunism and Jewish
deconstructiveness" and attributed Heine's world view to a "material-

ism of half-Young Hegelian, half-Saint-Simonian origins disguised as Pantheism." As for the influence of German culture and customs on Heine's inner being, Bartels claimed that no evidence of such influence could be found.[24]

In the face of such campaigns against Heine, even many German and Austrian Jews began to have their doubts about Heine, and some of them joined the anti-Heine forces. The best-known example of this trend is Karl Kraus (1874–1936), who, in his 1910 essay "Heine und die Folgen," laid the responsibility for the general degeneration of language and the ever-expanding liberal passion for journalistic mass influence squarely on Heine's shoulders. Kraus's apodictic judgment: "Without Heine, no *feuilleton*—that is the French disease he has introduced here."[25] Similar judgments were later made by Friedrich Gundolf and Rudolf Borchardt.

Not all German liberals let themselves be trapped by the reigning anti-Heine sentiment, however. Gustav Karpeles, Johannes Proelß, and Paul Nerrlich continued in the tradition of Franzos, offering a liberal view of Heine in their publications of the 1880s and 1890s. Meanwhile, many Jewish liberals, disgusted by the degrading debate over the various Heine memorials and inspired perhaps by the first stirrings of Zionism, decided to reclaim for the Jewish cause that poet German nationals had cast out from German cultural life. Examples of this trend include M. Bienenstock's 1910 study *Das jüdische Element in Heines Werk* [The Jewish Element in Heine's Work] and Georg L. Plotke's 1913 work *Heine als Dichter des Judentums* [Heine as Poet of Jewry].[26] And yet such voices raised in defense of Heine only sharpened the debate, since praise for Heine as a Jew and a liberal actually supplied the German nationalist camp with more anti-Heine ammunition. A relative lull in the polemical storm came only in the middle 1920s, when the consolidation of the Weimar Republic brought with it an atmosphere in which left-wing liberalism was once more allowed to show its face. To be sure, the Weimar Republic represented in this area merely a brief intermezzo, endangered by the fact that the same tolerance that permitted the appearance of left-wing liberalism also allowed the rise of a new wave of anti-Semitism.[27] Men such as Ludwig Marcuse, who at this time were arguing for a greater appreciation of Heine, ended up remaining exceptions rather than the rule.

On the part of the nationalist camp, the merciless storm of abuse against Heine continued unabated during the Weimar years. *Der Stürmer* [The Storm Trooper] had already labeled Heine "the Jewish pig from Montmartre" in 1926 and went on to express its indignation that the money of good German taxpayers was being spent for the upkeep of a grave where "a first-rate lout rots."[28] The bourgeoisie may have merely smiled at such phrases in 1926, if they took any notice of them, and yet this same bourgeoisie would, because of the lack of a liberal consciousness, run in droves to join the National Socialists after 1929. When in January 1933 the transfer of power to Hitler finally took place, there was no longer room for Heine in Germany. Aside from his "Lore-Ley," which was in any event designated an anonymous folksong, both Heine and his work could be seen only from the official standpoint of someone like Bartels, a standpoint that critics such as Ewald Geißler and Eduard Fuchs slavishly followed over the course of the next few years.[29] A positive assessment of Heine from a German perspective was possible after 1933 only in exile, while in Germany Heine suffered the same fate of all other German Jews, that is to say, total liquidation.

After Auschwitz and the founding of a Jewish state in the British protectorate of Palestine, the whole question of Heine as a German Jew must be seen in a new light. Auschwitz throws such a long shadow over the entire expanse of German-Jewish history that anyone who approaches the topic with both a critical-historical perspective and an intuitive sense of the dismaying questions such a history raises is immediately caught up short by feelings of unease, feelings that no one should attempt to brush aside. After these events the case of Heine can no longer be thought of as a purely academic matter, especially for Germans. Rather, it must be seen as a case that constantly raises questions concerning the course of German history, a history replete with countless failures, including, among others, the failure to develop a truly liberal consciousness. In the face of such issues, it would be inappropriate simply to move ahead with one's own personal or political agenda. When dealing with such questions, there can be no sense of relief that the guilt is now too remote to concern us, no sense that the work of mourning is completed or that one has finally come to terms with the past. Here, everything remains unsettled, at least for those who are inspired by liberal ideals, who continue to hope for a renewed German-Jewish dialogue, and who work at making amends for that which can hardly be mended. Seen in this light, the case of Heine remains for all those deeply affected by it a subject whose tensions and inner contradictions grow rather than recede the deeper one delves into it. For Heine is not an average liberal, but rather a German-Jewish liberal whose nature one cannot begin to comprehend until one has developed a better understanding of the triple symbiosis at work here, the symbiosis of German, Jew, and liberal. When one speaks of Heine, then, one should also think through this aspect of his work. In this way Heine has managed to bequeath to the Germans a highly exasperating legacy. That is especially true for those intellectuals who, unsure about their own national and social identity, experience uneasiness when faced with the enormity of the crimes committed against the Jews between 1933 and 1945 by the Nazis, an uneasiness that unfortunately cannot be dispelled merely by good intentions alone.

Thus, it seems essential that both Jewish and non-Jewish Germans who deal with Heine should approach their subject with special caution, in effect resisting the temptation to appropriate Heine for German, Jewish, or liberal goals as part of larger strategies of legitimation. Those trying to come to terms with Heine's works should always bring to their readings an understanding of Heine's tripolar identity, not merely for the sake of any vague sense of historical justice, but rather for the sake of a better understanding of fundamental questions of personal identity, an understanding that might help one avoid the traps of ideological one-sidedness to which other Heine critics have been prone. After all, Heine constantly thematized such questions in his own work. In this respect he has remained the most important author for those affected by such questions of identity, an author who, because of his tripolar identity, is able to challenge all forms of naive self-certainty. He forces his readers constantly to reexamine all deeply cherished convictions, requiring of them a double or even triple perspective. In the end, he often exasperates his readers by confronting them on the highly personalized level of their own identities. Heine's goal, it would seem, is to ensure that his readers are never left in peace. For he is a writer who not only illustrates for his readers the collapse of the German-Jewish symbiosis and the failure of German liberalism,[30] he also forces his readers, through a series of incisive formulations, to confront their own problematic status as bourgeois intellectuals, a status based on the privileged nature of their social and ideological position. With Heine, nothing can be subsumed into those higher unities of a national, religious, or castelike nature which promise their adherents a cosy sense of security. Everything with Heine has the status of unfulfilled demands; everything remains a challenge not to reconcile oneself prematurely with harsh realities, but rather to move against such realities with a critical and/or utopian perspective.

And yet it is not only German readers who have failed to appreciate Heine's human and political legacy. The Israelis should also one day
come to terms with Heine, once their main energies are no longer solely
directed toward their struggle for national preservation. They must develop a better relationship to that part of their history (or perhaps pre-
history) which stood under the sign of a sympathetic appropriation of
Western European liberalism. Continuing to characterize this process
of liberalization as merely an ominous sign of the assimilation that hindered the development of a truly Jewish sense of identity would be as
shortsighted as rejecting for the same reasons the European Enlightenment as a whole.

Such problems are far from being the only ones to arise in this area,
for Heine did not leave his exasperating legacy merely to the liberals
among Germans and Israelis; he left it as well to liberals of all the Western nations. From the example of Heine one can learn that liberalism
does not necessarily mean simply egoism, the desire to succeed, self-
realization, culinarism, a hedonistic craving for pleasure: in short, ego
boosting. It can also mean political engagement, a social conscience,
and solidarity with the oppressed peoples of this world, as well as a biting social criticism. For who, if not Heine, actually lived through all of
these stages, often to the point of excess, while showing that he was
capable of actually drawing a lesson from them? In his early German
phase he played off his own unfettered subjectivity against the restrictions of the Metternichean restoration and the anti-Semitism of his surroundings; that is to say, he provided ample opportunities for scandal,
he provoked the established greats of his time, he wore his Romantic
discontent on his sleeve; in a word, he showed that a German-Jewish
liberal could only prove a constant source of embarassment in this kind
of a society. In his first Parisian years, on the other hand, he swore
allegiance to an equally provocative form of subjectivism. Inspired by
the ideals of Saint-Simon, he abandoned himself to the dream that the
highest form of freedom consisted in the enjoyment of nectar and ambrosia, of music, comedy, and the dances of laughing nymphs. It should
come as no surprise, therefore, that during this period Heine was relatively indifferent to concepts such as equality, community, religious
ties, *camaraderie*, or *fraternité*. In fact, he often made fun of such ideals,
seeing the telos of his life more in terms of an unshackled eroticism and
a privileged notion of personal freedom. Only during his later Parisian
years, when he was made bitterly aware through personal experience of

the transitory nature of all things of the flesh, did his opinions change. Spurred by his own physical pain, he once again turned his thoughts to the Jews, the blacks, and other oppressed peoples and classes and in the end placed the notion of ethical necessity above his earlier liberal dream of erotic-culinary privilege.

The changes Heine went through served to spare him from the ideological shallowness so common among the liberals or Young Germans of his time,[31] a shallowness that led many to concentrate solely on the struggle for broadening their own personal freedoms. In the process, many tended to forget the misery of all those still struggling for the basic necessities of life, that is to say, all those who could not even afford the luxury of intellectual and personal freedom. One should therefore not claim Heine as an advocate for a notion of freedom based merely on the expansion of certain privileges. Underlying his work, especially that of his earliest and latest periods, there is often a highly discerning dialectical perspective, one that is able to keep both the changes in the ideological superstructure and the relationships found within the material base in sight. It was this perspective that saved Heine from that form of parasitic liberalism which puts its trust in progress defined in terms of unfettered freedom, a liberalism that, in the euphoria of this purely individualistic conception of freedom, loses all sense for the ideas of solidarity, the common good, or the material needs of others, in effect equating freedom with the divestiture of all previous ties, norms, and responsibilities. Such a position leads inevitably to an ideal of the liberal as "the man on the fence," someone who no longer involves himself in social issues, no longer allows himself to be used for political purposes, and rejects anything that might stand in the way of his own self-realization as being tainted with ideology.

This position has become increasingly popular among Western liberals since the mid-1970s. In this camp it is fashionable to label Heine, in conformity with the liberals' own predisposition, an intellectual "on the fence" and to emphasize his tendencies toward "noncommittalness." As Robert C. Holub expressed it in 1982, such liberals, especially in the United States and the Federal Republic, use Heine's works merely as a means to "legitimate the dominant society, while at the same time moving against both the critical tendencies of the Left and the Left's view of Heine."[32] For them, Heine, like all "good liberals" in their opinion, can never be "grasped," can never be "pinned down." He is someone who, through his skillful opportunism, managed to evade all ideological labels and strictures. And if we are to believe these liberal interpretations, that is precisely what was admirable about Heine: in this sense he serves as a role model for today's intellectuals who, faced by a totalitarian or a technocratic world, find as well that their only refuge lies in the private or aesthetic sphere. One such right-of-center liberal captures this mood exactly when he says of Heine that "he was a man who preferred to live in peace with the powers of this world, in order that he would be able to encounter those adventures that were properly and immediately his: artistic adventures."[33]

When we are asked today to determine whom we should defend Heine from, the answer would be not the anti-Semites, but rather the false heirs of Heine's liberalism, heirs who want to interpret Heine in terms of their own privileged positions or their own opportunism. In moving against such false heirs, one cannot merely invoke Heine's love of freedom; one must also invoke his understanding of difference, oppression, and suffering. This understanding enabled Heine intermittently to rise above traditional notions of bourgeois liberalism, in effect approaching those utopian socialist visions of society in which the freedoms of the privileged are no longer achieved by exploiting and oppressing the underprivileged. When Heine mixed his critical views with a utopian perspective, he was no longer functioning as one more bourgeois liberal among many; here he was a Left Hegelian German, a Utopian Socialist Frenchman, and a Jew striving for emancipation. With this triple role came a keener perspective on the existing conditions of his time, a perspective superior to that of most of his liberal contemporaries. The self-assured nature of their national allegiances may not have hindered some attempts at social criticism or reformist aspirations, yet in their efforts one notices the lack of a specifically revolutionary potential, not to speak of the lack of a utopian perspective. Today, when reading Heine, one should bring precisely this perspective to bear on the text.

NOTES

1. Jost Hermand, *Streitobjekt Heine: Ein Forschungsbericht 1945–1975* (Frankfurt am Main: Athenäum Fischer, 1975), pp. 21ff.
2. See Fritz J. Raddatz, *Heine: Ein deutsches Märchen* (Hamburg: Hoffmann & Campe, 1977).
3. Jürgen Habermas, "Heinrich Heine und die Rolle der Intellektuellen in Deutschland," *Merkur* 448 (1986): 453–468.

4. Theodor W. Adorno, "Die Wunde Heine," *Noten zur Literatur,* in *Gesammelte Schriften,* vol. 11 (Frankfurt am Main: Suhrkamp, 1974); Ludwig Rosenthal, *Heinrich Heine als Jude* (Frankfurt am Main: Ullstein, 1973); Hans Mayer, *Außenseiter* (Frankfurt am Main: Suhrkamp, 1975).

5. Jeffrey L. Sammons, *Heinrich Heine: The Elusive Poet* (New Haven and London: Yale University Press, 1969), p. 451.

6. Walter Grab, "Heine und die deutsche Revolution von 1848," in *Der späte Heine 1848–1856,* ed. Wilhelm Gössmann and Joseph A. Kruse (Hamburg: Hoffmann & Campe, 1982), pp. 147–173.

7. Hermand, *Streitobjekt,* pp. 16–18.

8. Hugo Bieber, "Recent Literature on Heine's Attitude toward Judaism," *Historica Judaica* 10 (1948): 175–183; see also Israel Taback, *Judaic Lore in Heine: The Heritage of a Poet* (Baltimore: Johns Hopkins University Press, 1948).

9. See Hermand, *Streitobjekt,* pp. 127–130; and Sammons, *Elusive Poet,* pp. 446–465. One of the better newer studies dealing with this topic is Michael Werner's "Heinrich Heine: Über die Interdependenz von jüdischer, deutscher und europäischer Identität in seinem Werk," in *Juden im Vormärz und in der Revolution von 1848,* ed. Walter Grab and Julius H. Schoeps (Stuttgart: Burg, 1983), pp. 9–28.

10. Jost Hermand, "Eine Jugend in Deutschland: Heinrich Heine und die Burschenschaften," in *Jahrbuch des Instituts für deutsche Geschichte der Universität Tel Aviv* 4 (1982): 111–135.

11. Heinrich Heine, *Werke-Briefwechsel-Lebenszeugnisse,* 27 vols., Säkularausgabe (Berlin: Akademie; Paris: Editions du Centre National de la Recherche Scientifique, 1970), 20:106. Bracketed translations from the German here and throughout this chapter supplied by Paul Levesque.

12. Cited in Heinrich Heine, *Jüdisches Manifest,* ed. Hugo Bieber (New York: Mary S. Rosenberg, 1946), p. 112.

13. Jost Hermand, "Gewinn im Verlust: Zu Heines Geschichtsphilosophie," *Text und Kritik* 18/19 [Heinrich Heine Special Issue] (1982, rev. ed. of 1968 issue): 56.

14. Heinrich Heine, *Sämtliche Schriften,* ed. Klaus Briegleb, 6 vols. (Munich: Hanser, 1968–76), 6:480–481.

15. See Hermand, "Gewinn im Verlust," pp. 61–63.

16. Peter U. Hohendahl, *Literarische Kultur im Zeitalter des Liberalismus 1830–1870* (Munich: C. H. Beck, 1985), pp. 160–165.

17. Jürgen Brummack, ed., *Heinrich Heine: Epoche-Werke-Wirkung* (Munich: C. H. Beck, 1980), pp. 320–323.

18. Translated from Wilhelm Dilthey, "Heinrich Heine," in his *Gesammelte Schriften,* ed. Ulrich Hermann (Göttingen: Vandenhoeck & Ruprecht, 1970), 15:205–244.

19. Translated from Karl Goedeke, *Grundriß zur Geschichte der deutschen Dichtung* (Dresden: Ehlermann, 1881), 3:437–465.
20. Translated from Heinrich von Treitschke, *Deutsche Geschichte im 19. Jahrhundert* (Leipzig, 1928), 3:694 and 4:409.
21. Translated from Xantippus [Franz Sandvoß], *Was dünket euch um Heine? Ein Bekenntnis* (Leipzig, 1888). See also Brummack, *Epoche-Werke-Wirkung*, p. 293.
22. Heinrich Heine, *Sämtliche Werke*, ed. Ernst Elster (Leipzig and Vienna: Bibliographisches Institut, 1887, 1888), 3:205–207.
23. See Brummack, *Epoche-Werke-Wirkung*, pp. 325–326.
24. Translated from Adolf Bartels, *Geschichte der deutschen Literatur* (Leipzig: Eduard Avenarius, 1902), 2:351, 343.
25. Translated from Karl Kraus, *Werke*, ed. Heinrich Fischer, 14 vols. (Munich: Kösel, 1952–64), 8:189.
26. See Sammons, *Elusive Poet*, pp. 454–455.
27. See Walter Grab and Julius H. Schoeps, eds., *Juden in der Weimarer Republik* (Stuttgart: Burg, 1986).
28. Translated from Hermann Glaser, *Spießer-Ideologie*, 2d ed. (Freiburg: Rombach, 1964), p. 91.
29. Hartmut Kircher, *Heinrich Heine und das Judentum* (Bonn: Bouvier, 1973), pp. 12–13.
30. See preface to Jost Hermand and Gert Mattenklott, eds., *Jüdische Intelligenz in Deutschland* (Hamburg: Argument, 1988).
31. Jost Hermand, "Jungdeutscher Tempelsturm: Zur Austreibung des Poetischen aus der Literatur," in *Das Junge Deutschland*, ed. Joseph A. Kruse and Bernd Kortländer (Hamburg: Hoffmann & Campe, 1987), pp. 65–82.
32. Translated from Robert C. Holub, "Zwischen allen Stühlen: Zum Bankrott der liberalen Heine-Legende," *Text und Kritik* 18/19 (1982, rev. ed. of 1968 issue): 117.
33. Translated from Raddatz, *Ein deutsches Märchen*, p. 137.

WORKS CITED

Adorno, Theodor W. "Die Wunde Heine." *Noten zur Literatur*. In *Gesammelte Schriften*, vol. 11. Frankfurt am Main: Suhrkamp, 1974.

Bartels, Adolf. *Geschichte der deutschen Literatur*. Leipzig: Eduard Avenarius, 1902.

Bieber, Hugo. "Recent Literature on Heine's Attitude toward Judaism." *Historica Judaica* 10 (1948): 175–183.

Brummack, Jürgen, ed. *Heinrich Heine: Epoche-Werke-Wirkung*. Munich: C. H. Beck, 1980.

Dilthey, Wilhelm. "Heinrich Heine." In Wilhelm Dilthey, *Gesammelte Schriften*, ed. Ulrich Hermann. Göttingen: Vandenhoeck & Ruprecht, 1970.

Glaser, Hermann. *Spießer-Ideologie*. 2d ed. Freiburg: Rombach, 1964.

Goedeke, Karl. *Grundriß zur Geschichte der deutschen Dichtung*. Dresden: Ehlermann, 1881.

Grab, Walter. "Heine und die deutsche Revolution von 1848." In *Der späte Heine 1848–1856*, ed. Wilhelm Gössmann and Joseph A. Kruse. Hamburg: Hoffmann & Campe, 1982.

Grab, Walter, and Julius H. Schoeps, eds. *Juden in der Weimarer Republik*. Stuttgart: Burg, 1986.

Habermas, Jürgen. "Heinrich Heine und die Rolle der Intellektuellen in Deutschland." *Merkur* 448 (1986): 453–468.

Heine, Heinrich. *Jüdisches Manifest*. Ed. Hugo Bieber. New York: Mary S. Rosenberg, 1946.

———. *Sämtliche Schriften*. Ed. Klaus Briegleb. 6 vols. Munich: Hanser, 1968–76.

———. *Sämtliche Werke*. Ed. Ernst Elster. Leipzig and Vienna: Bibliographisches Institut, 1887, 1888.

———. *Werke-Briefwechsel-Lebenszeugnisse*. 27 vols. Säkularausgabe. Berlin: Akademie; Paris: Editions du Centre National de la Recherche Scientifique, 1970.

Hermand, Jost. "Eine Jugend in Deutschland: Heinrich Heine und die Burschenschaften." *Jahrbuch des Instituts für deutsche Geschichte der Universität Tel Aviv* 4 (1982).

———. "Gewinn im Verlust: Zu Heines Geschichtsphilosophie." *Text und Kritik* 18/19 [Heinrich Heine Special Issue] (1982, rev. ed. of 1968 issue): 65–82.

———. "Jungdeutscher Tempelsturm: Zur Austreibung des Poetischen aus der Literatur," in *Das Junge Deutschland*, ed. Joseph A. Kruse and Bernd Kortländer. Hamburg: Hoffmann & Campe, 1987.

———. *Streitobjekt Heine: Ein Forschungsbericht 1945–1975*. Frankfurt am Main: Athenäum Fischer, 1975.

Hermand, Jost, and Gert Mattenklott, eds. *Jüdische Intelligenz in Deutschland*. Hamburg: Argument, 1988.

Hohendahl, Peter U. *Literarische Kultur im Zeitalter des Liberalismus, 1830–1870*. Munich: C. H. Beck, 1985.

Holub, Robert C. "Zwischen allen Stühlen: Zum Bankrott der liberalen Heine-Legende." *Text und Kritik* 18/19 [Heinrich Heine Special Issue] (1982, rev. ed. of 1968 issue): 117–128.

Kircher, Hartmut. *Heinrich Heine und das Judentum*. Bonn: Bouvier, 1973.

Kraus, Karl. *Werke*. Ed. Heinrich Fischer. 14 vols. Munich: Kösel, 1952–64.

Mayer, Hans. *Außenseiter*. Frankfurt am Main: Suhrkamp, 1975.

Raddatz, Fritz J. *Heine: Ein deutsches Märchen*. Hamburg: Hoffmann & Campe, 1977.

Rosenthal, Ludwig. *Heinrich Heine als Jude*. Frankfurt am Main: Ullstein, 1973.

Sammons, Jeffrey L. *Heinrich Heine: The Elusive Poet*. New Haven and London: Yale University Press, 1969.

Taback, Israel. *Judaic Lore in Heine: The Heritage of a Poet*. Baltimore: Johns Hopkins University Press, 1948.

von Treitschke, Heinrich. *Deutsche Geschichte im 19. Jahrhundert*. Leipzig, 1928.

Werner, Michael. "Heinrich Heine: Über die Interdependenz von jüdischer, deutscher und europäischer Identität in seinem Werk." In *Juden im Vormärz und in der Revolution von 1848*, ed. Walter Grab and Julius H. Schoeps. Stuttgart: Burg, 1983.

Xantippus [Franz Sandvoß]. *Was dünket euch um Heine? Ein Bekenntnis*. Leipzig, 1888.

MICHAEL WERNER

Crossing Borders between Cultures:
On the Preconditions and Function
of Heine's Reception in France

I t may seem rather like carrying coals to Newcastle
to point, in a country like the United States, to
problems that arise from the clashing and merging of cultures. Yet to relate problems of acculturation to processes of literary reception has not
up to now been customary. And in fact, the theme of Heine's reception
in the West poses fundamental questions of transnational acculturation. How do modern national cultures work on and through "foreign"
cultural artifacts, artifacts lying outside their horizon of understanding?
What factors determine their reception? Is it determined by the artifact
itself, the object of reception, or the receiving culture? If, as one ex-
pects, both the reception object and the reception culture are involved,
how do these two domains relate to each other? These complex relations point, of course, far beyond the particular case of Heine, and they
should not be elaborated here as only more or less speculative generalities. On the other hand, however, Heine philology has suffered from the
fact that the problem has not been perceived as such. Was it not Heine
who served as living proof for the obvious supposition that one can successfully mediate between cultures? Is his work not a textbook case of
the translatability, of the boundary-transcending international traffic of
cultural artifacts? The evidence that Heine's reception in France made
him well known there, however, doesn't by itself say much about the
specificity of the process. And, if we recall Heine's more or less intense
relationship with the Parisian literary activity of his day, we might create the (not necessarily correct) impression of a fully achieved literary
and social integration, as though Heine had been an immediately recognized magnate among the French literati of the July Monarchy.[1]

Translated by Andreas Kriefall

Abandoning a familiar cultural environment with its specific points of reference exposes one to a process of reorientation that, especially for a writer in a country with a foreign language, can bring about far-reaching changes. Conversely, even cultures that are for the most part open and receptive to foreigners generally submit the outsider to acculturation pressures, if only for the simple reason that self-assertion may not be possible in the long run without a mastery of the appropriate internal social and linguistic codes. Heine's case is especially apt for a consideration of the fundamental dimension of such problems. In studying them, I wish in each instance to juxtapose the double perspectives of historical biography and work reception to view the problematic in all its complexity.

One can sum up Heine's reception in France[2] in the following somewhat simplified paradox: failure during his lifetime, though he participated actively at the center of literary life; and success after his death, once he had to a certain extent fallen in line and little distinguished him from the "average" German writer. Actually, this paradox obscures the harmonies and tensions between Heine's strategies for conquest or retreat and the general circumstances of the reception of German literature in France during the nineteenth century. Furthermore, the level of Heine's recognition in France has markedly fallen since the end of World War II. Today a relatively intense academic interest[3] continues in the face of the rather depressing fact that for the broader public Heine has become an unknown great.

Heine was not the first German writer to settle in Paris for the long run. In the second half of the eighteenth century, for instance, the assimilation of Friedrich Melchior Grimm (1723–1807) and Baron von Holbach (1723–1789) was so complete that hardly a single French lexicon of the time designated them as Germans. During the Empire and the Restoration a colony of middle-class Germans already existed in Paris, and it boasted a number of German authors and literarily active intellectuals. One thinks of Jacobins such as Georg Forster, C. F. Cramer, and Michael Huber; of K. F. Reinhardt, K. B. Hase, and Julius Mohl; and of G. F. Depping and Maximilian Donndorf.[4] It was well known that, one year before Heine's arrival, Ludwig Börne had made his home in Paris. The novelty in Heine's emigration, however, lay in the fact that in this case a German writer, after a short time of self-searching, very deliberately set about conquering the Parisian literary market without giving up his German identity—indeed, aiming on the contrary to promote it to a certain extent.

Several biographical factors seem to have predestined Heine to a change of cultural context. First of all, of course, his German-Jewish descent from the start provided for a certain cultural polysemy. If we define culture as the system that imparts meaning to the objects of everyday life and of the abstract ideational world, then one can observe how Heine, during the time in Berlin when he became more conscious of his German-Jewish identity, underwent a series of cultural displacements. It is no accident that his first plans to emigrate emerged during this phase. That is not meant to imply that the Parisian exile would have necessarily resulted from the double German-Jewish heritage: in any case, this double identity became significant only when it was felt to be a painful split. And it would be just as foolish to represent Heine as some kind of "German by descent," who as a Jew only waited for the chance to cast off the German perspective on things. By referring to the potential polysemy of a bicultural tradition, I merely wish to emphasize that Heine's German-Jewish descent must have made it easier for him to distance himself, to relativize his native cultural context, to register breaks in cultural self-understanding—in short, to be open to new cultural systems and the problem of mediating between them.

A second, equally important sociohistorical-biographical factor was the failure of his professional-social integration into the society of the German restoration. The problematic, which I have analyzed in diverse ways in the past,[5] can in its general features be taken for granted: the futile efforts to convert his law study, undertaken solely as a breadwinning occupation, into a state appointment or a position as a lawyer; the miscarrying of his journalistic activity in Munich; and the unsuccessful attempts at a university career in Munich and Berlin—to which one should add that the problem lay not only in the unreceptiveness of Restoration society, but probably also in Heine's own lack of will to succeed or, rather, desire to adapt. In any case, the upshot of his very imperfect integration into German society was that Heine could set out on the journey to France in 1831 without any substantial material entanglement in German affairs and without any personal ties beyond a few friends and family. Though he was already thirty-two years old, his social baggage consisted of little more than a university degree and a few early literary successes.

This biographical background brings us to the third precondition of emigration: Heine's decision to undertake a writing career. Here again the essential facts are well established: the failure of his plans for a bourgeois career forced Heine, who initially by no means wanted such a thing, to venture into the insecure existence of a writer living by the earnings of his pen. The narrow literary market of the Biedermeier period could scarcely feed professional writers and literati, especially if, like Heine, they had become accustomed to middle- or upper-middle-class living standards but at the same time were unwilling (or unable) to hire themselves out as journalistic day laborers. Thus it must have seemed enticing to Heine, the German writer, to acquire through the emigration to Paris both a journalistically interesting and exploitable environment and a more broadly developed and profitable French literary market.

The material conditions of a literary career were not the only basis for Heine's plan to integrate himself, however. Like most of the German liberals of the time, he experienced the ideological pressure of a downright mythical image of France, which strongly demanded conformity—or, at the very least, commentary. Paris was for liberal circles the center of the modern world, a "Jerusalem of freedom," as Heine himself put it, the real location of a symbolic awakening to a better future, the promise of an earthly salvation of humanity. In this sense, the conquest of the Parisian scene signified participation in a suprapersonal historical process, admission into the circle of the "chosen" who were allowed to fight for this salvation.

The mythical exaltation of the city of Paris was completed on a more concrete plane through its big-city aura. As the most heavily populated city on the European continent at that time (in 1830: 850,000 inhabitants), Paris offered a concentration of urban life and civilization unknown in Germany, a mind-altering experience of space and time. The "culture shock" of arriving in Paris had been described again and again by German travelers, especially since the French Revolution.[6] Foremost in this impression was the feeling of an acceleration of time, brought about by a combination of historicopolitical revolutionary experience and antiprovincial urbanity. In addition, there was the sense of an intense spatial focalization: one stood in Paris at the heart of a homogenous, centralized nation-state, which furthermore considered itself the cradle of political, social, and cultural modernity. For Heine, who had, on the one hand, always felt drawn to the metropolis from the small city of Düsseldorf and who had, on the other, experienced the July Revolution as a liberation from historical stagnation and restoration, such a combination of temporal acceleration and spatial centering was particularly meaningful.

It was precisely this symbolic-mythic exaltation that made the attraction of this image of Paris and Heine's expectations of it not entirely unproblematic. A process of disillusionment soon set in, first in the realm of politics, then in the appraisal of French culture (especially high literature). Such distancing is partly a natural process: the rejection of the generalizing perspective of the tourist, the dissolution of stereotypes before the multifarious reality of daily life, inimical to generalities. Besides, one should not forget that Heine's rational distancing was compensated by a deepened emotional devotion to the cheerful everyday life of France (naturally, among other things, also in the form of his life companion, Mathilde), to the "geliebte Pflaster der Boulevards" ["the beloved pavement of the boulevards"].[7] But let us not jump too far ahead; instead, let us turn again to Heine's integration strategy.

The precondition for this strategy was, first, to create social contacts, contacts that could provide access to informal groups and connections, "lobbies" and influential circles of cultural life. In Heine's case these were, during the first years, the Saint-Simonians, the group gathered around the newly established *Revue des deux mondes*, and the circle of *Europe littéraire* (in which Heine did indeed find his first French publisher, Eugène Renduel). Interestingly, Heine abandoned this group strategy relatively quickly. As early as 1832 the arguments about (and among) the Saint-Simonians had given him cause for reflection in this regard. All too often membership in such groups entailed unwonted liabilities, quite apart from the fact that Heine was by nature averse to dissolving his personality in a collective identity. Furthermore, the developments in *Europe littéraire* in 1833, as the paper took more and more of a legitimist Catholic turn, called for caution. Consequently, Heine relied more on personal relations with individual representatives of different groups. He had allies and friends among the Saint-Simonians (Chevalier, Carnot, Duveyrier), among more conservative circles (Mallac, Nisard, Mignet) and newspapers (*Journal des Debats, Le Constitutionnel, Le Temps*), among the moderate republican opposition (Odilon-Barrot), and later also among the early Socialists (Blanc, Sand, Leroux), and others.[8] The common denominator of these relationships was a certain aristocracy of the spirit, a feeling of understanding each other with few words because these individuals thought they had seen through to the essence of their new epoch. National considerations played practically no role in this feeling; their approach to the world was assumed to be, in typical French fashion, universal and supranational: the interests of all humanity were at stake.

Such a network of personal relationships was, however, only conditionally effective if one hoped to convert it into direct sales success in the marketplace. In itself heterogenous, it could sustain no continuous pressure or one-sided demands. Decisive for real success were, on the one hand, the fundamental conditions of the market and the expectations of the public and, on the other, the characteristics of the "product" that Heine was in a position to offer to fulfill those expectations.

In the France of the July Monarchy the overall business outlook for German cultural imports was relatively good. The process of relativizing social norms, which had begun in the eighteenth century, was already rather far advanced: French national culture no longer seemed unquestionably the best, the most tasteful, the most civilized, and so on, or, at the very least, it no longer seemed to exist alone. The *encyclopédistes* had opened a view of the historical specificity of neighboring cultures. Madame de Staël had attempted to add to the work of the *idéologues* by pushing toward alternative standards of judgment beyond francocentric cultural imperialism. The German Jacobins in Paris had awakened interest in German philosophy (Kant) by pointing —forty years before Heine—to the complementarity of French political revolution and German philosophical revolution.[9] François Guizot had, under the empire, made himself the advocate of German pedagogy. After 1815 a continually increasing interest in German scholarship (philosophy, philology, history, law, geography, etc.) developed, which grew by leaps and bounds after the July Revolution, when a whole series of intellectuals more closely acquainted with German affairs entered into power.

So it came about that around 1830—contrary to typical images before then—several competing images of Germany were current in France. We may juxtapose at least two of these basic images: first, the literary Romantic Germany, introduced to public consciousness most notably by de Staël and then supported with relatively numerous translations of German literature (Goethe, Schiller, Lessing, Jean Paul, E. T. A. Hoffman, Z. Werner, and others); and second, the philosophically and scientifically learned Germany of the new universities, an area where things had developed intensely since de Staël's book on Germany. This Germany exercised considerable attraction and prompted a number of young intellectuals (Cousin, Lerminier, Comte, d'Eichthal, Quinet, Michelet)[10] to make special trips there. Later, in the second half of the century, it was to play a fundamental role in the self-understanding of France.

This learned image of Germany possessed a special dynamic even at the beginning of the July Monarchy. The reform of the basic teaching system by Guizot and Cousin and the well-known signs of crisis associated with it (tension between church and state) explain among other things why the realm of learning should prove to be a sector of French cultural and spiritual life especially sensitive to German influence. At this point little distinction was made between German philosophy and German philology—though after 1850, that was increasingly the case. Both subjects were considered areas in which the German mind had set itself up as an example and raised international standards. Naturally, this scholarship could not be imported to France on these terms, since the French still considered themselves the leading European nation, especially in cultural matters. But the growing prestige of German work in the humanities, and soon also in the natural sciences, served to an increasing extent as an authority-establishing argument in debates within France itself. At the time, "objective" knowledge about Germany and German circumstances was minimal, a fact that made the French allusions to German matters easier, since one didn't have to enter into particulars. Still, the tendency was unequivocal: ever more knowledge of the Germans, and in the elite institutions such as the Collège de France and especially the Ecole Normale Supérieure, the preoccupation with German learning became a solid component of teaching and research.[11]

If I revalue here the relative importance of a scholarly-philological image of Germany as against the well-known Romantic one, it is because in my opinion the tensions between these two strains of reception vitally determined Heine's effect in France. Except for *De la France* (the translation of *Französische Zustände* [French Affairs], which appeared in 1833), Heine's first French publications out of the *Reisebilder* [Pictures of Travel] are closest to the realm of the literary Romantic image of Germany. In the press's reviews of both volumes of *Reisebilder/Tableaux de voyage*, first published by Renduel in 1834, the prevailing impression was of Heine as a charming, witty, and formless representative of German fantasy. The political explosiveness of the texts, which had been written about the German situation before 1830, passed largely unnoticed in France. At best, Heine could count on a certain kind of literary-political reception, since German Romanticism possessed a particular valence in the internal French debates over the progress of (French) Romanticism. From this perspective the positive discussions of Heine by exponents of the French literary scene (Léon Gozlan and Hippolyte Carnot) [12] are of special significance. Finally, it is worth noting that in the case of *Tableaux de voyage* a series of reviewers raised the question whether Heine ought to be classified as a French (non-German) German or as a typical representative of the German nation.

With the series of articles on German literature and philosophy and the projected series of books *De l'Allemagne* (1833 and 1835, respectively), [13] Heine published his first writings conceived specifically for the French market, which possessed strategic importance in his plans for conquest. He consciously set about entering the French debates over an authentic image of Germany. The established professional Germany experts (including some of Heine's own competitors) were in part sharply attacked (Cousin) and in part ignored (Lerminier, Quinet). The article on German literature, with its political interpretation of the German "Romantic School," was officially supposed to stay clear of French polemics, according to Heine's own words—although one might still investigate to what degree he could be responding indirectly to representatives of a French "historical school" like Lerminier. But the sections on philosophy and religion in Germany explicitly addressed the internal French discussion. To avoid any doubt on this score, Heine stressed in his preface to *De l'Allemagne* that he was committed to working against the view of German philosophy spread by de Staël, the "grandmother of the doctrinaire." Through de Staël he wanted to strike at the "doctrinaire," that is, the liberal-conservative group around Guizot and Rémusat, and the "grand master of the university," Cousin, to whom Heine also dedicated a special polemical supplement. [14]

Thus Heine was no longer engaging in a literary debate about Romanticism, but was involved in an ideological conflict with eminently political side effects. Before the July Revolution, Cousin had deduced the legitimacy of the French Charter from Hegel's philosophy of history. After the July Revolution he then rose up to become one of the leading intellectual personalities of the new monarchy. The importance of his role in France would be difficult to overestimate: "Grand-Maître de l'Université" (that is, the key figure of the educational system), director of the Ecole Normale Supérieure, later minister of education (1840), leading member of the Academy of Sciences, and long-time president of the national board of examiners for philosophy—his influence on educational structures can be felt in France to this day. Through his position in the Ecole Normale Supérieure he governed an institution designed for the formation of an intellectual elite that had strategic importance for the control of the new education and teaching system. Several significant intellectual personalities, such as Amédée Jacques, Jules Barni, Etienne Vacherot, and Paul Janet, were introduced to German philosophy and philology there by Cousin and his first generation of pupils.[15]

To push his own interpretation of German philosophy against Cousin's thus meant that Heine had to proceed against the dominant, state-sponsored image of Germany. To build up his position as a Germany expert, he had to enter the French discussion, and he did so by launching a subversive critique within the dynamic and explosive part of the debate about Germany: the philosophical-scientific image of Germany, the interpretation of the intellectual-scientific awakening in Germany, the "German Revolution" of the mind. Thus, Heine's target in De l'Allemagne was not really de Staël any longer, but—to put it sharply—the July Monarchy itself.

In a paragraph of the article series on German literature in 1833 Heine had already hinted as much when he wrote:

> Having spoken here of German philosophers, I really must correct an error about German philosophy which I find all too common in France. To wit, since certain Frenchmen have been occupied with Schellingian and Hegelian philosophy, have shared the results of their studies in the French language, and indeed have applied them to French circumstances: since then the friends of clear thinking and freedom have complained that the most ludicrous daydreams and sophisms are being introduced, with which minds will be confused, and every lie and every despotism disguised with the appearance of truth and justice. In a word, these noble persons, concerned for the interests of liberalism, complain about the shameful influence of German philosophy in France. But this does poor German philosophy an injustice.[16]

Heine set himself against those who wanted to appeal to Hegel and Schelling instrumentally as a means of politically supporting the "party of stasis" ["parti de la résistance"]. Even if one saw similar things happening in Germany, at least with the late Schelling,[17] that altered nothing of the revolutionary substance of idealist philosophy, which could be translated into social and political emancipation. His main argument against Cousin, whose ignorance of German conditions Heine sought to ridicule, consisted of his claim that he as a German must after all possess a more authentic knowledge of German philosophy than Cousin. And so Heine quoted extensively in his appendix from a criticism of Cousin by the Hegelian Hinrichs, in which Hinrichs accuses the Frenchman of not having understood Hegel correctly. In doing so, however, Heine neglected to consider that the essential issue wasn't a correct, authentic understanding of Hegel or Schelling at all, but the instrumental use of German philosophy (and its obvious, inherent authority) in the internal power struggles of France. Cousin was not the incompetent, silly outsider and lone combatant that Heine pictured him to be. On the contrary, he was the center of the most influential group in French intellectual life and a major player on the political stage. For higher officials in the teaching system, for professors on the academic boards of examination, for students at the Ecole Normale Supérieure, he had propagated the image of a serious Germany, working methodically for the advancement of knowledge, whose language one had to acquire if one wished to remain at the forefront internationally and whose (in many ways) exemplary educational system it would be wise to adopt in France or to adapt to the French context.

The Cousin circle's answer to Heine's frontal assault was not long in coming. On June 25, 1835, a Cousinian—presumably the publisher Hébert[18]—took the field against Heine in a detailed review of *De l'Allemagne* in the *Journal général de l'Instruction publique*, the quasi-official newspaper of the teaching system. His surprising central argument is that the Frenchified, basically un-German Heine lacks the necessary seriousness to discuss things as important and fundamental as German philosophy. Indeed, he is less popular in Germany than in France, because "in Germany, content comes before form; ideas are gauged severely, and readers are no more dazzled by the showiness of sentences than they are amazed by the clash of antitheses. False knowledge there is soon disrobed of its borrowed dress and thrashed in the public amphitheater. Among us, by contrast, it is accorded impunity, and perhaps that is why Monsieur Heine has changed homelands."[19]

Heine had assumed that he had to express himself in the typical "French" manner in order to be heard in France, so he popularized things, simplified, prepared them in a palatable fashion, even spiced them up with esprit and jokes, all to beat the French, so to speak, at their own game. Now they answer him that one cannot as a German speak in such a manner about the earthshakingly great German mind. Some of these arguments had been similarly leveled against Heine by German republicans (Börne), but their function here is different: the point is to shut Heine out of the internal French discussion over profound German metaphysics, which was required to secure a new French (postrevolutionary) identity.

For this reason, the reviewer opposes especially fiercely Heine's final prophecy of a violent revolution in Germany:

> But what above all makes us believe that the times predicted by the prophets are still remote and that the Teuton Robespierres and Dantons are not yet sharpening the blade of the guillotine is the very nature of the German genius. Among the German peoples, thought kills action, the brain develops at the expense of the arm. . . . One shouldn't conclude from this disposition to enervating reveries that they are condemned to remain immobile in the midst of European movement, but the revolution in deeds has been so well prepared for by the revolution in ideas that it will be accomplished without too violent an upheaval, without too painful a sacrifice, and it will be much more worthy than our '93 of being compared to an *innocent idyll*.

And in conclusion, we find this clear allusion to Heine's attack on Cousin:

> This playful gaiety, these sharp sallies are not at all shocking or out of place in accounts of travel; but must he carry into the study of philosophical questions, into the appraisal of the most serious of men, a lack of restraint in his attacks which approaches cynicism? Must he borrow from pamphleteers their habits of denigration, their passions and insults? Let M. Heine, instead of trying to imitate the French, and thereby falsifying the nature of his talent, take a more calm and serious attitude, let him give his brilliant faculties a less frivolous, less

sterile direction, and I know two great peoples who would be proud, one, for having seen him born, the other, for having adopted him.[20]

There is no room for Heine's revolutionary politicizing of German philosophy in the internal French discussion of the 1830s. There, on the contrary, one is interested in a scientific-philosophical image of Germany, which, on the one hand, aids the ideological legitimization of postrevolutionary consolidation in France and, on the other, remains useful through its "otherness" as a rhetorical way of depoliticizing the debate.

The point here is that in Cousin we have a typical representative of French rhetorical culture, who at bottom has little in common with the free and objective progress of learning in the tradition of Humboldt. For Cousin, the brilliant reformulation of well-known ideas (i.e., basically the Vulgate) was always more important than philological critique and hermeneutics. And institutionally-politically, he aimed at compromise and moderation (for instance, also toward the Church). Only for some of his pupils such as Jules Simon (1814–1896), Jules Barni, and Etienne Vacherot did the relation to German philosophy, especially to Kant, develop a certain revolutionary potential. During the 1830s, however, a contradiction developed between the reference to the abstract progress of German learning and the actual practice of the Cousin school. In this respect, Heine was thoroughly correct in denouncing the French "reception" of German philosophy through Cousin. But this problem was simply not the decisive one. Decisive, on the contrary, was that Heine's representation of German philosophy ran up against a practically closed front of refusal. The publication of *De l'Allemagne* to a certain extent disqualified him from the forward-looking elements of the French intelligentsia, from those open to German intellectual life. Heine could not establish himself as an authority in discussions of the scholarly-philosophical-philological image of Germany, could not participate in its expansion, but stood instead opposed to it, relegated in the end to the (politically "safe") literary Romantic sectors, to which he was explicitly tied by the Cousin school. As an author of *Tableaux de voyage* he counted, but not as a thinker and philosophical exegete.

The opposition of the professional Germany experts makes the commercial failure of *De l'Allemagne* more understandable. Between 1835 and 1841 only 622 copies of both volumes were sold (from an edition of 1,000).[21] It was not the publisher Renduel who erred in his appraisal of the market, when in 1833 he settled the general contract counting on the likelihood of several editions; the Germany theme was at the time doubtless a promising one. It was rather Heine who miscalculated, who either did not rightly perceive the dominant position of Victor Cousin in the French debate about Germany or who overestimated his own energies and powers of influence in this area.

In the second half of the 1830s no further opportunity existed to alter this situation in any fundamental way. Only with the rise of the early Socialists did a new starting point present itself, because in them a new, antigovernmental, anti-Cousin front emerged, which also hoped to draw on German philosophy and science. But characteristically, Heine appeared too frivolous even to Louis Blanc (on this point Blanc adopted as his own the arguments of his opponents, the Cousin circle).[22] And Pierre Leroux, in his attacks on Cousin beginning in 1841, sought ammunition not so much in Heine—from Heine he merely derived a few arguments for his antiatheistic Hegel criticism—but, paradoxically, in Schelling, the representative of restoration.[23] Thus, the new connection with the early Socialists posed no feasible alternative, and consequently Heine's attempts to push for a new edition of *De l'Allemagne* during the 1840s had little chance of success.

So the reactivation of Heine's reception in France succeeded not because of the theoretical writings, but because of the lyrics and verse epics, that is, the Romantic image of Germany.[24] With the translation of *Wintermärchen* [Winter's Tale] and especially of *Atta Troll* in *Revue des deux mondes*, Heine made a new start. In the foreword to his French readers he presented it as characteristic of his fantastic poem that it would breathe the inner life of mysterious Germany ("qu'il respirera dans ce poëme fantastique la vie intime de la mystérieuse Allemagne");[25] in other words, he put himself squarely in the Romantic tradition. The translation of *Nordsee* [The North Sea] by Nerval in 1848 as well as the constant efforts of Saint-René Taillandiers in the *Revue des deux mondes* in the 1850s (translations of parts of *Romanzero, Doktor Faust, Götter im Exil* [The Gods in Exile], etc.), and the (unauthorized) new edition of *Reisebilder* by Victor Lecou in 1853 opened the way for the new reception that began in 1855 with the French edition of Heine's work by Michel Lévy.

Even the Lévy edition was out of balance, however. The *Reisebilder* went through ten editions through 1895, *Lutèce* had nine through 1871, the poetry collection *Poèmes et légendes* five (through 1880), and *De l'Allemagne* only four (through 1872). The *Reisebilder* remained the most successful piece almost to the end of the century, at which point—parallel to the development in Germany, though much later—the lyric poet, the author of the *Buch der Lieder* [Book of Songs], came to the fore. Altogether, though, the Romantic Heine predominated. Clearly, he did not fit in the center of French representations of German Romanticism; rather, he belonged on the periphery, with his attributes of esprit, joke, aggressiveness, ironic distance, lack of seriousness, and so on. His relation to the Romantic image of Germany thus remains partly contradictory; Heine functions through a certain opposition to that image, at whose center one might sooner expect authors like Hölderlin or Novalis.

This contradiction is further sharpened by the question of national identity, which in Heine's case is always especially acute: it appears to have functioned according to variations in French self-definition. One can see Heine as a naturalized Frenchman because he fought against the fanatical Teutons and for German-French understanding; he is a good German, so to speak, because he is basically French. This point of view acquires significance during times of intensified crisis, such as the Franco-Prussian War of 1870–71 and World War I and II. But the making of this anti-German, French citizen Heine in France can proceed smoothly only when the fronts are clearly drawn, when a French liberal democracy stands against an aggressive German nationalism. When, however, France itself is gripped by national chauvinism, as for instance in the Dreyfus era, then Heine, the Jew and the democrat, is denied recognition. Conversely, emphasis on Heine's Francophilia can also reduce his importance in times of real interest in the German neighbor, when the periodically recurring questions resurface about the strange "riddle of Germany," France's radical opposite, the Other. In such phases Heine appears to be too atypical, too un-German. It has been especially in the last few decades, since the *Buch der Lieder* has no longer been considered a typical Romantic collection of lyrics, that this point of view has prevailed. Both of these views—the anti-German acceptance of the citizen democrat and the lack of interest in the rationalistic critic of Romanticism—are significantly constitutive of France's self-appraisal and its relation to its German neighbor.

Before drawing general conclusions, let us turn once again to the problem of Heine's individual acculturation. The miscarriage of his attempt to integrate himself by force into the French cultural exchanges of 1835–36 converged, as we know, with a personal crisis: the intensification of his relationship to Mathilde and the threat to his professional existence in Germany through governmental decrees, to name only the most prominent factors. From a Rastignac who set out to conquer Parisian society by storm, he became a man shaken by a mid-life crisis, a sobered master of his material, preferring to withdraw from the general bustle; he was seen only sporadically in the salons and the high-society balls, and he chose his friends very carefully. Such phases of disillusionment are a normal part of the acculturation process and are basically a sign of psychic stability. Still, it seems to me that the role of the acculturation problem in Heine's personal crisis in the mid-1830s and in its eventual overcoming has not up to now been correctly understood. His choice of Mathilde, the child of the lower class, which closed certain circles in Parisian society to him, coincided with a re-definition of his relation to French culture. From that point it was no longer primarily the contemporary high culture of France that inter-ested him. He felt a marked distance between his own poetological posi-tion and that which seemed to him to be pompous rhetoric in the work of writers and poets such as Lamartine, Hugo, Vigny, and even Musset. At the same time, he preserved a more intimate relationship to trivial literature (Alexandre Dumas, Pierre Jean de Béranger, Alphonse Royer, Eugène Sue) and to high literature disguised as trivial (Balzac, Gautier, Sand)—that is, he remained tied to the lower genre of the French novel, whose closeness to reality he obviously preferred.[26]

Thus Heine directed his literary-political engagement exclusively at Germany, at what was topographically distant but affectively close, while he stood clear of French discussions.[27] On the basis of this new division in his work, he also made his peace with Cousin, whose con-tributions to the spread of German philosophy he had come to value, as well as Cousin's role in keeping church and state distinct.[28]

Heine endured the tension of a double cultural reference. He neither went down the road of hyperassimilation, nor did he fall back into an exiled isolation. His strength consisted of maintaining—vis-à-vis Ger-many—distanced, critical ties to German culture, made possible pri-marily by the language, but also by personal emotional attachments (family, friends, acquaintances) and by material relations to the German public, to the literary market. At the same time—vis-à-vis France—he did not let himself be blinded by hasty generalizations, and he discovered, after a phase of mythic-symbolic overestimation and a concomitant crisis of disillusionment, a more differentiated position, in which he distinguished between different levels and in which his basic sympathy for the French "heiterer Morgen" ["bright morning"][29] mixed with his consciousness of insurmountable boundaries, of his own otherness.

As we saw, however, the achievement of this private balance offered no guarantee that his work would strike a responsive chord in France. After the failure of his early integration strategy he wisely switched priority to the German market, and as far as the French market was concerned, his efforts were limited to tailoring his German texts for the French public with a more or less careful modification of details. The originality of his position, however, lies in the fact that putting priority on Germany was by no means unproblematic. Heine wrote to Germany from Paris, from outside, and in time this approach necessarily altered his perspective. His Germany, "Land der Rätsel und der Schmerzen" ["land of riddles and of pain"],[30] assumed an increasingly imaginary character, while he developed an increasingly realistic relation to French culture. One might point to works like *Atta Troll* or to the late poems as examples of this trend, and perhaps also partly to the development of Heine's language. His position between cultures tended toward the accentuation of an ever more idiosyncratic poetic world, which withdrew from the dominant tendencies of the day.

The conclusions of this double study of reception object and reception culture can be summarized as follows. First, both the literary Romantic and the scholarly-philological images of Germany are products of French economic conditions, expressing internal French realities and imperatives. Second, the processes of reception necessitate labels; they cannot be provoked *ex nihilo*. Ideally, these labels emerge from a congruence between the actual attributes of the reception object and the needs of the reception culture (though even then a functional reinterpretation is generated by the new context). Usually, however, a more or less violent process of adaptation and appropriation takes place, and for that reason there follow different reception histories divided among different discursive fields. Third, the labels that defined Heine's work as an object of reception to French culture were his identities as a German Romantic, as a representative of French thought, as a fighter for democracy and progress. These identities were only provisionally reconciled with each other. Fourth, Heine's reception in France ran fundamentally against the grain. His early acculturation strategy was not taken seriously. He was thought of more often in times of crisis than in phases of productive neighborliness. The German poet in Paris, the advocate of the French cosmopolitan spirit, thus became in a peculiar way the victim of German-French projections. Fifth, Heine was also a problem detector in France. With seismographic precision, his reception manifested breaks, not only in bourgeois society or in the self-understanding of the revolutionary intellectual, but in German-French cultural exchange. Sixth, in France one should no longer be content smugly to acknowledge Heine's repeated declarations of love for the French people; rather, one should work through the misfires and failures of Heine's reception, precisely because they signal divergences and problems in the German-French relation that are very real and still with us today. Finally, I must add in closing that the academic reception, too, has fallen short of its true goal so long as it fails to generate an urgently needed retranslation of Heine's work by a respected French publisher.

NOTES

1. According to Friedrich Hirth, *Heine und seine französische Freunde* (Mainz: Kupferber, 1949).
2. About Heine's contemporary reception in France, see Hans Hörling, *Heinrich Heine im Spiegel der politischen Presse von 1831–1841* (Frankfurt am Main: P. Lang, 1977), as well as the commentary volumes of the Düsseldorfer historisch-kritische Ausgabe, as far as they are available: Heinrich Heine, *Sämtliche Werke*, ed. Manfred Windfuhr (Hamburg: Hoffmann & Campe, 1973–).
3. Cf. Beatrix Müller, *Die französische Heine-Forschung 1945–75* (Meisenheim: Hain, 1977); also Michael Werner, "Heine-Forschung in Frankreich 1975–1982," in *Interferenzen: Deutschland und Frankreich*, ed. Michael Werner (Düsseldorf: Droste, 1983), pp. 80–91.
4. Dates for these writers are: Forster (1754–1794), Cramer (1752–1807), Huber (1727–1804), Hase (1780–1864), Mohe (1800–1876), and Depping (1784–1853).
5. See especially Michael Werner, *Genius und Geldsack: Zum Problem des Schriftstellerberufs bei Heinrich Heine* (Hamburg: Hoffmann & Campe, 1978).
6. See Günter Oesterle, "Urbanität und Mentalität: Paris und das Französische aus der Sicht deutscher Parisreisender," in *Transferts: Relations*

interculturelles dans l'espace franco-allemand, ed. Michel Espagne and Michael Werner (Paris: Editions Recherche sur les Civilisations, 1988), pp. 59–82.

7. Heinrich Heine, *Sämtliche Schriften,* ed. K. Briegleb, 6 vols. (Munich: Hanser, 1968–76), 5:416 (*Lutezia,* article LI). Bracketed translations from the German and the French here and throughout this chapter are supplied by Andreas Kriefall.

8. Michel Chevalier (1806–1879), Hippolyte Carnot (1801–1888), Charles Duveyrier (1803–1866), Désiré Nisard (1806–1888), Auguste Mignet (1796–1884), Camille Hyacinth Odilon-Barrot (1751–1873), Louis Blanc (1811–1882), George Sand (1804–1876), Pierre Leroux (1797–1871).

9. See Alain Ruiz, "A l'aube du kantisme en France: Sieyès, Karl Friedrich Reinhard et le traité pour la paix perpétuelle (hiver 1795–1796)," *Cahiers d'Etudes Germaniques* (1980): 147–193.

10. Victor Cousin (1792–1867), Eugène Lerminier (1803–1857), Auguste Comte (1798–1857), Gustave d'Eichthal (1804–1886), Edgar Quinet (1803–1875), Jules Michelet (1798–1874).

11. From the start, the library of the Ecole Normale Supérieure subscribed to practically all of the important German old-philological journals: *Rheinisches Museum* (1827), *Neue Jahrbücher für Philologie und Pädagogik* (1831), *Philologus* (1846), *Hermes* (1866); of the 189 journals listed for the library in 1915, 59 were from Germany and 7 from Austria (according to an unpublished presentation by P. Petitmengin in the seminar of the research group "Transferts culturels franco-allemands," at the Ecole Normale Supérieure on May 28, 1988). From 1832, German instruction there was conducted by Karl-Benedikt Hase, the Sachsen-born director of the handwriting department at the royal library.

12. The reception of *De la France* was essentially determined by the theme of a "foreign" German view of French conditions. Gozlan's dates are 1803–1866, and Carnot's are 1801–1888. See Heine, *Sämtliche Werke,* 6:688–689.

13. The announcement of the book series *De l'Allemagne* is dated December 26, 1833 (Heinrich Heine, *Werke, Briefe, Lebenszeugnisse,* 27 vols., Säkularausgabe [Berlin: Akademie; Paris: Editions du Centre National de la Recherche Scientifique, 1970], 21:78–80). It was not until 1835, however, that the two volumes appeared.

14. See Heine, *Sämtliche Werke,* 8:26off, for Heine's preface, including his comment on de Staël on p. 262. The supplement addressed to Cousin was dropped in the 1855 edition, but it was retained in the *Romantische Schule.*

15. See Heinz Wismann, "Modus interpretandi: Analyse comparée des études platoniciennes en France et Allemagne au 19ème siècle," in *Philologie und Hermeneutik im 19. Jahrhundert 2,* ed. Mayotte Bollack and Heinz Wis-

mann (Göttingen: Vandenhoeck & Ruprecht, 1983), pp. 490–512. Dates for some of Cousin's less famous pupils are: Barni (1818–1878), Janet (1823–1899).

16. Translated from Heine, *Schriften*, 3:437; also *Sämtliche Werke*, 8:190 (cited according to the German edition of *Zur Geschichte der neueren schönen Literatur in Deutschland* [1833]). In moving this passage to the *Romantische Schule* (1835), Heine made clear that he had been thinking of Cousin. He continued there: "Denn erstens ist das keine deutsche Philosophie, was den Franzosen bisher unter diesem Titel, namentlich von Herren Victor Cousin, präsentiert worden. Herr Victor Cousin hat sehr viel geistreiches Wischiwaschi, aber keine deutsche Philosophie vorgetragen." ["Because first of all, it simply isn't German philosophy which has been presented to the French till now by that name, by Mr. Victor Cousin, to be specific. Mr. Victor Cousin has introduced a great deal of brilliant gobbledygook, but no German philosophy."] Ibid.

17. Heine, *Schriften*, 3:437–438; or *Sämtliche Werke*, 8:191.

18. The review is signed "H." See *Journal général d'instruction publique*, 1834–35 (June 25): 338–340.

19. Translated from ibid., p. 338.

20. Translated from ibid., pp. 339–340.

21. For the corresponding figures for the Renduel edition and their sources, see Werner, *Genius und Geldsack*, p. xxx.

22. See Blanc's letter to Heine of September 24, 1840 (Heine, *Werke, Briefe, Lebenszeugnisse*, 25:288).

23. On this subject, see Michael Werner, "À propos de la reception de Hegel et de Schelling en France pendant les années 1840," in *De Lessing à Heine: Un siècle de relations littéraires et intellectuelles entre la France et l'Allemagne*, ed. Jean Moes and Jean-Marie Valentin (Paris: Didier, 1985), pp. 277–291.

24. To be sure, Heine the lyric poet also had to contend with the accusation that he lacked seriousness; notice in this regard the comment of Marie d'Agoult (in "Daniel Stern"): "What a shame! If he wanted to be serious, what a great poet he could become!" Translated from *Revue des deux mondes*, December 1, 1844.

25. Heine, *Sämtliche Werke*, 4:161.

26. For Heine's comments on French lyric and meter, see the article "Retrospective Aufklärung," as well as the disparaging judgment of Lamartine in a draft of his will, contained in Heine, *Schriften*, 5:479, 6/1:547. Dates for some of these popular French authors are: Alexandre Dumas (1802–1870), Pierre Jean de Béranger (1780–1857), Alphonse Royer (1803–1875), Eugène Sue (1804–1857).

27. An exception may be found in the discussions of Balzac and Sand in articles for the *Allgemeine Zeitung* (1840), which were, however, conceived for the German public, as well as the letters *Über die französische Bühne*, already written in 1837, in which Heine manifests the change in his allegiance.
28. Heine, *Schriften*, 5:498–500.
29. This feeling becomes especially clear and is sworn to as his legacy in the wills of 1843, 1846, 1851 (Heine, *Schriften*, 6/1:534, 536, 542).
30. From the will of September 27, 1846 (Heine, *Schriften*, 6/1:536).

WORKS CITED

"H." Review of Heine's *De l'Allemagne*. *Journal général d'instruction publique*, 1834–35 (June 25): 338–340.

Heine, Heinrich. *Sämtliche Schriften*. Ed. K. Briegleb. 6 vols. Munich: Hanser, 1968–76.

———. *Sämtliche Werke*. Düsseldorfer historisch-kritische Ausgabe. Ed. Manfred Windfuhr. Hamburg: Hoffmann & Campe, 1973–.

———. *Werke, Briefe, Lebenszeugnisse*. 27 vols. Säkularausgabe. Berlin: Akademie; Paris: Editions du Centre National de la Recherche Scientifique, 1970.

Hirth, Friedrich. *Heine und seine französische Freunde*. Mainz: Kupferber, 1949.

Hörling, Hans. *Heinrich Heine im Spiegel der politischen Presse von 1831–1841*. Frankfurt am Main: P. Lang, 1977.

Müller, Beatrix. *Die französische Heine-Forschung 1945–75*. Meisenheim: Hain, 1977.

Oesterle, Günter. "Urbanität und Mentalität: Paris und das Französische aus der Sicht deutscher Parisreisender." In *Transferts: Relations interculturelles dans l'espace franco-allemand*, ed. Michel Espagne and Michael Werner. Paris: Editions Recherche sur les Civilisations, 1988.

Ruiz, Alain. "A l'aube du kantisme en France: Sieyès, Karl Friedrich Reinhard et le traité pour la paix perpétuelle (hiver 1795–1796)." *Cahiers d'Etudes Germaniques* (1980): 147–193.

Werner, Michael. "À propos de la reception de Hegel et de Schelling en France pendant les années 1840." In *De Lessing à Heine: Un siècle de relations littéraires et intellectuelles entre la France et l'Allemagne*, ed. Jean Moes and Jean-Marie Valentin. Paris: Didier, 1985.

———. *Genius und Geldsack: Zum Problem des Schriftstellerberufs bei Heinrich Heine*. Hamburg: Hoffmann & Campe, 1978.

———. "Heine-Forschung in Frankreich, 1975–1982." In *Interferenzen: Deutschland und Frankreich*, ed. Michael Werner. Düsseldorf: Droste, 1983.

Wismann, Heinz. "Modus interpretandi: Analyse comparée des études platoniciennes en France et Allemagne au 19ème siècle." In *Philologie und Hermeneutik im 19. Jahrhundert 2*, ed. Mayotte Bollack and Heinz Wismann. Göttingen: Vandenhoeck & Ruprecht, 1983.

EGON SCHWARZ

Heine, Don Quijote, and the Generation of 1898

*H*eine in Spain—the temptation is great to turn the question around and ask about the significance of Spain for Heine. After all, German Romanticism, whose ungrateful offspring Heine was, exhibits an almost obsessive attachment to things Spanish, from the romances to Gracián, from the *novela picaresca* to Calderón, from translation to imitation. Heine's taste ran in somewhat different directions, but it is obvious that, inspired by Herder, whom he revered, and by August Wilhelm Schlegel and Ludwig Tieck, about whom he was ambivalent (to put it mildly), Heine assigned a more than peripheral role to Spanish history and lore in his work. "Spain is constantly on my mind; I am irresistibly drawn to Madrid. Sometime I want to read *Don Quijote* in the Mancha."[1] It is a pity that he was prevented by an illness from visiting Spain in 1837. He had hoped for "rich literary results" from this trip in the form of "a series of extensive articles," probably to be named *Spanische Zustände* [Spanish Affairs], in analogy to his earlier *Französische Zustände* [French Affairs].[2] Yet even though he lacked the benefit of such firsthand acquaintance, there is abundant evidence of Heine's fascination with, and poetic evocation of, Spanish history and culture: the tragedy of *Almansor*, set in Granada; the epic *Atta Troll*, with its Spanish allusions; such poems as *Disputation* [Disputation], *Der sterbende Almansor* [The Dying Almansor], and *Der Mohrenkönig* [The King of the Moors], set in the Alpujarras; the specter ballad *Don Ramiro*; the ironic poem *Donna Clara*, mocking the infatuation of a Christian lady for an anonymous youth who turns out to be the son of Rabbi Israel of Saragossa; the triptych *Almansor*; the utopian epics *Bimini*, with Juan Ponce de León as the central character, and *Vitzliputzli*, about Hernán Cortez's conquest of Mexico; and the long cycle *Hebräische Melodien* [Hebrew Melodies], about the Toledoborn poet Jehuda ben Halevy. These works amply testify to Heine's abiding involvement with Hispanic culture, mostly of the period of the *Reconquista,* and incite the curiosity of the reader to delve more deeply.

I must resist such temptation in the interest of my announced topic, except perhaps to say that these Spanish affinities may be adduced to explain, at least in part, the extraordinary impact Heine had on the poetry of Spain. "There is probably no German poet," Jost Hermand writes, "who had made his way into foreign lands as quickly as Heinrich Heine. Already in the fifties and sixties of the nineteenth century . . . his fame reaches such dimensions that it begins to compete with that of Goethe; indeed, it threatens to obscure the renown of the great Weimaranian."[3] This observation is especially true of Spain, which Hermand lists among the countries where Heine's popularity abounded prodigiously. Claude Owen's bibliographies on Heine in the Spanish-speaking regions comprise more than five hundred pages and thousands of entries, a vast territory that has not yet been fully explored.[4]

It was especially Heine's lyrical poetry that found fertile soil in nineteenth-century Spain, for reasons that it is neither possible nor necessary to elucidate here because this rewarding task has already been performed for us.[5] Suffice it to say that an increasing number of young poets enthusiastically seized on Heine to break out of the carapace of academic ossification and sterile rhetorical pathos into which not only Spanish poetry but the Spanish language itself had been pressed by midcentury. Heine's perceived freshness, brevity, and suppleness of expression, as well as his simplicity of style, seemed the proper remedy for this malaise, and its adoption caused enormous *furore* among both friends and foes. It was the celebrated author Emilia Pardo Bazán who perhaps expressed the phenomenon most poignantly: "Heine . . . is not like Goethe with his *Faust* who is more admired than understood in Spain; rather, his [Heine's] poems are models for our lyrical poetry, and it is in large part to them that we owe the adequate expression of our feelings, inclinations, and disappointments. He lives more in our souls than on Parnassus." Bazán also makes clear which part of Heine's production had the greatest influence: "What one reads of Heine . . . are not his *Französische Zustände,* nor his *De l'Allemagne* and *Atta Troll,* but his charming and disconsolate love songs," since what "we see in Heine is above all the incomparable poet of eroticism."[6]

It is precisely because of this preponderance of Heine's influence as a poet that I turn to the less-investigated reception of his prose in Spain.

If I narrow the focus to Heine's various attempts at interpreting *Don Quijote,* the great Spanish masterpiece, it is not only because of constraints of time and space, but also because of the unending fascination the novel had for the Generation of 1898 and its successors as well as for Heine himself. He regarded it as the ultimate literary achievement that created the modern European novel. In his view, Cervantes, Shakespeare, and Goethe constituted an unsurpassed poetic triumvirate, a kind of secular cultural trinity.[7] He returned to the novel repeatedly in his writings and subjected it to a quasi-religious exegesis, discovering in, or reading into, its depths parallels to his own life and times. It is not an exaggeration to say that Don Quijote, the book as well as the character, albeit for different reasons, were of similar significance for Heine and his readers among the Generation of 1898 in Spain. Nevertheless, mine will not be the customary "reception study." Even though all my Spanish witnesses were familiar with Heine and his writings on *Don Quijote,* each one went his own independent way. Rather, one must look on Cervantes' novel as one of the great European myths that every generation needed to reinterpret for itself. Just as Heine inherited the rich legacy of Quijote interpretations from his Romantic forebears and reshaped it for his own purposes, the Spanish writers took cognizance of his ideas only to form their own. It is within this continuum that the encounter between these Spanish writers and Heine must be placed.

Three times in the course of his oeuvre Heine attempted to come to an understanding of *Don Quijote:* in 1828, at the age of thirty, in "The City of Lucca," Part Three of his *Italienische Reisebilder* [Pictures of an Italian Journey]; then again in his famous treatise *Die romantische Schule* [The Romantic School], first published in French in 1833; and finally, in an introduction he wrote for an anonymous edition of *Don Quijote* in 1837.[8] It was in this introduction that Heine accorded *Don Quijote* and its author his most extensive treatment. Yet on repeated occasions Heine deprecated this piece, which he wrote for a new edition of *Der sinnnreiche Junker Don Quixote von La Mancha* commissioned by the Verlag der Classiker. On May 3, 1837, for example, he confesses to his regular publisher, Julius Campe, that it was "the worst I ever wrote." In this letter and again a week later, in a letter to the same correspondent, he enumerates the reasons for what he terms its bad style: illness, pressure from the publisher, and the need for money.[9]

We can only speculate why he insists on denigrating this work. It could be because he wanted Julius Campe to understand why he had accepted a commission from another publisher; he could also have had in mind the lengthy biographical and historical digressions that such an introductory piece required and that tend to give it a somewhat rambling appearance; and it may further have been because he repeats verbatim entire passages from the earlier discussion of *Don Quijote* contained in his *Italienische Reisebilder*.[10] It is there that Heine views his life, as it were, in the mirror of the much-admired novel. In the casual, almost frivolous manner characteristic of many of his writings, he endeavors to grasp the spiritual forces emanating from the book whose aura enthralled him throughout his life. Because of the lighthearted tone in which they are offered, one hesitates to apply these interpretations to Heine's actual biographical personality. It suffices to recognize in them a literary device, a series of allegorical self-projections with the aid of which the poet attempted to make visible a pervasive pattern, a cohesive design governing his life's work. Cervantes' *Don Quijote* thus becomes a grandiose ordering principle for Heinrich Heine, an authority that legitimizes the past and adumbrates the future.

To emphasize its unique place in his life, Heine reveals that it was the first serious book he read in his childhood after reaching literacy. By poetically evoking the natural surroundings in which his "little heart" ["mein kleines Herz"] absorbed "the great adventures of the intrepid knight" ["den großen Abenteuern des kühnen Ritters"], by conjuring up the blossoming spring, the caressing song of the nightingale, the rays of the sun playing on the trees, the flowers, the waterfall, and so on, he suggests that the first impressions he received from the novel were inextricably intermingled with those of an idyll without pain and malice. Yet it would be a mistake to dismiss the age-old topoi composing this expurgated picture as clichés. The attentive reader soon recognizes that this scene and the following stages of Heine's characterization of his relationship to *Don Quijote* function as a palimpsest, that the plot elements from the novel and the botanical and meteorological commonplaces he associates with one another are meant to be understood as surface phenomena. Beneath, the true text begins to emerge, evoking venerable mythological verities, telling the story of the naiveté of childhood and, on a still deeper level, the innocence of Eden where everything is what it seems. "I was a child," Heine reminisces, "and did not know the irony that God had infused in his creation and that the poet had imitated in the printed version of his miniworld" ["Ich war ein

Kind und kannte nicht die Ironie, die Gott in die Welt hineingeschaffen, und die der große Dichter in seiner gedruckten Kleinwelt nachgeahmt hatte"].[11] This is one of the telltale sentences that intimates what *Don Quijote,* the prototype of all great literature, is for Heine: a holy scripture with the aid of which he succeeds in raveling not only his own life, not only the meaning of contemporary events, but the trajectory of all mankind.

The next stage is inevitably the fall from grace, the expulsion from paradise. The roses prove to have thorns, the landscape changes and is now dominated by cliffs, the struggle with a hostile reality has begun: "Everywhere I see a disguised winter" ["Überall sehe ich einen verkappten Winter"]. With this phrase Heine announces a change in the emotional climate. Together with the harmony of early childhood, the idyllic images of the novel have vanished, and in the "Introduction," where Heine describes the same sequence, *Don Quijote* has even become "a most unedifying book" ["ein sehr unerquickliches Buch"], which, in the turbulent years of adolescence, the youth avoids: "and whenever it lay in my path, I pushed it indignantly aside" ["und lag es in meinem Wege, so schob ich es unwillig zur Seite"]. It takes the rest of his life as a grown man to understand the inexhaustibility of the book and to fathom its meanings in an infinite effort at approximation. "Every five years of my life I have read *Don Quijote* with alternatingly changing impressions" ["ich erinnere mich, daß ich in jedem Lustrum meines Lebens den *Don Quixote* mit abwechselnd verschiedenartigen Empfindungen gelesen habe"].[12]

We must not be led by the seeming flippancy of the parallels with which he intertwines fiction and fact into failing to take seriously Heine's underlying social commitment. In his earlier piece on *Don Quijote* he speaks with deadly conviction about politics, capable of echoing across the centuries, as when he proclaims: "how German philosophers and historians torment their brains to defend any despotism, no matter how insipid and loutish, as reasonable and legitimate" ["wie deutsche Philosophen and Historiker ihr Gehirn abmartern, um jeden Despotismus, und sei er noch so albern and tölpelhaft, als vernünftig oder als rechtsgültig zu verteidigen"]. In his more or less biographical introduction to Cervantes, obvious and direct associations of his own life with scenes in the novel would have been inappropriate, but in a much more personal and partly fictional travelogue such as the *Italienische Reise-*

bilder, Heine is less reluctant to intersperse some intimate beliefs and fundamental philosophical reflections among the elements he recapitulates from the plot:

> Perhaps you are right and I am nothing but a Don Quijote, and the reading of all kinds of miraculous books has confused my head, as they did the Manchegan hidalgo's. Perhaps Jean Jacques Rousseau was my Amadis of Gaul, Mirabeau my Roldan or Agramanth, and I have studied too deeply the heroic exploits of the French paladins and the Round Table of the National Convention. To be sure, my madness and the fixed ideas that I drew from books are of a nature contrary to the madness of the Manchegan; he wanted to restore the perishing age of chivalry, whereas I want to annihilate everything that has remained from that epoch. . . . My colleague took windmills for giants, while I see in today's giants nothing but bragging windmills; he regarded leather wineskins as mighty magicians, whereas I detect in our present-day sorcerers merely leathery winebibbers.[13]

We cannot accompany Heine page after page as he turns Don Quijote's adventures on their head in order to imbue them with meaning for his involvement in the cultural and political life of his own time. It is enough to make clear that he endows the novel with vast allegorical powers to derive from them his insights into the mechanisms of contemporary as well as long-range history. In the succinct discussion to which he subjects the novel in *Die romantische Schule,* the triadic structure of his exegetic practice, alluded to earlier, leaps to the eye. It has enabled Heine scholars to discern the similarities of Heine's aesthetics and hermeneutics with the allegorical schemes of interpretation elaborated by the early church fathers. The parallels extend to the last details of Heine's procedure and diction, in apparent contradiction of his overt rejection of Romantic spiritualism and its medieval Christian premises. By quoting from a text that establishes this dependence, we can avoid following the meandering path of Heine's *Don Quijote* interpretations:

> In the first stage Heine . . . is still guided by the literal historical meaning of the work. On this level it is understood as the author's intended mockery of an anachronistic attempt at restoring medieval chivalry. . . . The second interpretation elaborates a timeless moral message: the contrast Don Quijote-Sancho Pansa [*sic*] is a more gener-

ally conceived satire of Idealism in the sense that Don Quijote incorporates the failure of "idealistic enthusiasm," whereas Sancho Pansa must be regarded as the incarnation of selfish "realistic sense." In a third stage, finally, the same constellation is elevated to an allegory of mind and matter, revealing the mystical meaning of the ultimate questions concerning human salvation and damnation. In Heine's version this mystical meaning has to do no longer with Christian truth, such as the doctrine of Fall and Redemption, but with his fundamental anthropological conception of Spiritualism and Sensualism. The interpretive method is theological and Christian; the conclusion is skeptical and materialistic.[14]

There is hardly a passage, no matter how well disguised, in which Heine does not relate *Don Quijote* to his own vital interests. But at the same time, other interpretive sections are capable of a more general application, and it is to be suspected that his Spanish readers could most easily adapt these to their own concerns. Thus, for example, they keep quoting Heine's verdict that in Cervantes one must revere the creator of the modern novel; that he revitalized it by introducing the faithful depiction of the lower classes into a genre that had dealt exclusively with the aristocracy; that Cervantes, as a Catholic poet, possessed the great epic calm that overarches his writings like a crystalline heaven and that this calm is concomitantly part of the Spanish national character. It is unlikely that these nationalists would not have applauded Heine's declaration that "the Spaniards merit the glory of having brought forth the best novel" of world literature ["Den Spaniern gebührt der Ruhm, den besten Roman hervorgebracht zu haben"].[15] They also must have shared Heine's assumption that every detail in the novel is of allegorical significance,[16] and they took visible delight in his interpretation of certain episodes, such as his defense of Don Quijote against "the base rabble who, adorned with colorful silken robes, noble phrases and ducal title, mocked a man who far surpassed them in mental strength and noble spirit" ["Wir verachteten den niedrigen Pöbel, der, geschmückt mit buntseidenen Mänteln, vornehmen Redensarten und Herzogstiteln, einen Mann verhöhnte, der ihm an Geisteskraft und Edelsinn so weit überlegen war"]. Like Heine, they were convinced that in spite of its fantastic character the novel is based in concrete reality, which is why it could achieve its folksy popularity.[17] Heine's identification of Don Quijote with idealistic enthusiasm and of Sancho Panza

with common sense—and especially the superiority he sometimes assigns to the first over the second—pleased the Spanish writers no end.[18]
On other occasions, it is true, he seems to arrive at the opposite evaluation, but that, too, can hardly have escaped the attention of the Spanish
writers.

Passages like the following must also have stirred the hearts of a
generation that had assumed the task of fathoming the depth of the
Spanish soul: "Did the profound Spaniard," Heine asked, "intend to de-
ride human nature even more deeply? Did he wish to allegorize in the
figure of Don Quijote our spirit and in the figure of Sancho Pansa our
body so that the entire poem in the end represents the great mystery
in which the questions regarding mind and matter are being discussed
in their awesome truth?"[19] Heine remarks that Don Quijote and Sancho Panza continuously parody each other but ultimately complement
one another so wondrously that together they constitute the real central
character,[20] and this hint made the Spaniards hail him as the initiator of
the psychological approach to Cervantes.

Thinking of themselves as Romantics, they must have been struck
by Heine's paradox that the German Romantics had produced the best
translation of a novel in which their own madness was mocked in the
most amusing manner, since they were caught in the same insanity
that inspired the noble Manchegan to engage in his follies. After all, the
German Romantics also wished to restore medieval chivalry, to revive
a dead past.[21] And at least the historically minded among the Spaniards must have been intrigued by the conclusion Heine drew from this
thought—namely, that it was just as thankless a folly to bring back to
life a spent past as to introduce the future into the present prematurely
and thereby run afoul of all the weighty interests of the day.[22]

The example of the German poet must have vindicated the Spaniards' own practice of changing their minds from time to time and
of trying out contradictory explanations of *Don Quijote*. Such an instance is Heine's statement in the *Romantische Schule* that Cervantes'
humoristic irony was a way of evading the censorship of the Holy Office.
This claim contrasts with his assertions in the "Introduction" that
the Spanish novelist was a faithful son of the Catholic church, that it
was not the Inquisition that kept him from discussing the Protestant
thoughts of his time, and that there were no antiauthoritarian overtones in his works. Cervantes, as an obedient soldier of his Majesty,

had been only too glad to sacrifice his individual freedom to Castilian national pride.[23]

Having said this much about the reception, putative as well as documented, of some of Heine's thoughts, I should like to cast a glance at the condition in Spain toward the end of the nineteenth century which made these thoughts so welcome in a place and a time far removed from their origins. Let me briefly recall some of the concerns articulated by the members of the so-called Generation of 1898. I have no ambition to replicate the findings and surmises of the plethora of books and articles on the subject but shall be content with reiterating that 1898 was the year of the Spanish-American War. The loss of Cuba and the Philippines completed the dismantling of the once vast Spanish overseas empire. These developments had, of course, no more than symbolic significance, since peninsular decadence and stagnation in every conceivable sphere of human endeavor had been long in evidence and was not the making of one year's events. Even after the war was over, most Spaniards remained unaroused. They were content with plodding along in their customary manner. But the precipitous military defeat alerted a group of already critical young intellectuals and literati even more painfully to the fact that their homeland had desperately fallen behind other European societies with which they were wont to compare themselves, that it was what today would be termed an underdeveloped society in need of modernization.[24]

The countryside that the ninety-eighters loved passionately was in the hands of powerful *caciques* who ruled with ruthless arbitrariness over an increasingly destitute peasantry and in favor of the still feudally oriented, landed aristocracy. In the cities the weak bourgeoisie maintained a far-from-democratic parliamentary system that practiced the well-known game of tweedle-dum and tweedle-dee, alternating not only between two rather indistinguishable parties, the Conservatives and the Liberals, but even switching back and forth perennially between the same political figures, Cánova and Sagasta. On the intellectual level this charade was duplicated by the traditionalists and the modernizers, also called *casticistas* and *europeizantes,* a contest that operated exclusively in the realm of spiritual values. None of the participants in these oppositions was seriously interested in changing the status quo kept immobile by the undisputed power of the latifundists, a petrified Catholic church, and the military establishment—a status quo that was only slightly disturbed by the distant rumblings of an incipient industrial capitalism and the stirrings of the working classes, urban and rural. These were circumstances that resembled, *mutatis mutandis,* the conditions in Germany fifty years before, enough to make Heine's musings seem quite timely. In our days a similar phenomenon obtained when the Euro-Communists of Spain began quoting the diagnoses of Karl Kautsky at a time when they had lost all relevance in the society for which they had been coined in the first place.[25]

The reception of German culture was put to varied ideological uses in nineteenth-century Spain. At the risk of oversimplifying a complex situation, one could say that there was a conservative trend that equated things German with strength and discipline, law and order, and cultivated them to counteract the "liberalism," "atheism," and "lasciviousness" with which influences from France were associated since the French Revolution. But there also existed another perception of Germany, inspired by German philosophy, education, religious tolerance, and progress—accomplishments that liberal forces were eager to oppose to the oppressive preponderance of French influences on Spain in general. These tendencies culminated in the adoption of *Krausismo,* a philosophy aiming to combine Catholicism and Protestantism into a coherent whole. Under the guise of this reconciliation, Krausism served to introduce the liberalism of Protestant thought into Spain, a country that still lived under the dominance of a medieval Catholic hierarchy. It is clear that the Generation of 1898 by and large belonged to this liberal camp, that it was influenced by Krausism and the institutions of teaching and research that had sprung up in its wake, and that Heine fit very well into the divisions between the Catholic and Protestant value systems.

Broadly speaking, Heine's historical situation resembled that of the Generation of 1898 in several respects. Like them, he had to mediate between French and German thought. Like Spain, Germany, the culture with which Heine was mainly identified, had seen glorious times in the distant past and had fallen into disarray and impotence, Marx's *deutsche Misere.* By the time the Generation of 1898 came around and included in its many interests the writings of Heine, Germany had risen to new heights, militarily, economically, and culturally. It had defeated France and was widely admired in the world, but at the same time it was not devoid of threatening features. Heine must have appeared to these Spanish intellectuals as a forerunner of the new greatness, as a critic and warning prophet who had predicted and helped bring about his country's rejuvenation.

At any rate, in the sociointellectual climate of fin-de-siècle Spain a small coterie of dissatisfied literati, who soon called themselves ninety-eighters, launched a campaign in favor of a variety of reforms. In their novels, poems, and plays, but even more so in journalistic writings and political manifestos, they laid the foundation for a new consciousness. They are thus universally credited with rekindling the great intellectual forces that renewed the cultural life of Spain and helped reintegrate it into the European configuration of cultures as an equal participant.

We need not be concerned today with the question who did and who did not belong to the ninety-eighters' inner circle. We cannot assert that they were very clear about their aims and methods, nor is it possible to proclaim the unanimity of their views: their later developments and polarizations, their disparate alignments within the spectrum of Spanish society, their diametrically opposed partisanship in the dictatorial regimes of Primo de Rivera and Francisco Franco prove the contrary. But for a while their reform-mindedness, their preoccupation with Spain, their love of its countryside and old cities, the pain they expressed about its loss of rank and prestige, their agony over its decadence, and their indignation at the irresponsible superficiality of their contemporaries gave them a kind of cohesion. What is more, their visions of a better future, their originality and wealth of ideas, and especially their eloquence and productivity assure them a permanent place in the history of Spanish culture.[26] It can be said that, together with other movements,[27] the Generation of 1898 initiated, in analogy to the French *renouveau catholique* and perhaps German Expressionism, a profound renaissance of Spanish culture.

For all of these reasons it is of interest to ascertain, first, how they dealt with one of the main figures of the Spanish tradition, Miguel de Cervantes Saavedra, and, second, what role Heine played in these cultural readjustments. The first of these questions has been dealt with repeatedly: "Don Quijote, the mythical personage par excellence for Spaniards," Werner Brüggemann writes, for example, "becomes the center of attention for the Generation of 1898 in its quest to understand the Spanish national character, the meaning of Spanish history and culture, as well as the peninsula's relation to Europe and the world." The preponderant importance assigned to the novel links the ninety-eighters to the German Romantics, for whom "Cervantes . . . possessed, as it were, canonical eminence."[28]

The Spanish writers of the Generation of 1898 all knew Heine and his ideas on *Don Quijote*. José Martínez Ruiz, for instance, better known by his pen name *Azorín*, mentions two sources in which he found Spanish versions of Heine's "Introduction" to *Don Quijote*. In a 1914 article entitled "Heine and Cervantes" he lists the translations by D. S. Restrepo in the Spanish-language journal *Hispania* published in London and an earlier one by Augusto Ferrer which had appeared in the September 30, 1877, issue of *Revista Contemporánea* in Madrid. Azorín then goes on to describe the merits and shortcomings of these versions. But it is not from them that he learned of Heine's piece. According to his own admission, he first read it in a French edition of Heine's complete works published in 1867. A note by its editor, Michel Lévy, alerted him to the fact that Heine had belittled his own essay. He quotes Lévy's commentary to the effect that "the reader will certainly accept only in part the poet's judgment." Azorín disagrees emphatically. "Not only do we not accept even in part Heine's verdict, but, far from it, we hold the poet's pages about the *Quijote* to be the most beautiful, fundamental, and deeply felt that have ever been written," he says, explicitly excluding Rousseau, La Fontaine, Victor Hugo, Turgenev, and Flaubert from this superlative.[29]

For Azorín, Heine's interpretation represents the most modern point of view, containing many of the ideas that have become part and parcel of the prevailing consensus, and he recapitulates, with the help of abundant citations, the ones that seem to him the most important. What is more, Azorín is conscious of a phenomenon that explains why it is difficult to trace borrowings from Heine in the Spanish writings concerned with Cervantes, why it is more appropriate to draw parallels between Heine and the Spanish interpreters of *Don Quijote* than to pinpoint precisely the ideas derived from him. Heine's aperçus, Azorín declares, "have all become extremely popular; having left the poet's pen, they dispersed all over the world, and today we encounter them, worn out, aged, debilitated, in journalistic articles and long-winded academic speeches, without the vibrancy and the fire with which the poet had endowed them."[30]

Azorín's own work is replete with reminiscences, vignettes, articles, and fragments of articles on Cervantes. Some of them have been collected under the ironic title *Con permiso de los Cervantistas* [By Leave of the Cervantes Scholars].[31] But the gist of his interpretation is contained in *Ruta de Don Quijote,* where, following in the footsteps of the fantastic knight like Unamuno, he evokes the suggestive territory of the province of La Mancha, intertwining historical and topographical detail. The wanderer "feels overwhelmed, stunned, by the unchanging plains, by the endless, transparent sky, the inaccessible distance." Mythifying the landscape, he prepared the ground for transforming Alonso Quijano, a normal inhabitant of Spain, into Don Quijote, the mythical embodiment of the country, ready to arise again and again, a "crazy, unreasoning, and impetuous phantasma, suddenly exploding into action only to relapse once more into unproductive stagnation." In Azorín's view this cycle is, "condensed, the eternal history of Spain." "How is it possible not to feel something mysterious, a desire that we cannot explain, an undefined, inexpressible yearning that rises in our spirit?"[32] The landscape has become the correlative of the soul, and a literary figure the incarnation of the national character. From here it is but a small step to the psychological interpretation of Don Quijote, and Azorín explicitly credits Heine with having invented this all-important method of exegesis. Acknowledging his debt, he concludes his little treatise, "Heine and Cervantes," by effusively thanking the German poet for what Azorín terms Heine's "wonderful pages." By emphasizing—quite out of context—that Heine is *"persecuted* [Azorín's italics] in his homeland where he does not even have a single monument," he creates the impression that he is offering the German writer an asylum in the more congenial cultural spheres of Spain.[33]

Ramiro de Maeztú was also an admirer of Heine. Maeztú referred to the German on various occasions and wrote on the conflict between Heine and Börne and on Heine's relationship to Goethe.[34] In a chapter of his book *Don Quijote, Don Juan y La Celestina: Ensayos en Simpatía,* entitled "The Critics of Don Quijote," he dedicates a paragraph to Heine, no more, but even this meager reference makes it clear that he is sympathetically familiar with Heine's ruminations on *Don Quijote.*[35] In another chapter, "Spain and the 'Quijote,'" he recalls that in the wake of 1898 various interpretations linked Don Quijote to the national disaster, distilling from it the lesson that one must not be a Don Quijote, that one should not engage in adventures and entertain illusions that of necessity end badly. Maeztú avers that he disagreed then with this conclusion and still does so now, decades later. He does not deny that

Don Quijote contains significant directions for the nation, but to profit from them it is necessary to view "the national novel par excellence," as he calls the work, historically. When it appeared early in the seventeenth century, its "historical function" was "to prepare the spirit of the Spaniards for a renunciation of undertakings that could no longer be undertaken anyway." The sixteenth century was a time of superhuman efforts on the part of Spain, and the novel marked the moment when a stop had to be put to these excessive endeavors. Spain was a nation that had desired too much. But then it fell into the other extreme of desiring nothing. It lost all historical initiative, lapsing into a profound quiescence. In the twentieth century the need is no longer one of disenchantment and disillusion; on the contrary, it is necessary to find another ideal. Moreover, Don Quijote is a book of love. But "love without strength cannot move anything, and to take good measure of our own strength we need to see things as they are. Truthfulness is an indispensable duty. Confusing windmills with giants is not merely a hallucination, it is a sin."[36]

Such views may differ from and even have little to do with Heine's. But since they are expressed in the chapter immediately following the section in which Maeztú discusses Heine, the "madman who woke up from his revolutionary madness to discover that Europe had not changed all that he had hoped for from the movements of 1848," one realizes that there is something analogous in the two approaches. It is immaterial whether Maeztú's pronouncement that "Cervantes was not nor wanted to be a reformer of the country's institutions" is a direct echo from Heine. The similarity lies not in the content, but in the method. The manner of the exegesis is the same. Maeztú's warning against reading Quijote "as if it had been written outside of time and space, for readers who are likewise located in a realm of eternity," and his exhortation to "place it in its historical perspective" is profoundly Heinean.[37] It recognizes the complex ambivalence of the book's symbolism, exploiting it, as Heine had done, to give it relevance for the political moment in which both the interpreter and his society find themselves.

The most eloquent and prolific spokesman of the ninety-eighters in the matter of Cervantes was probably Miguel de Unamuno. As far as Heine is concerned, Unamuno was well informed. He is said to have penned eighteen hundred poems that bear the imprint of Heine's characteristic strophe.[38] In his Cancionero, a kind of poetic diary, Unamuno pays tribute to Heine as a source from which he imbibed the German language, and what is at least equally important, Unamuno acknowledges Heine as a model for his ecumenical humanism. These are his often-quoted lines:

> Heine de mis mocedades
> donde aprendí mi alemán
> judío de toda patria
> hijo de la humanidad.

> [Heine of my early years
> from whom I learned my German
> Jew of all fatherlands
> son of all mankind.][39]

Nevertheless, Unamuno was apparently less interested in Heine's poetry than in his critical writings, such as the essay *Zur Geschichte der Religion und Philosophie in Deutschland* [On the History of Religion and Philosophy in Germany], in which Heine warns against the demonic forces of Teutonic pantheism which might someday result in an outbreak of brutal Germanic belligerency. These ideas may have influenced Unamuno's sharp criticism of Imperial Germany during World War I.[40]

With regard to *Don Quijote,* Unamuno did not need anybody's guidance; he proved quite capable of forging his own strong, albeit shifting, opinions. Still, there are significant points of convergence between his and Heine's views. In contrast to a long interpretive tradition that assumed an "intentional" Cervantes, proceeding from the supposition that the novelist's intention had to be reconstructed as a first step toward an understanding of his work, both Heine and Unamuno postulated a Cervantes whose creation was largely unconscious and thus more attuned to the future, more open to a flexible interpretation.

Thus when Unamuno praises the last chapter of the novel, in which Don Quijote is cured of his madness and reverts to being Alonso Quijano once more, it is entirely in what he took to be Heine's spirit. The words with which Unamuno extols this transformation as a portent of Spain's regeneration sound like a transposition into prose of his verses about Heine quoted above: "He achieved a kind of renunciation of his Spanishness; he touched on the universal spirit, the human being that sleeps in the interior of all of us."[41] The fact that Unamuno later shifted his attention from Alonso Quijano back to Don Quijote does not detract from this parallelism.

Another bond of unison that connects him with Heine is to be found in the role Unamuno assigns to Don Quijote's idealism, which, as he proclaims, "drags behind it, however much they resent it, all the Sanchos" of this world.[42] This statement is so close to Heine that it almost seems like an echo of the German poet's comparison between the relative strengths of the knight and the squire: "Material Sense," Heine mocks, "must trot . . . behind Enthusiasm; despite his better knowledge he and his donkey must share all the reverses that so often beset the noble knight; indeed, Ideal Inspiration possesses such sweeping powers that Material Sense . . . must always follow it around automatically."[43]

Unamuno's utterances in which he expresses a preference for Alonso Quijano over Don Quijote stem from 1895, before the crucial date that gave the movement with which he associated himself its well-known name. Ten years later, when the significance of the year 1898 had generally sunk in, Unamuno resolutely distances himself from his erstwhile condemnation of the mad knight. In the last chapter of his famous book *Del sentimiento trágico de la vida* [Of the Tragic Sense of Life] of 1905, he calls his rejection of Don Quijote in favor of Alonso Quijano a blasphemy and his book *Vida de Don Quijote y Sancho* [The Life of Don Quijote and Sancho], in which he retracts and indeed reverses this predilection, "his cult of Quixotism" and "a national religion."[44] Instead of the Europeanization of Spain, he demands a Hispanization of Europe. But this reversal notwithstanding, there are unmistakable similarities to Heine even in the new orientation, such as the idea that Cervantes was not really aware of the full meaning of his novel and the demand that Don Quijote be separated from his creator. "It is all-important," Unamuno decrees with the same fervor with which he had exclaimed "Death to Don Quijote" in the last chapter of *Del sentimiento trágico*, "that the plague of the Cervantophiles and Cervantists be replaced by the holy legion of the Quixotists. We need Quixotism as much as we have a surfeit of Cervantism."[45]

One result of his rejection of the artistic unity of the novel in favor of an extrapolation of the characters as independent mythological entities is Unamuno's emphasis on their inherent polarization and ultimate fusion into one. This approach again resembles Heine. In Unamuno's version Don Quijote is the "spiritual knight" and the squire becomes "carnal Sancho": "Oh, practical Sanchos, positive Sanchos, material Sanchos!" Unamuno laments. "When will you hear the silent music of the spiritual spheres?" But the contrasting symbols do not remain isolated forever. Like Heine's opposites, they meet and unite as basic forces in the human existence. "The greatest and most comforting aspect of their life together," Unamuno continues, "is that it makes it impossible to conceive of one without the other, and far from being opposite poles . . . they were and are not two halves of an orange but one and the same being seen from two sides."[46] And let me repeat what Heine says in a similar context: "The two characters who call themselves Don Quijote and Sancho Panza parody each other constantly and yet they complement one another so wondrously that they constitute the real hero of the novel."[47] It does not matter whether this is a direct Heinean echo or proof that Heine's thought has been totally absorbed into the cultural dialogue of the day, as Azorín surmised. The point is that it runs through Unamuno's writings like a red thread.

José Ortega y Gasset, born in 1883, cannot strictly be regarded as belonging to the same generation. But since he and his age group continued the work of their predecessors in the same spirit of "national regeneration," they have been dubbed "the second generation of 1898."[48] In his work Heine crops up now and then on insignificant occasions. Only in an examination of the Romantic affinities of his generation does Ortega seem to establish a somewhat more intimate link between Heine and himself. "We gave in to the illusion," he writes, "of no longer being Romantics, emotionally and literarily. But we need only compare ourselves with the young people of today in order to feel how much we are still in the tow of our Romantic grandfathers. Long ago Heine claimed—even if somewhat unclearly—not to belong fully to the Romantics anymore."[49] Other references at least testify to the fact that Heine figures in Ortega's "ideario."

Nevertheless, Ortega's approach to Cervantes, best documented in his *Meditaciones del Quijote* of 1914, is informed by a desire to cast aside interpretive influences that came to Spain from abroad. He sees it as his task "to replace the foreign ideas by a national interpretation vitally concerned with the Spanish destiny and the meaning of the trajectory of Spanish history."[50] It is doubtless for this reason that he dismisses the contributions of some non-Spanish authors who have written about *Don Quijote,* explicitly including Heine, as "brief elucidations" that shed only "momentary and insufficient light" on the

problems raised in the novel. "For those men," Ortega opines, "the Quijote was only a glorious curiosity: for them he was not, as he was for us,
the problem of their very fate."[51]

Despite such disclaimers, it has been said that Ortega still draws,
in his complex meditations about the meaning of the novel for Spain,
on impulses emanating from Heine, both in method and in substance.[52]
With Heinean intensity he examines the problem of irony: "Of whom is
Cervantes making fun?"[53] This question could easily have been asked
by Heine, and he actually came close to posing it. Ortega's preoccupation with the novel's psychological opposites, alternately forming patterns of polarization as well as undergoing processes of fusion into a
composite entity, is also deeply Heinean. This chapter is not the place to
reconstruct or criticize Ortega's thought on Spain. No social scientist
can predict with accuracy the development of a society, and specula-
tions about a nation's "essence" and "mission" are best left to writers
and philosophical essayists like Ortega. But this role is one of the many
Heine also played: a philosophical essayist. It is this coincidence that
probably accounts for the similarities that can be detected in their
styles.

Indeed, "similarities of style" may be the best formula to describe
the loose bond that connects Heine's cultural and political essays with
the writings of many of the ninety-eighters, at some of whom we have
just cast a glance. They knew Heine, they admired and were inspired
by him, whom they quote and praise, and they were influenced by his
inimitable combination of lightness and profundity, brilliance of formulation, and incessant stream of ideas. It is the same mix that left
a comparable mark on Nietzsche, whose impact on the Generation of
1898 might also merit another look.

There is no doubt that the reception of the products of one culture
in another is fraught with peril and precariousness. It can indeed be
called the sum total of all the misunderstandings inevitably caused by
the transfer from one linguistic milieu with its peculiar traditions to
another. Until recently, Spain was so distant from Germany that the
shape such transfers took on their way from one of these spheres to the
other was often grotesque. Examples abound. With its often arbitrary
selection, its whimsical transformations, and its paradoxical results,
the German stimulus was "usually distorted by the time it reached
Spain."[54] The fate of Heine does not deviate from this pattern. It is especially true of his poetry, whose deeply ironic and equivocal character

was rarely recognized in Spain. But it is much less apparent in the reception of Heine's thoughts on Cervantes. After all, *Don Quijote* is as Spanish a product as there can be, and its reimportation from the German Romantics and their successor Heinrich Heine was exempt from the customs duties ordinarily exacted. Heine's attempts at interpreting the novel and its characters by and large struck a sympathetic chord and provided many impulses for further meditation. There is no reason to disagree with Heine, who attributed much of the "interpretive fertility" the novel exhibited to Cervantes himself. "The pen of a genius is always greater than he himself; it reaches out far beyond his temporal intentions, . . . without his ever becoming conscious" of this difference, Heine declared,[55] thus enunciating a principle that has become fundamental to all reception histories. Had he been able to witness the rich interchanges that ensued between his thoughts and those of the Spanish ninety-eighters, he could have added another facet to his maxim, namely, that the place has to be right and the time ripe for certain of the innumerable vibrations emitted by every masterful work of art to become audible messages.

NOTES

1. Translated from Heinrich Heine, *Werke-Briefwechsel-Lebenszeugnisse,* 27 vols., Säkularausgabe (Berlin: Akademie; Paris: Editions du Centre National de la Recherche Scientifique, 1970), 21:171. The original letter of November 21, 1836, to August Lewald reads: "aber immer liegt mir Spanien im Sinne und es zieht mich unwiderstehlich nach Madrid. Ich will mal den Donquixote in der Mancha lesen." Within the chapter all translations from non-English sources are provided by the author, except where otherwise noted. Where useful or necessary, these sources are cited in the original either within the chapter or in the notes.

2. Heine, *Werke,* 21:179 (letter to Baron Johann Georg von Cotta of January 29, 1837).

3. Translated from Jost Hermand, *Streitobjekt Heine: Ein Forschungsbericht, 1945–1975* (Frankfurt am Main: Athenäum-Fischer, 1975), p. 167.

4. Claude Owens, *Heine im Spanischen Sprachgebiet,* Spanische Forschungen der Görresgesellschaft, Zweite Reihe, 12. Band (Münster: Aschendorff, 1968); and Owens, *Heine im Spanischen Sprachgebiet: Eine kritische Bibliographie,* Sonderdruck aus Spanische Forschungen der Görresgesellschaft, Erste Reihe, Gesammelte Aufsätze zur Kulturgeschichte Spaniens, 27. Band (Münster: Aschendorff, 1973).

5. I refer to, among others, the important article by Udo Rukser, "Heine in der hispanischen Welt," *Deutsche Vierteljahrsschrift für Literaturwissenschaft und Geistesgeschichte* 30 (4) (1956): 474–510; and my own "Reception of German Culture in Spain," *Yearbook of Comparative and General Literature* 14 (1965): 16–36.

6. Translated from Emilia Pardo Bazán, "Fortuna española de Heine," *Revista de España* 110 (1886): 491–496.

7. Heinrich Heine, "Einleitung zum Don Quichotte," in *Sämtliche Schriften*, ed. Klaus Briegleb, 6 vols. (Munich: Hanser, 1968–76), 4:163. The relevant passage reads as follows: "Cervantes, Shakespeare und Goethe bilden das Dichtertriumvirat, das in den drei Gattungen poetischer Darstellung, im Epischen, Dramatischen und Lyrischen, das Höchste hervorgebracht." ["Cervantes, Shakespeare, and Goethe constitute the poetic triumvirate that has brought forth the greatest in the three genres of literary representation: the epic, the dramatic, and the lyrical."]

8. For Heine's first reading of *Don Quijote*, see "Italienische Reisebilder," in Heine, *Schriften*, 2:478–529. For the second, see "Die romantische Schule," in Heine, *Schriften*, 5:357–504 (for an English translation, see Heinrich Heine, *The Romantic School and Other Essays*, ed. Jost Hermand and Robert C. Holub [New York: Continuum, 1985]). And for the last, see "Einleitung zum Don Quichotte," in Heine, *Schriften*, 4:151–170.

9. For these letters, see Heine, *Werke*, 21:204 (the original reads: "das Schlechteste, was ich je geschrieben habe"), and ibid., 210.

10. Cf. "Italienische Reisebilder," in Heine, *Schriften*, 2:487–529; and "Einleitung zum Don Quichotte," in 4:151–170.

11. Heine, *Schriften*, 2:522.

12. Ibid., 2:524; 4:153.

13. Ibid., 2:525; translated from ibid., 2:525–526.

14. Translated from commentary by Norbert Altenhofer, editor of Heinrich Heine, *Die romantische Schule* (Frankfurt am Main: Insel, 1987), pp. 232–234.

15. These dicta can be found in the "Einleitung zum Don Quichotte," Heine, *Schriften*, 4:161–167. The citation about "the best novel" is found on p. 164.

16. Ibid., p. 169.

17. Ibid., pp. 152, 169.

18. This interpretation is given in *Die romantische Schule*, Heine, *Schriften*, 3:430–431 (in English, see Heine, *Romantic School*, pp. 56–68).

19. Translated from *Die romantische Schule*, in Heine, *Schriften*, 3:431 (in English, see Heine, *Romantic School*, p. 68). The original reads as follows: "Oder hat der tiefsinnige Spanier noch tiefer die menschliche Natur verhöhnen wollen? Hat er vielleicht in der Gestalt des Don Quixote unseren

Geist, und in der Gestalt des Sancho Pansa unseren Leib allegorisiert, und
das ganze Gedicht wäre alsdenn nichts anders als ein großes Mysterium,
wo die Frage über den Geist und die Materie in ihrer gräßlichsten Wahrheit
diskutiert wird?"

20. "Einleitung zum Don Quichotte," Heine, *Schriften,* 4:165.

21. *Die romantische Schule,* Heine, *Schriften,* 3:429 (in English, see Heine,
Romantic School, p. 66).

22. "Einleitung zum Don Quichotte," in Heine, *Schriften,* 4:154.

23. Cf. *Die romantische Schule,* Heine, *Schriften,* 3:429 (and in English, Heine,
Romantic School, p. 66); and the "Einleitung zum Don Quichotte," Heine,
Schriften, 4:159.

24. See Carlos Blanco Aguinaga, *Juventud del 98* (Madrid: Emilio Rubin, 1970),
p. 294, where the author speaks of Spain's "desarrollo caótico del capital-
ismo de país subdesarrollado" ["chaotic development of the capitalism of
an underdeveloped country"].

25. See John Kautsky, "Karl Kautsky and Euro-Communism," *Studies in Comparative Communism* 14 (Spring 1981): 3–44.

26. See also Borja de Arquer, *La generación del 98 hoy* (Barcelona: Ramón
Sopena, 1968).

27. I.e., the so-called *Krausismo* and its offshoots, the Institución Libre de Ense-
ñanza, and the Junta de Ampliación de Estudios. For a detailed treatment,
see Juan Lopez Morillas, *El krausismo español* (Mexico City and Buenos
Aires: Fondo de cultura económica, 1956).

28. Translated from Werner Brüggemann, *Cervantes und die Figur des Don
Quijote in Kunstanschauung und Dichtung der deutschen Romantik,* Spanische Forschungen der Görresgesellschaft, Zweite Reihe, vol. 7 (Münster:
Aschendorffsche, 1958). Passages cited are found on pp. 331 and 310. I owe
the discovery of many of the quotations in this chapter to this work.

29. Translated from José Martínez Ruiz [Azorín], "Heine y Cervantes," in *Obras
Completas,* ed. Angel Cruz Rueda (Madrid: Aguilar, 1947), pp. 951–960.
The original version of the translated passage (on "Heine's verdict") is on
p. 952.

30. Ibid., p. 955.

31. Azorín, *Con permiso de los Cervantistas* (Madrid: Biblioteca Nueva, 1948).

32. Translated from *Ruta de Don Quijote,* in Azorín, *Obras Completas,* 36,
210, 101.

33. See "Heine y Cervantes," in Azorín, *Obras Completas,* p. 955.

34. See "Desde Bilbao: Heine y Boerne," in *El nuevo mundo* (Madrid), November 10, 1910; and "Wilson, Goethe y Heine" in *España y Europa* (Buenos
Aires: Espasa-Calpe, 1947), pp. 138–141.

35. See Ramiro de Maeztú, *Don Quijote, Don Juan y La Celestina: Ensayos en*

Simpatía (Buenos Aires and Mexico City: Espasa-Calpe Argentina, 1939).

36. First quotation translated from ibid., p.63; second two from p.74; and the last from p.77.

37. First citation translated from ibid., p.62; the second from p.69; and the final two from p.73.

38. According to Owens, *Heine im Spanischen Sprachgebiet*, p.298.

39. Cited in ibid., p.299.

40. See Gerhart Mayer, "Unamunos Beziehungen zur deutschen Dichtung," *Germanisch-Romanische Monatsschrift* 17 (1961): 197–210. Mayer quotes from Unamuno's October 15 article "La pureza del idealismo"—available in "De esto y de aquello" [Of this and that], in Miguel de Unamuno, *Obras Completas*, 16 vols. (Madrid: Aguado, 1950–58), 3:427—in which he uses obviously Heinean terminology to voice his sharp criticism of Germany: "Through this pantheism or rather this pagan pan-Germanism . . . all abuses are justified in the name of victory and power."

41. Translated from Miguel de Unamuno, "La tradición eterna," in *Ensayos* (Madrid, 1916), 1:37.

42. Translated from Unamuno, "El caballero de la triste figura: Ensayo iconológico," in *Ensayos*, 2:128.

43. Translated from *Die romantische Schule*, in Heine, *Schriften*, 3:430–431 (in English, see Heine, *Romantic School*, pp.67–68). The original reads: "denn der reale Verstand . . . muß . . . hinter der Begeisterung einher trottieren; trotz seiner besseren Einsicht muß er und sein Esel alles Ungemach teilen, das dem edlen Ritter so oft zustößt: ja, die ideale Begeisterung ist von so gewaltig hinreißender Art, daß der reale Verstand, mitsamt seinen Eseln, ihr immer unwillkürlich nachfolgen muß."

44. Translated from Unamuno, *Obras Completas*, 4:704.

45. Translated from Unamuno, *Ensayos*, 5:217.

46. Translated from Unamuno, *Obras Completas*, 4:295.

47. From the "Einleitung zum Don Quichotte," in Heine, *Schriften*, 4:165. The original reads: "Was nun jene zwei Gestalten betrifft, die sich Don Quixote and Sancho Pansa nennen, sich beständig parodieren und doch so wunderbar ergänzen, daß sie den eigentlichen Helden des Romans bilden."

48. See Arquer, *La generación del 98 hoy*, p.83.

49. Translated from the German edition of José Ortega y Gasset, *Gesammelte Werke in vier Bänden* (Stuttgart: Deutsche Verlagsanstalt, 1955), 2:306.

50. Translated from a citation in Brüggemann, *Cervantes und die Figur des Don Quijote*, p.342.

51. Translated from José Ortega y Gasset, *Meditaciones del Quijote* (Madrid: Calpe, 1921), p.114.

52. See Brüggemann, *Cervantes und die Figur des Don Quijote*, p.342. Brüggemann alludes to the "Heinean intensity" with which Ortega speculates

about the "meaning" of *Don Quijote* and on p. 345 actually speaks of a "Weiterbildung der Gedankengänge Heines" ["a continuation of Heine's thoughts"] on the part of Ortega.

53. Translated from Ortega, *Meditaciones*, p. 114.

54. Schwarz, "Reception of German Culture in Spain," p. 36.

55. Translated from "Einleitung zum Don Quichotte" in Heine, *Schriften*, 4:154. The original reads: "die Feder des Genius ist immer größer als er selber, sie reicht immer weit hinaus über seine zeitlichen Absichten, und ohne daß er sich dessen klar bewußt wurde, schrieb Cervantes die größte Satire gegen die menschliche Begeisterung."

WORKS CITED

Arquer, Borja de. *La generación del 98 hoy*. Barcelona: Ramón Sopena, 1968.

Blanco Aguinaga, Carlos. *Juventud del 98*. Madrid: Emilio Rubin, 1970.

Brüggemann, Werner. *Cervantes und die Figur des Don Quijote in Kunstanschauung und Dichtung der deutschen Romantik*. Spanische Forschungen der Görresgesellschaft, Zweite Reihe, Bd. 7. Münster: Aschendorf, 1958.

Heine, Heinrich. *Die Romantische Schule*. Ed. Norbert Altenhofer. Frankfurt am Main: Insel, 1987.

——. *The Romantic School and Other Essays*. Ed. Jost Hermand and Robert C. Holub. New York: Continuum, 1985.

——. *Sämtliche Schriften*. Ed. Klaus Briegleb. 6 vols. Munich: Hanser, 1968–76.

——. *Werke-Briefwechsel-Lebenszeugnisse*. 27 vols. Säkularausgabe. Berlin: Akademie; Paris: Editions du Centre de la Recherche Scientifique, 1970.

Hermand, Jost. *Streitobjekt Heine: Ein Forschungsbericht, 1945–1975*. Frankfurt am Main: Athenäum Fischer, 1975.

Kautsky, John. "Karl Kautsky and Euro-Communism." *Studies in Comparative Communism* 14 (Spring 1981): 3–44.

Lopez Morillas, Juan. *El krausismo español*. Mexico City and Buenos Aires: Fondo de cultura económica, 1956.

Maeztú, Ramiro de. "Desde Bilbao: Heine y Boerne." *El nuevo mundo* (Madrid). November 10, 1910.

——. *Don Quijote, Don Juan y La Celestina: Ensayos en Simpatía*. Buenos Aires and Mexico City: Espasa-Calpe Argentina, 1939.

——. "Wilson, Goethe y Heine." In *España y Europa*. Buenos Aires: Espasa-Calpe, 1947.

Martínez Ruiz, José [Azorín]. *Con permiso de los Cervantistas*. Madrid: Biblioteca Nueva, 1948.

——. *Obras Completas*. Ed. Angel Cruz Rueda. Madrid: Aguilar, 1947.

Mayer, Gerhart. "Unamunos Beziehungen zur deutschen Dichtung." *Germanisch-Romanische Monatsschrift* 17 (1961): 197–210.

Ortega y Gasset, José. *Gesammelte Werke in vier Bänden*. Stuttgart: Deutsche Verlagsanstalt, 1955.

——. *Meditaciones del Quijote*. Madrid: Calpe, 1921.

Owens, Claude. *Heine im Spanischen Sprachgebiet*. Spanische Forschungen der Görresgesellschaft, Zweite Reihe, 12. Band. Münster: Aschendorff, 1968.

——. *Heine im Spanischen Sprachgebiet: Eine kritische Bibliographie*. Sonderdruck aus Spanische Forschungen der Görresgesellschaft, Erste Reihe, Gesammelte Aufsätze zur Kulturgeschichte Spaniens, 27. Band. Münster: Aschendorff, 1973.

Pardo Bazán, Emilio. "Fortuna española de Heine." *Revista de España* 110 (1886): 491–496.

Rukser, Udo. "Heine in der hispanischen Welt." *Deutsche Vierteljahrsschrift für Literaturwissenschaft und Geistesgeschichte* 30 (4) (1956): 474–510.

Schwarz, Egon. "The Reception of German Culture in Spain." *Yearbook of Comparative and General Literature* 14 (1965): 16–36.

Unamuno, Miguel de. *Ensayos*. Madrid, 1916.

——. *Obras Completas*. 16 vols. Madrid: Aguado, 1950–58.

LUCIANO ZAGARI

Permanence in Change:
Heine's Reception in Italian Culture
through Two Centuries

The title of this essay should direct the attention of the reader right from the start to the singular role ascribed to Heine time and again in Italian cultural life.[1] Heine's presence in several stages of his Italian reception was not simply that of one great poet and writer among many. A basically militant reception saw him as the exemplary figure of an intellectual whose overall appearance exercised an important influence on cultural life in Italy, of course with different functions at different times. And even when Heine the writer seemed to supplant Heine the intellectual—as in the period after World War I or today in our movement away from ideologies—this reorientation succeeded under the auspices of a polemical, but no less militant, attitude.

Only after the establishment of the new kingdom in 1861 can one speak of an appreciable reception of Heine in Italy. Receptions by translators, such as Bernardino Zendrini[2] and Giuseppe Chiarini;[3] by writers, such as Giosuè Carducci,[4] Arrigo Boito, and Carlo Dossi; and in general by "intellectuals," such as Tullo Massarani,[5] were much more common than theoretical literary discussions of his texts in the narrower sense of the term.

The "modernity" of Heine was for the most part understood as an interweaving of contradictory moments. *Dissonance* was and remained for a long time the soon-clichéed *parole*. Thus one admired, on the one hand, the enchanting melodiousness of the *Buch der Lieder* [Book of Songs] and, on the other hand, the finesse of Heine's iconism, clear and polished as smooth as a diamond, image and melody almost without assertion, springing forth directly from subjectivity, such that even subjectivity itself seems to merge almost entirely into the lyrical creative process. No less stimulating and exciting was Heine's effect as a multi-faceted writer of wit, of sarcasm to the point of self-satirization. The way Heine united relativization, desecration, and demystification with the purity of the song of a nightingale was archmodern. The reader was supposed to have the impression of taking part in the secularization of traditional values, but without having to give up any claim to a binding aesthetic radiance in modern, prosaic life. This reading accommodated a principal concern of moderate, bourgeois, progressive culture of so-called Third Italy, a culture that among other things strived for a less academic form of literary communication (within bounds), hoping in this way to find access to the international culture and "way of life" without having to make a complete and radical change.

In particular, Heine's unusual talent for creating new myths or varying old ones had a guiding influence. In a culture that no longer possessed any direct access to the dimension of mythos (or, rather, that possessed such access only in the form of a classical or romanticizing decadence), poems such as "Auf Flügeln des Gesanges" [On Wings of Song], "Die Lore-Ley" [The Lorelei], "Geoffrey Rudèl and Melisande of Tripolis," *Karl I* [Charles I], as well as Heine's American poems, gave fresh impetus, especially to Giosuè Carducci's late Romantic epics. It is no coincidence that his translations of Heine were included in the complete edition of Carducci's poems, among them "Der König von Thule" [The King of Thule], "Der Grab im Busento" [The Grave in Busento], and "Der Pilgrim vor St. Just" [The Pilgrim before St. Justin]. These translations were even celebrated—strange as it may sound to our ears—as the paradigm for a modern form of mythical writing.

No less effective, however, were poems of a different orientation, such as "Die schlesischen Weber" [The Silesian Weavers], or certain scenes and female figures veristically reminiscent of the big city. A chapter in itself, furthermore, could be devoted to the effect of Heine's prose as a paragon of mixed-pitch writing, impossible to categorize in any traditional genre, artistically demanding, colored subjectively to the point of a *capriccio* timbre, yet at the same time flexible enough to serve any communicative purpose. Here again Carducci comes to mind. He unexpectedly interrupts the academic scholarly course of his discussion of Italian and European literature with imaginative recollections of his childhood—deviating completely from the Italian tradition of this academic writing. Or he expresses his opinion in political-personal polemics against the Manzoni disciples or the pettiness of life during the Third Italy. In his commemorative address for Garibaldi, Carducci tells of the reawakening of the folk hero after a thousand years, following a model that strongly calls to mind Heine's Kyffhäuser legend, admittedly without penumbral overtones.

Heine was experienced as a fighting comrade in other circles as well —for instance, by the "Scapigliati," the Italian variation of a predecadent but realistically minded *Bohème*. He was seen as a prophet of a more freely moving culture that was itself prepared to grapple with a petty, colorless reality, often in the shape of a realistic moody performance of arabesques or a fanciful ironic self-projection. Arrigo Boito, later the Verdi librettist, wrote a *Re Orso* [King Bear] that would have been unthinkable without Heine's *Atta Troll*.

In general, Heine, the first German-French (i.e., modern European) intellectual, pointed toward new thematic and formal paths with his interest in the big city and in the great political, philosophical, and social currents of the time. In comparison, say, to Goethe or Schiller, Heine had a more immediate effect, because he was on our side, so to speak, no longer on the Olympus of pure, contemplative art and ontological values. The subjectivistic adventure into which Heine's renunciation of Romanticism and his personal engagement flowed was taken as a model for a pose that made it possible for the new protagonist of modern culture and reality—namely, the lacerated subject in an antagonistic world—to show the public his unhealed and untransfigurable wounds openly and unabashedly. In 1895 the mediocre composer Pietro Mascagni referred to *William Ratcliff* to express this torn capriciousness, in the midst of the high tide of naturalism (with the delay typical of many opera composers).

Oddly enough, and yet not by coincidence, the change of generations at the beginning of the twentieth century brought with it an eclipse of Heine, not among educated readers generally, but certainly in the circles of those writers and intellectuals claiming to be modern. That Futurists and Avantgardists in the decade surrounding World War I ignored *the* linguistic genius—who, although he undermined the language of literary tradition, nevertheless still seemed to orient himself even in his most daring poetic journeys of discovery by the mainland of tradition— need not amaze us. But that Decadents and Symbolists pushed Heine aside as obsolete is ascribable to the lack of knowledge of Heine's later poems at that time. What would a D'Annunzio, a Pascoli, a writer from the group of the Crepuscolari have done with the "Lore-Ley" or with "Du bist wie eine Blume" [You Are like a Flower]?

Heine's poems, which at least seemed to take words and the art of dissonance seriously, must have seemed obsolete to writers who—schooled in the French Symbolists, in Wagner, in the Russian narrators, in Ibsen, or in the pre-Raphaelites—dared to set out into the regions of vague intimations and suggestive paraphrases. Even such an important procedure, for Heine as well as for the Italian representatives of symbolistic Decadence, as the deformation of venerable models did not lead to any close contact. Parody, travesty, pastiche, demystification remained foreign to writers who hoped to extract the shiver of a timeless contact with the inconceivable heart of the matter, that is, those who strived after an artistically tense deepening of the old art forms in an oversubscription to classical contours. Now the dissonant effects in Heine's works seemed more like harmless attempts to smuggle the old tradition of consonance in a new form into the new cultural life. Even the laceration of the subject seemed to demand a still-complete substance as a prerequisite for this subject. Still, Heine's name came up again and again. Enrico Thovez, a representative of a modern classicism, who wanted to open himself up carefully to the demands of a modern lyric poetry, gave Heine a place in his personally tinted review of modern poetry. Giuseppe Antonio Borgese, the romancer and mischievous scholar of German (later the son-in-law of Thomas Mann), found a fruitful theme in Heine's problematic personality and lasting influence.[6]

Finally, in 1921, none other than Benedetto Croce entered the discussion on Heine.[7] For Croce, Heine possessed only *one* authentic tone, that of "celia," that is, of a childlike receptivity and responsiveness able to extract from the seriousness of life the charm of an almost flirting naiveté through the fresh immediacy of his impressions and imagery. Engagement, irony, polemics, proximity to reality, the art of dissonance: these were brushed aside by Croce with a drastic gesture as poetically irrelevant and child*ish* (rather than childlike). Such a drastic division between "poetry" and "nonpoetry" corresponds, by the way, to Croce's aesthetics. But shouldn't such a highly individual judgment be dismissed as a rather orthodox application of theoretical axioms?

These heresies of Croce caused much offense in professorial circles and in the educated bourgeois reading public of the time and are indeed to be understood today as a part of his "militant" accounting of what was for him still the "modern" culture. Croce wanted to ward off in this way the pathological aspect of this culture without having to shut himself off from the eternally valid creative power of many nineteenth-century European authors, who had still demonstrated in their works— at least occasionally—the power to wrest beautiful, intact, even classical fruits from the poisonous substance of modern development. Croce's judgment also corresponded largely, as already intimated, to the new, not yet critically articulated trend in the taste of Italian cultural life. The courage to call the naked emperor naked, however, could be summoned up only by a Croce. In essence, his essay played at that time a role in Italy not unlike Karl Kraus's polemics against Heine's language in the German-speaking countries. In actuality, then, excepting outdated provincial readers and unaware professors, Heine was finished in Italy until the end of World War II.[8] The fact that an honor was bestowed on him which was otherwise reserved for Goethe among the German lyric poets—namely, that the best translations of Heine were collected in one edition and made available to a wider public—seems today more like a deferential embalming of the once-vivacious poet.[9]

The supposed mummy awoke to new life in the first years after the end of World War II. Heine's rebirth in Italy was due more to German scholars than to the wider reading public. It had to do primarily with the ideological discourse about the possibility of a new role for German culture in Europe after the twilight of the gods— the false gods. In the search for a "different" Germany, the traditional partiality for Goethe, Romanticism, and Neoromanticism yielded to interest in the line of Lessing and Enlightenment, *Sturm und Drang*, Goethe still and again, Büchner, Thomas Mann, Expressionism, and Brecht. The fact that Heine was included in this sequence was, to be sure, attributable not so much to a newly oriented reading of his poetic texts, but rather to the preeminence accorded Heine the intellectual. Once again Heine assumed the militant role of an exemplary figure, a figure that had a stimulating effect on the self-comprehension of the new, progress-oriented intellectual in postwar Italy.

There is permanence in flux, especially since the polarities of explicit polemics against Croce were the main characteristic of the overall re-acceptance of Heine. But before turning to the details of this move away from Croce, let us consider certain essays that continue the Crocian line of thought, essays that, in spite of their negative view of Heine, have nevertheless de facto assisted in opening up the field for the new interpretation or have engaged this interpretation critically or constructively. Elena Croce directed attention to the journalist Heine—doubtless emulating her father but also under the influence of Kraus's remarks about Heine's ominous role in the corruption of the German language.[10] Last but not least, because of her restrictive comments, the dispute concerning "Heine as lyric poet," having become unproductive, was laid aside, while more thorough investigations into the problematic activity of the journalist, that is, the intellectual Heine, became current.[11]

Only in 1963 did a subtler and freer follower of Croce's, the Turinian German scholar Leonello Vincenti, dedicate a paper to Heine's satirical poems.[12] Without exploding Croce's critical concept, Vincenti valued texts in which engagement, refraction effects, and intellectually complex forms of literary-communicative composition proved themselves to be poetically productive, even structurally decisive. The decades-long interest in Heine's lyrical oeuvre by Ferruccio Amoroso receives in this context unmistakable importance. This great, highly individualistic Heine translator, representative of Crocian aesthetics, with an almost exaggeratedly gifted sense for intellectual play, wit, and sarcasm, carried out the audacious undertaking of placing a new and totally differently constructed and inspired transcription of Heine's entire corpus alongside the old translations of Carducci, Zendrini, and Giuseppe Chiarini (the last two oscillating between traditional lyrical language and a preference for prosaic refraction effects).[13]

Amoroso holds systematically to the metric rhythm not just of each verse and line, but also of each foot—a virtuoso masterpiece, since the meter of Romance language does not provide for a scansion of individual feet. In his rendering, at times somewhat spurious-seeming, Amoroso brought about important hermeneutic changes in the familiar image of the spontaneous, nonchalant, even limelit rhymester Heine: the Italian reader was suddenly confronted with a self-consciously formal artist who coined refined images according to rules that at times estrange and at times fascinate. Only with Amoroso's transcription did it become clear to the Italian reader not schooled in German that Heine belongs to the series of modern language artists, balancing between the triumph and erosion of the lyrical word rendered absolute.

It is only against this backdrop that one can do justice to the full significance of the Marxist-oriented new interpretation of Heine. In the turn to ideological critique, not only literary critics but even historians and philosophers investigated Heine's ideological role.[14] Among literary scholars, it was most notably Paolo Chiarini who established a reorientation of Italian Heine research, articulated in numerous papers.[15] His research attained special prominence in relation to the lack of interest of German studies in the Federal Republic and the somewhat orthodox contributions of Heine research from the Democratic Republic.

The pairs of oppositions Chiarini worked out in the 1950s and 1960s possess a completely different historical precision than those characteristic of the more psychological impressionist-oriented Italian reception of Heine a hundred years ago. Heine, this Moses on the border of the Promised Land, is situated for Chiarini between Romanticism and Realism, but also between Marxism and Decadence. Chiarini wishes to have Heine's "suffering and greatness" understood as categories that ought to throw light on a decisive historical occurrence, that is, the conflict-ridden and laborious "pathologization of subjectivity." In Heine's work this process was being not conclusively eliminated, but rather transformed into a vehicle—obstinate, to be sure—of new collective functions.

The coherence of the seemingly crooked path, so typical for Heine's creations, was to be found not so much in individual achievements but rather more in Heine's ability, aimed at the future, to express the important factors in the development of modern culture and modern society. Heine's contradictions and oscillations were seen as important moments along the way, giving him the capability to survey the oscillating and contradictory powers of past, present, and future in play on the stage of Europe at the time—without the necessary outcome of the fight (necessary at least in the eyes of Heine and his modern Marxist-oriented researchers) being clearly evident. Chiarini extols the almost prophetic vision of Heine, who recognized the societal powers that had to lead to the triumph of the bourgeoisie and then later of Communism. But even more important were the courage and the openness that made it possible for Heine to capture the multiplicity of social currents and countercurrents in the words of his own works.

Giorgio Tonelli, a Pisan German scholar and philosopher, later employed at American universities, tried to bring important corrections to bear on this image.[16] He refused to see the years in which Heine observed the *juste milieu* and the general capitalist development in France with a more benevolent eye as mere dialectical preparation for the discovery of the role of the proletariat and of Communism. The fact that many of Tonelli's individual readings threaten to tear apart the tightly woven net of ideological interpretations of *Atta Troll* and *Deutschland: Ein Wintermärchen* [Germany: A Winter's Tale] was resented by many Heine researchers in the mid-1960s (including the present writer). Today this view would probably be seen as an advantage. What decisively reduces the usefulness of this book, however, is the identificational, reductive, often hairsplitting way in which Tonelli attempts to elucidate the hidden and half-hidden innuendos that Heine sprinkled through his political-satirical poems. At the end there is hardly a trace to be found of the playfulness of the engaged yet simultaneously *fanciful* poetic projection.

Among the contributions to ideologically critical Heine research, a short essay by Ferruccio Masini assumes an exceptional place.[17] According to this study, Heine's irony served not only to unmask Philistine lifestyle in general, but more specifically to desecrate the lie behind the ontological demand of poetry itself. Thanks to Heine's lifelong efforts to relativize tradition and himself ironically, we now have (to use Nietzsche's term somewhat anachronistically) a kind of *genealogy* of forms, which, by the way, could only introduce a corresponding undermining of values.

Even as the socioideological interpretations of Heine in the 1950s and 1960s were breaking new ground, the demand to refer back to the poetic texts became ever more urgent—not in spite of but actually because of the new results. It was just this demand, felt particularly among friends of Heine, that called for a truly radical surveying of the selection criteria and value judgments in Heine studies which had long since become cliché. In this regard the work of Vittorio Santoli and Ladislao Mittner is fundamentally significant. Santoli united Croce's influence with strong impulses from the critique of style so detested by Croce.[18]

Santoli's works signified a decisive turn in the critical study of the actual structures of Heine's lyrical oeuvre (especially the *Buch der Lieder*). Santoli investigated Heine's multifaceted style not by appealing to any preconceived ideological world view or standard of aesthetic evaluation, but by studying the morphological nature of the poetry to expose the multiplicity of the methods and levels of style used. To sketch this clear profile, Santoli did not flinch at the assumption of a calculated one-sidedness that could only shock historically or socio-ideologically oriented Heine researchers of the day.

Heine's texts were torn out of their synchronic context and were confronted directly with the poetic categories of the Baroque (primarily with that of *meraviglia* [surprise]). This unique point of departure enabled Santoli to investigate thoroughly the structurally formative power of Heine's irony in all of its various forms of expression to cast light on the literary density of these poems. Paradoxically, Santoli succeeded, despite the proximity of the *Book of Songs* to texts from the seventeenth century in his reading, in working out the modernity of Heine's lyric structures. These structures were not to be seen only as the documents of the crisis of the Classical-Romantic understanding of art. Rather, Heine's lyric forms had epoch-making effects because of his novel use of the art of words in the midst of a reality increasingly alien to art, a reality that nevertheless was more and more dependent on the magic of artistic-communicative effects.

Ladislao Mittner proceeds from different methodological assumptions in his work on Heine.[19] His framework is a robust socioideological reconstruction of Heine's position between France and Germany, with what is at first a somewhat estranging overemphasis on certain weaknesses of Heine's character. At second glance, however, it becomes evident that Mittner is not on the lookout for biographical or psychological motives. Rather, the indication of concrete details is supposed to articulate more fully a pure dialectics of abstract socioideological positions. If Mittner finds the root of Heine's anguish in the wound of being torn between wanting to be German and not being able to be so—an aged cliché—and if he underlines Heine's subjective, moody reactions to the conflicts of the time, it is only to emphasize more vividly the pathological subjectification characteristic of many of the texts of this supposed opponent of Romantic subjectivity in its penumbral dimension and structural function. In this pathological subjectification, however, the crystallization of the repulsive aspects of modern reality and struggle (admittedly also of play) itself comes to the fore, along with the poetic gesture that has become a rigid attitude and cliché.

Mittner sees the poet Heine more at the crossroads of Rococo and Decadence than at the crossroads of Romanticism and Realism. He analytically depicts the process that metamorphoses and simultaneously undermines the traditional world of images. The language of images, especially because it befits Heine's share in the one-dimensionality of surviving forms, is removed to a thin atmosphere of solitary absoluteness in his poems, which in its eerie solitude far from life seems self-ironical, that is, modern and discordant.

Mittner is able to infer from Heine's ever-popular deformation effects a deeper relationship to three different representatives of French art of the times: from the form art of Gautier, to Berlioz's preference for that which Heine once called "stacked-up impossibilities," to the frivolous lightness of Offenbach—Heine tread every thinkable path that could lead his writing to the edge of Decadence, all the way to the extreme case of what we could in Mittner's critical language call "apocalypse without apocalyptical format." Strangely enough, it is just those extreme fruits of the productive perversion of traditional lyrical language—Heine's later poems—which remained relatively difficult for Mittner. Thus it is certainly not inappropriate to take the beloved image of Heine as Moses on the border of the Promised Land and reapply it in this case to the patriarch of Italian German studies.

In the 1960s I tried to produce a specialized contribution to a newly oriented critical contact with Heine's poetic texts. The topic I chose was a relatively little-known cycle from the *Romanzero*, namely, "Pomare."[20] The study concerns first of all the false gods of modern big-city life as they appear before the eyes of the perplexed but sympathetic reader in Heine's verse and prose texts. Desecration and resanctification, in multiple interweavings, form the two main structures of the Pomare cycle. The desecration questions only within certain limits, however; the myth-creating power of the poetic word radiates from the corrupt, inhumane life in the modern Babylon, finding suitable expression—for the first time in German literature—in the paradoxical form of a parareligion of fetishized flesh. In this world of cardboard and tinsel, where everything has a repulsive, superficial, faked effect while exhibiting the explosive power of the indisputably real, a fetishized Eros celebrates his shameless triumph in the scintillating shape of clichés. For the modern reader, the border between masterly play, satire, and erosion of the firm contours of epic-lyric form might not always be readily recognizable. This virtuosity is, however, in the long run the appropriate vehicle for a profound experiment on the edge of a newly understood function of poetic language.

In the early 1970s Chiarini continued his studies of the politically engaged Heine, no longer in the form of a total interpretation, but rather by laudably translating Heine's most important polemical-ideological texts on culture, society, and politics into Italian and by furnishing the three separate volumes with profound and unsettling introductions.[21] Especially productive is his analysis of Heine's essay on Börne, since it was here for the first time that the essay was dispatched not just as the product of a semiprivate feud, but rather as the main testimony to Heine's efforts to recognize the unbroken thread of a meaningful, unified development in the almost impenetrably entangled problematics of the time.

As we look back on them today, these three well-argued papers assume a unique documentary relevance, since it was just at this point—when a zenith in the socioideologically oriented Heine research was reached—that the inner difficulties and contradictions began to stand out clearly, contradictions that would gradually lead the Italian Heine researchers (foremost among them Chiarini himself) down far-reaching new paths. Gradually, the constellation, the synergeia, as it were, became problematic.

Admittedly, during the prime of the ideologically oriented Heine research in Italy, these studies had made, out of every contribution to the historical definition of Heine the intellectual, a simultaneous, implicit contribution to the self-definition of the progressive Italian intellectual. That is especially true for some crucial points in the debate about Heine at that time: for Heine's words about the German *misère,* a debate that had the effect of somewhat exaggerating the problem of Germany's (and Italy's) foiled accession to the French or English road toward a modern form of social and political organization; and for Italian intellectuals' insight into the (dialectically) necessary development toward the victory of the proletariat and the Communists.

The critical debate also brought to light Heine's sense of the historically necessary, and therefore meaningful, contradictions in the forming of a modern intellectual, that is, the outmoded demand for autonomy, "organic membership" of the line of political-historical progress, but also uneasiness at the pressure to take on the role of mouthpiece for the tendencies of party politics. Just as important was the critical awareness of Heine's inner struggle between his inextinguishable belief in the individual, even subjectively colored role of art and artists and his tendency to oppose the new representative role of the "modern" writer and intellectual. Heine's greatness was measured either explic-

itly or silently by his capacity for experiencing and poetically articulating in the first person these and similar contradictory factors and
antinomies, determined by the objective development of modern social
and cultural powers and oppositions at an intellectual level in semi-
dialectical anticipation of a modern form of humanism.

Eventually, however, the unbroken thread of the interpretation has
slipped out of even the most careful hands, since the system of values by
which Heine's achievements were being measured—namely, the interpretation of social and cultural history as a teleological, unambiguous
roadway of progress—seems to have become unstable. It does not mean,
nevertheless, that the individual results of such a fruitful stage in the
history of Heine research should suddenly be thrown overboard. The
points mentioned, freed from the straitjacket of an "objective" knowledge value and a modern humanist optimism, remain at the center
of hermeneutic work concerning Heine. Today it is more a matter of
sketching the profile of each of these points with more historical clarity
and of appreciating them as a poetological or ideological self-projection
by the poet and intellectual Heine.[22]

Mazzino Montinari, publisher of the historical-critical Nietzsche
edition, contributed to the clarification of this complex of questions
with a differentiated interpretation of Heine's "Confessions."[23] Montinari (who also worked on the Heinrich Heine secular edition) em-
ploys his usual extreme precision and proximity to the texts to expound
highly complex motifs. He not only calls attention, as a matter of biographical relevance, to Heine's return to the belief in a personal God and
to his questioning of a linear or dialectical progress—to which the two
great strengths of man (the capacity to suffer and to enjoy) threatened to
fall victim. He also depicts a meaningful stage in an individual process
of political, philosophical, and poetic development, characterized by its
inability to be reduced to one preconceived formula.

In 1984, Maria Fancelli examined Heine's partial reception of Saint-
Simonianism in a detailed analysis of the relevant passages in *Die
romantische Schule* [The Romantic School].[24] Chiarini himself contributed actively to the reorientation of Heine research in Italy at the beginning of the 1980s. In his most recent papers he thematizes not only
the current problematic role of the intellectual Heine, but especially
this poet's peculiar way of writing on the threshold of Decadence.[25] Prerequisite for this new phase of his Heine studies is a more flexible reconstruction of his political-ideological context. In this way Chiarini is

able to elaborate on the many-layered relevance of even Romantic anti-capitalism for the construction of a modern self-consciousness on the part of the German intellectual. This approach goes far beyond the traditional association of Romanticism with the reactionary consequences of German *misère*. Chiarini now sees the reciprocal relationship between political positioning and a sense of the social in Heine, even going so far as to intimate a theory of needs.

The polemics that Heine directed against the artistic epoch and against functional literature engaged in party politics are now often seen as merely symptomatic. According to Chiarini, the cleft between the world of (aesthetic) form and that of (social and cultural) forms in the (modern) world had structural effects even in Heine's works, similar to those in Baudelaire or later in Rimbaud and the French Symbolists. Knowledge of the power of absolute, unique form, lost by historical necessity, is attributed to the beginning of a new determination of and for form. Subjectivity—robbed of its claim to objective, world-changing, or world-affirming obligations and simultaneously delegitimized in its claim to voice an ahistorical, transtemporal truth of inwardness—became a source for an older Heine of a highly modern art form: the art of pathological self-disintegration that develops between phantasmagoria and play with eroded forms, on the edge of death. It is precisely these traits that are seen as historically more significant than the many "engaged" positions of the poet and politician.

As I demonstrate in my own most recent Heine papers,[26] Heine knew in his later years of the dubiousness of any superficial humanism in modern culture. He also knew, however, how misleading the idea was that the modern intellectual could, by the power of the poetic word alone, conjure up a *new* humanity. In many of the poems from Heine's middle period we still find myths about the emancipation of the flesh and of all humanity as structurally significant forces. Even though the tone is dominated by the ironic desecration of false myths and the polemical game, with a multifaceted style and with the clichéed lyrical jargon of tradition, the loss of archetypal freshness was at that time still to be understood as anticipation of a utopia on this side of the world, which passed as a secularized form of humanism. In his late period, however, Heine knew that every form of poetic language threatens to degenerate into an idling machine, whether that language aims at communicating with the public, depicting ontological epiphany, or expressing subjectivity. Yet it is just such an unbridled proliferation of language robbed of every "natural" function which pushes language to a new type of independence and power.

Should this new development be understood as an anticipation of the Symbolist-Decadent use of language? Only a differentiated answer can do justice to this complex phenomenon. Heine's late poems have, after all, little in common with the linguistic magic wrought by that network of words aiming to indicate suggestively the world of the inexpressible.

Admittedly, the line from "Für die Mouche" [For Mouche] which reads, "The pronounced word is without shame," sounds almost like a manifesto of the Decadent understanding of the role of poetic language. Heine makes a virtue here out of linguistic necessity. A deluge of words and images is characteristic of his late poems. Yet words and images are at the disposal of the "dead poet" only because they have been robbed of their ability to express and their individual-universal stamp. They lead a spectral life in the "dead brain" of the poet, celebrate in him "sweet orgies" as mummies from an extinct world where everything has already happened and already been formed. Poetry is now possible only as a game of variations and glosses to a world of revenants. Iconolatry seems at first glance to be the most fitting definition for such poems, in which only iconic moments reign. If one were to examine more closely the actual function of these word constructions, however, one would rather be tempted to speak of iconoclasm, since any myth-creating transitive power of the language of images has been lost.

If we were to stop here, the picture of Heine's late poetry would be vastly distorted. A myth is conjured up in these texts, that is, the myth of a simultaneously skeptical and idolatrous cult of the word. The true utopia of the sick poet is that of the flood of words and images as real dreamscapes. What seems only coquettish mimicry of a myth-forming or myth-exposing poetic language *is* itself the new myth. There is no longer any possibility for the development of the thematic myth (as in the fountain of youth on Bimini, the archetype of Jewish poetry in "Jehuda ben Halewy," or the pre-Flood American world in *Vitzliputzli*); but indeed, that should not and cannot be possible anymore. Poetry remains only a continuous, further poeticizing, eternal prelude (as the construction of *Vitzliputzli* and *Bimini* irrefutably confirm). The poet's tightrope walk above the abyss of emptiness leads him to open up new landscapes on the verge of (but not beyond) silence. This ghostly triumph of word and image depicts a striking rite that is supposed simultaneously to conjure up as well as control the gaping emptiness of the inexpressible. It is only in this sense that Heine's late poetic language can be understood: as a two-dimensional reflective surface uniquely significant to Heine, within the limits of a Decadent poetry that thematizes itself on the border between linguistic magic and linguistic skepticism.

The growing interest of Heine researchers in close textual but not intrinsic interpretations can be measured by the numerous papers attempting to bring to light and critically examine the many-layered texture of Heine's prose and poetry between iconicity and cliché, between mythogenesis and *divertimento*, between adaptation to and challenge of the "normal" boundaries of the expectations of the average reading public. As early as 1972, Maria Fancelli, independently resuming the initial methodological steps of Vittorio Santoli, investigated dimensions and motives in the "Florentinische Nächte" [Florentine Nights] in a stylistic and textual criticism.[27] Lia Secci dedicated three papers to the bacchantian in Heine, that is, to the mythogenesis of the boundless vitality in the conventionalized and stylized forms of ballet.[28] Abrogation of sin and rehabilitation of flesh: these two themes have an uncannily spectral attractive power over the reader in the fleshless and bloodless schematic world of the fictitious ballet, on the boundary between mythos and cliché, between emancipatory engagement and mundane *divertissement*.

It is self-evident that in this context the *Book of Songs*, in its structures and varying stages of reception, should attract the attention of Heine researchers. Ida Porena, for example, uses implied critical interpretation in Schumann's musical arrangements of some of the poems from the *Book of Songs* to show how close the young lyric poet himself repeatedly comes to the edge of cliché.[29] For the modern reader, the charm of this daring game lies precisely in the fact that the sovereign superiority of the poetic phrase is repeatedly brought into question but is, however, never lost.

With recourse to the heuristic instruments of semiotics, as well as reception history, Alberto Destro interpreted the *Book of Songs*, and especially the "Lyrisches Intermezzo," not as a random sequence of sometimes melodically ingratiating, sometimes satirically brusque individual texts, but rather as a unity that had been thought through strategically.[30] This text in its entirety was meant to have an ironic enlightening effect on readers—an effect obtained by the constant shifting between images meant to fulfill readers' expectations of contemporary lyric poems and other images meant to frustrate these purposefully awakened expectations in the form of a sudden twist at the end of the poem. In this way distance was to be created, and the staunch emotional world of the reader was to be forced to waver.

In a second thesis Destro elucidates the horizons of expectation of the average readership between Romanticism and Biedermeier more concretely by using paperback books, almanacs, and even second- and third-rate literary magazines to elicit the leading topoi of the day in their thematic, metaphorical, and formal aspects.[31] An exhaustive confrontation—between the function of these popular topoi and the manner of their representation on the one hand and their appearance in Heine's work on the other—led Destro to an unexpected but convincingly argued conclusion: the average German readers of the 1820s and 1830s would have to a large extent lacked the prerequisites needed for Heine's many-layered and penumbral strategy to have any effect on them beyond momentary impressions of alienation. Thus, in this respect the success of the *Book of Songs* would have actually been a failure or at least the fruit of a misunderstanding. Only much later did it become possible for new generations of readers to appreciate the *Book of Songs* as a pattern for a new path in the efforts poetically to overcome contemporary contradictions.

In recent years Destro has devoted himself to publishing the late Heine volume of the great Düsseldorf historical-critical Heine edition. Thanks to his friendliness, I had the opportunity to view the manuscript. In the introduction to the *Hebräische Melodien* [Hebrew Melodies] Destro raises the delicate issue of Heine's relationship to Judaism. In the late phase of his religious awakenings the poet was attracted by the Jewish past as a treasure (and reservoir) of innocent memories of customs, rites, atmospheres, viewed of course through the penumbra of longing irony. The dogmatic-institutional, as well as the ideological in the narrow sense of the word, remained the target of Heine's biting scorn. In the late poems, however, political considerations receded more and more, as did any programmatic and pragmatic reference to concrete relations. Priority was given to atmosphere and a private sphere that would have been unthinkable for the middle Heine. Both realistic and utopian future-oriented ideas withdrew to make room for the adjuration of half-buried relics of a legendary or even only familiar past in the poetic texts.

Jewish tradition would play a role in this semiemotionally charged and semi-ironic poetic adjuration: out of this tradition the substance of a presence without any perspectives for the future would be made. This approach was possible for the poet only in a (for him) typically oxymoronic way: in his late poems there was no talk of the reappearance of living archetypes. On the contrary, dead images were strung together in the form of inopportune travesty and inorganic divagation.

Especially revealing is the section on *Bimini*, which seems to attract more and more critical interest, even if with noticeable, cultural-historically significant delay. Destro, taking into account the most recent textually critical results, elaborates his main theses clearly. The actual portrayal of the paradoxical journey of discovery of Juan Ponce de León is given—in partial deviation from my aforementioned *Bimini* interpretation—an independent importance. In spite of the prevalence of the illusory rejuvenating power attributed to an inexhaustible, intransitive poetic language, the epic-lyrical arrangement of the almost-completed poem at least partially preserves its constructive function: the eternal prelude turns out in the end not to be as eternal as it at first seemed to this author. Various dimensions—which, to be sure, flow semi-inorganically into each other over and over again—are actually recognizable: the mythical, cliché-like portrayal of a plentiful utopian landscape; the progressive erosion of the original epic inception, which undermines the incessant process of identification between Juan Ponce de León and the sick, resigned "lyrical I," so that by the end of the poem the hero who at the beginning rode out so hopefully into the world no longer is capable of believing in any fountain of eternal youth; and the tragic-ironic identifying of the desired happiness of the magic fountain with the peace of death. Only in the many-faceted diversity of this arrangement does Destro recognize traces of the typical modes of dénouement of a utopian poetry that only gradually leads itself "ad absurdum."

A final note is appropriate here. From my depiction it is possible to conclude a certain asynchronism between the development of Italian and German Heine research, in reference to methodical starting points, questions posed, and concentration on certain themes. An especially illuminating example is offered by the general sequence I outlined above: a subsiding of interest in Heine's work; new interest—mainly socioideological and historical—in the intellectual Heine; and finally, return to the poetic texts with a colorful palette of divergent methodological starting points. Thanks to such an asynchronism,

Heine researchers of close proximity but in different countries reach results that deviate strongly from each other. It is through the resulting
opportunities for fruitful confrontations governed by the asynchronism
of the synchronous that one may hope for continuous renewed progress
in the international debate surrounding Heine.

NOTES

1. On Heine's reception in Italy, see A. Fiedler Nossing, *Heine in Italia nel
   secolo XIX* (New York: Vanni, 1948); L. Zagari, "Ritorno di Heine," *Nuova
   Antologia* 489 (1963): 513–530; L. Zagari, "Heine in der italienischen
   Kritik," *Heine-Jahrbuch* (1965): 51–63; J. Hermand, *Streitobjekt Heine:
   Ein Forschungsbericht 1945–1975* (Frankfurt am Main: Athenäum Fischer,
   1975). In these works other contributions to the study of Heine's reception
   are indicated.
2. See Heinrich Heine, *Il canzoniere,* trans. B. Zendrini (Milan 1866, 1913);
   B. Zendrini, "Enrico Heine e i suoi interpreti," *Nuova Antologia* 27 (1874):
   793–821; and 28 (1875): 5–26, 346–384, 848–894.
3. G. Chiarini, *Studi e ritratti letterari* (Livorno: Giusti, 1900), pp. 277–408,
   463–501; see also H. Heine, *Poesie,* trans. and intro. G. Chiarini (Bologna: 1883).
4. G. Carducci's essays on Heine have been collected in Carducci's *Edizione
   nazionale delle opere* (Bologna: Zanichelli, 1942, 1943), 23:93–148, and
   27:115–157.
5. T. Massarani, *Enrico Heine e il movimento letterario in Germania* (Milan,
   1857), rpt. in his *Studi di letteratura e d'arte* (Florence: 1873), pp. 181–316.
6. E. Thovez, "Il quirite e l'ebreo," in his "Il pastore, il gregge e la zampogna,"
   Dall'Inno a Satana alla Laus Vitae (Naples: Ricciardi, 1910), pp. 17–21. Bib-
   liographical references to Borgese's short articles can be found in L. Zagari,
   "Heine in der italienischen Kritik," p. 62.
7. B. Croce, "Heine," *La critica* (1921): 65–75, rpt. in his *Poesia e non poesia:
   Note sulla letteratura europea nel secolo diciannovesimo* (Bari: Laterza,
   1923), pp. 172–185. German translation available in *Heinrich Heine,* ed.
   H. Koopmann (Darmstadt: Wissenschaftliche Buchgesellschaft, 1975).
8. On Heine research in Italy between the two world wars, see the detailed bib-
   liographical notes in Zagari, "Ritorno di Heine" and "Heine in der italienischen Kritik."
9. Heinrich Heine, *Antologia lirica delle migliori traduzioni a cura di T. Gnoli
   e A. Vago* (Milan, 1935).
10. E. Craveri Croce, "Il giornalista Heine," written in 1953 and available in

E. Croce, *Romantici tedeschi e altri saggi* (Naples: Edizioni Scientifiche Italiane, 1962), pp. 155–185.

11. Later, under new aspects, influential reservations about the format of "Heine the poet" were voiced, unfortunately always only fragmentarily. See, for example, B. Tecchi's "Heine oggi," in his *Scrittori tedeschi moderni* (Rome: Edizioni di storia e letteratura, 1959), pp. 255–257.

12. L. Vincenti, "La poesia satirica di Heine," dated 1963 and available in his *Nuovi saggi di letteratura tedesca* (Milan: Mursia, 1968), pp. 231–280.

13. Heinrich Heine, *Poesie*, trans. Ferruccio Amoroso, 3 vols. (Milan-Naples, 1952, 1963, 1967).

14. For a look at some of the historical-ideological studies of Heine, see D. Cantimori, *Studi di storia* (Torino: Einaudi, 1959), pp. 655–664, and "Note heiniane," on pp. 779–781; L. Basso, "Heine e Marx," *Belfagor* (1956): 121–136; and E. Rambaldi, *Le origini della sinistra hegeliana: Heine, Strauss, Feuerbach, Bauer* (Florence: La Nuova Italia, 1966).

15. See P. Chiarini, "Per una biografia spirituale di Heinrich Heine: Appunti e proposte," in his *Letteratura e società: Studi sulla cultura tedesca da Lessing a Heine* (Bari: Adriatica, 1959), pp. 165–188; "Dolore e grandezza di Heinrich Heine," "Heine e le radici storiche della 'miseria' tedesca," and "Heinrich Heine fra decadentismo e marxismo," all in P. Chiarini, *Romanticismo e realismo nella letteratura tedesca* (Padova: Liviana, 1961), pp. 5–32, 35–50, and 81–102.

16. G. Tonelli, "Heine e la Germania; Saggio introduttivo e interpretativo," introduction to *Atta Troll* and *Deutschland: Ein Wintermärchen*, by Heinrich Heine (Palermo: Instituto di storia dell' Universita, 1963); available in German as *Heinrich Heines politische Philosophie (1830–1845)* (Hildesheim and New York: G. Olms, 1975). A decided non-Marxist like F. Amoroso viewed the whole complex of questions with a freer eye and in the long run did more justice to the many strands of Heine's political position, though not always through convincing proofs. See also Amoroso's introduction to his own translation of H. Heine's *Lutezia* (Torino: U.T.E.T., 1959).

17. F. Masini, "Il purgatorio ironico di Heine," in his *Itinerario sperimentale nella letteratura tedesca* (Parma: Studium Parmense, 1970), pp. 41–71.

18. See "Il neobaroccoo di Heine," in V. Santoli, *Fra Germania e Italia: Studi di storia letteraria* (Florence: Le Monnier, 1962), pp. 54–72; available in German in V. Santoli, *Philologie und Kritik* (Bern and Munich: Francke, 1971), pp. 133–151. See also H. Heine, *Il libro dei canti*, trans. A. Vago and intro. V. Santoli (Torino: Einaudi, 1962), pp. v–xxii.

19. See L. Mittner, "Violette e marmi nella lirica di Heine," *Studi Germanici* 3 (new release, 1966): 265–323; and "Heine," in L. Mittner, *Storia della letteratura tedesca* (Torino: Einaudi, 1971), 3/1:123–278.

20. "La 'Pomare' di Heine e la crisi del linguaggio 'lirico,' " in L. Zagari, *Studi di letteratura tedesca dell'Ottocento* (Rome: Edizioni dell' Ateneo, 1965), pp. 121–154.

21. The three texts are H. Heine, *Rendiconto parigino*, trans. and intro. by P. Chiarini (Bari: Laterza, 1972); H. Heine, *La Germania*, trans. and intro. by P. Chiarini (Bari: Laterza, 1972); and H. Heine, *Ludwig Börne*, trans. and intro. by P. Chiarini (Bari: Laterza, 1973). Chiarini's introductions may be found on pp. vii–xxv, vii–lxxv, and vii–xlvii of these editions, respectively.

22. Ugo Rubini devoted himself to numerous socioideologically oriented papers in the course of the 1970s and 1980s.

23. M. Montinari, "Heines 'Geständnisse' als politisches, philosophisches, religiöses und poetisches Testament," in *Interpretationen zu Heinrich Heine*, ed. L. Zagari and P. Chiarini (Stuttgart: Kleff, 1981), pp. 102–111.

24. M. Fancelli, "Elementi sansimoniani nella 'Romantische Schule' di Heine," in *Mito e utopia nel romanticismo tedesco*, ed. M. Freschi (Naples: Instituto Universitario Orientale, 1984), pp. 169–182.

25. See P. Chiarini, "Epigonentum und Übergangszeit: Eine Schreibweise zwischen Privatem und Politischem,' " in *Interpretationen zu Heinrich Heine*, ed. Zagari and Chiarini, pp. 39–58; and P. Chiarini, "Introduzione," in *Alle origini dell'intellettuale moderno: Saggio su Heine* (Rome: Riuniti, 1987), pp. ix–xv (Chiarini's Heine essays of the 1970s and 1980s are reprinted in this volume).

26. L. Zagari, "Einleitung," " 'Das ausgesprochene Wort ist ohne Scham': Der späte Heine und die Auflösung der dichterischen Sprache," both in *Interpretationen zu Heinrich Heine*, ed. Zagari and Chiarini, pp. 5–21 and 124–140.

27. M. Fancelli, "Heine minore: Le 'Florentinische Nächte,' " *Studi Germanici* 1–2 (new release, 1972): 51–70.

28. L. Secci, "Die Götter im Exil: Heine und der europäische Symbolismus," *Heine-Jahrbuch* (1976): 96–114; H. Heine, *Gli dei in esilio*, trans. and intro. L. Secci (Milan: 1978), pp. 9–28; and L. Secci, "Die dionysische Sprache des Tanzes im Werk Heines," in *Interpretationen zu Heinrich Heine*, ed. Zagari and Chiarini, pp. 89–101.

29. I. Porena, "Schumann, Heine und die 'Dichterliebe,' " in *Interpretationen zu Heinrich Heine*, ed. Zagari and Chiarini, pp. 74–78.

30. A. Destro, "L'attesta contraddetta: La svolta finale nelle liriche del 'Buch der Lieder' di Heinrich Heine," *AION-Studi Tedeschi* 1 (1977): 7–127.

31. A. Destro, "Das 'Buch der Lieder' und seine Leser: Die Prämissen einer mißlungenen Rezeption," in *Interpretationen zu Heinrich Heine*, ed. Zagari and Chiarini, pp. 59–73.

WORKS CITED

Basso, L. "Heine e Marx." *Belfagor* (1956): 121–136.

Cantimori, D. *Studi di storia.* Torino: Einaudi, 1959.

Carducci, G. *Edizione nazionale delle opere.* Vols. 23 and 27. Bologna: Zanichelli, 1942, 1943.

Chiarini, G. *Studi e ritratti letterari.* Livorno: Giusti, 1900.

Chiarini, Paolo. *Alle origini dell'intellettuale moderno: Saggio su Heine.* Rome: Riuniti, 1987.

———. "Epigonentum und Übergangszeit: Eine Schreibweise zwischen Privatem und Politischem." In *Interpretationen zu Heinrich Heine,* ed. L. Zagari and P. Chiarini. Stuttgart: Klett, 1981.

———. "Per una biografia spirituale di Heinrich Heine: Appunti e proposte." In *Letteratura e società: Studi sulla cultura tedesca da Lessing a Heine.* Bari: Adriatica, 1959.

———. *Romanticismo e realismo nella letteratura tedesca.* Padova: Liviana, 1961.

Craveri Croce, Elena. "Il giornalista Heine." In *Romantici tedeschi e altri saggi.* Naples: Edizioni Scientifiche Italiane, 1962.

Croce, Benedetto. "Heine." *La critica* (1921): 65–75.

———. *Poesia e non poesia: Note sulla letteratura europea nel secolo diciannovesimo.* Bari: Laterza, 1923.

Destro, A. "Das 'Buch der Lieder' und seine Leser: Die Prämissen einer mißlungenen Rezeption." In *Interpretationen zu Heinrich Heine,* ed. L. Zagari and P. Chiarini. Stuttgart: Klett, 1981.

———. "L'attesta contraddetta: La svolta finale nelle liriche del 'Buch der Lieder' di Heinrich Heine." *AION-Studi Tedeschi* 1 (1977): 7–127.

Fancelli, M. "Elementi sansimoniani nella 'Romantische Schule' di Heine." In *Mito e utopia nel romanticismo tedesco,* ed. M. Freschi. Naples: Instituto Universitario Orientale, 1984.

———. "Heine minore: Le 'Florentinische Nächte.'" *Studi Germanici* 1–2 (new release, 1972): 51–70.

Heine, Heinrich. *Antologia lirica delle migliori traduzioni a cura di T. Gnoli e A. Vago.* Milan: 1935.

———. *Il canzoniere.* Trans. B. Zendrini. Milan, 1866, 1913.

———. *La Germania.* Trans., ed., and intro. Paolo Chiarini. Bari: Laterza, 1972.

———. *Gli dei in esilio.* Trans. and intro. L. Secci. Milan, 1978.

———. *Il libro dei canti.* Trans. A. Vago. Intro. Vittorio Santoli. Torino: Einaudi, 1962.

———. *Ludwig Börne.* Trans., ed., and intro. Paolo Chiarini. Bari: Laterza, 1973.

———. *Lutezia.* Trans. F. Amoroso. Torino: U.T.E.T., 1959.

———. *Poesie.* 3 vols. Trans. F. Amoroso. Milan and Naples, 1952, 1963, 1967.

————. *Rendiconto parigino*. Trans., ed., and intro. Paolo Chiarini. Bari: Laterza, 1973.

Hermand, Jost. *Streitobjekt Heine: Ein Forschungsbericht 1945–1975*. Frankfurt am Main: Athenäum Fischer, 1975.

Koopmann, H., ed., *Heinrich Heine*. Darmstadt: Wissenschaftliche Buchgesellschaft, 1975.

Masini, Ferruccio. "Il purgatorio ironico di Heine." In *Itinerario sperimentale nella letteratura tedesca*. Parma: Studium Parmense, 1970.

Massarani, T. *Enrico Heine e il movimento letterario in Germania*. Milan, 1857.

————. *Studi di letteratura e d'arte*. Florence, 1873.

Mittner, Ladislao. "Heine." In *Storia della letteratura tedesca*, 3/1:123–278. Torino: Einaudi, 1971.

————. "Violette e marmi nella lirica di Heine." *Studi Germanici* 3 (new release, 1966): 265–323.

Montinari, Mazzino. "Heines 'Geständnisse' als politisches, philosophisches, religiöses und poetisches Testament." In *Interpretationen zu Heinrich Heine*, ed. L. Zagari and P. Chiarini. Stuttgart: Klett, 1981.

Nossing, A. Fiedler. *Heine in Italia nel secolo XIX*. New York: Vanni, 1948.

Porena, I. "Schumann, Heine und die 'Dichterliebe.'" In *Interpretationen zu Heinrich Heine*, ed. L. Zagari and P. Chiarini. Stuttgart: Klett, 1981.

Rambaldi, E. *Le origini della sinistra hegeliana: Heine, Strauss, Feuerbach, Bauer*. Florence: La Nuova Italia, 1966.

Santoli, Vittorio. "Il neobaroccoo di Heine." In *Fra Germania e Italia: Studi di storia letteraria*. Florence: Le Monnier, 1962.

————. *Philologie und Kritik*. Bern and Munich: Francke, 1971.

Secci, L. "Die dionysische Sprache des Tanzes im Werk Heines." In *Interpretationen zu Heinrich Heine*, ed. L. Zagari and P. Chiarini. Stuttgart: Klett, 1981.

————. "Die Götter im Exil: Heine und der europäische Symbolismus." *Heine-Jahrbuch* (1976): 96–114.

Tecchi, B. "Heine oggi." In *Scrittori tedeschi moderni*. Rome: Edizioni di storia e letteratura, 1959.

Thovez, E. "Il quirite e l'ebreo." In "Il pastore, il gregge e la zampogna," *Dall'Inno a Satana alla Laus Vitae*. Naples: Ricciardi, 1910.

Tonelli, G. "Heine e la Germania: Saggio intriduttivo e interpretativo." Introduction to *Atta Troll* and *Deutschland: Ein Wintermärchen*, by Heinrich Heine. Palermo: Instituto di storia dell' Universita, 1963.

————. *Heinrich Heines politische Philosophie (1830–1845)*. Hildesheim and New York: G. Olms, 1975.

Vincenti, L. "La poesia satirica di Heine." In *Nuovi saggi di letteratura tedesca*. Milan: Mursia, 1968.

Zagari, Luciano. "Einleitung" and "'Das ausgesprochne Wort ist ohne Scham':

Der späte Heine und die Auflösung der dichterischen Sprache." In *Interpretationen zu Heinrich Heine,* ed. L. Zagari and P. Chiarini. Stuttgart: Klett, 1981.

———. "Heine in der italienischen Kritik." *Heine-Jahrbuch* (1965): 51–63.

———. "La 'Pomare' di Heine e la crisi del linguaggio 'lirico.'" In *Studi di letteratura tedesca dell'Ottocento.* Rome: Edizioni dell' Ateneo, 1965.

———. "Ritorno di Heine." *Nuova Antologia* 489 (1963): 513–530.

Zagari, Luciano, and Paolo Chiarini, eds. *Interpretationen zu Heinrich Heine.* Stuttgart: Klett, 1981.

Zendrini, B. "Enrico Heine e i suoi interpreti." *Nuova Antologia* 27 (1874): 793–821, and 28 (1875): 5–26, 346–384, 848–894.

SUSANNE ZANTOP

Colonialism, Cannibalism, and Literary Incorporation:
Heine in Mexico

*"There comes our dinner hopping along!"—Hans Staden,
Faithfull Historie and Description of a Countrie of Wild/
Naked/Feirce Canniball Peeple Located in the New World
of America*

*It would be a grave error, nevertheless, to see in the
massacre of the European mission nothing but base
gourmandizing and purely culinary interests. This event, in
our opinion, manifests one of the most noble tendencies of
the human spirit: its propensity to assimilate to itself that
which it finds good. . . . The Papus intended only, when
they devoured the explorers of the white race, a sort of
communion with their civilization.—Alfred Jarry,*
Cannibalism, *1902*

As Heine's range of mobility narrowed with his in-firmity, the geographical range of his concerns
and interests widened. A list of the books he checked out from libraries
in the late 1840s and early 1850s indicates that histories of discovery
and conquest, of world travels and colonial endeavors form the bulk of
his reading during his years of confinement to the "mattress grave."[1] It
seems that Heine's own physical decline becomes the point of departure for his renewed preoccupation with the decline of whole peoples
and cultures, past and present, in Europe and its colonies. His concern
with assimilation and annihilation, or rather, with the dialectics of extinction and preservation contained in Hegel's concept of *Aufhebung*,
finds its most salient expression in his *Romanzero* (1851) and its most
poignant form in his poem *Vitzliputzli*. *Vitzliputzli* can indeed be considered the culmination of part one of the *Romanzero* triptych; Heine
himself granted it special status when he published it with a few other

poems in advance, in French.[2] Moreover, and more importantly, it contains *in nuce* Heine's theory of reception. This theory deserves closer scrutiny, since it both illuminates Heine's reception in Mexico and anticipates twentieth-century Latin American theories of culture. In more than one sense Heine's *Vitzliputzli* serves as a key to the reciprocal cultural transfer taking place between Europe and Latin America in the nineteenth and twentieth centuries.

      In *Vitzliputzli*, by means of a series of dramatic moments, Heine stages before us the appropriation of the New World by the Old. The first "act," entitled "Präludium," evokes Columbus's discovery of the New World in terms of a widening of the European visual horizon. But Heine does not simply assume the point of view of the explorer-ethnographer who glances curiously at a strange new world. He suggests that the European onlooker himself becomes the object of curiosity when a monkey stares back at him. As their gazes meet, Old World and New World not only mirror each other but become inextricably intertwined: spectator-subject and object of scrutiny change places.

This visual compenetration of realities is also represented as verbal and conceptual incorporation. As the poet-explorer asks himself, "Wo hab ich denn / je dergleichen schon gerochen?" ["Where have I once before this smelled such odors?"],[3] he attempts to make familiar that which is strange, hitherto unseen or unknown. He integrates it into lived experience, into existing images and concepts: the parrots prattle "wie Kaffeeschwestern" ["like old gossips"]; their eyes are framed by black circles, "brillenartig" ["like goggles"]. Likened to the old, the new is thus defined, domesticated, and contained.

Heine takes the verbal incorporation, which he reenacted before us, onto another plane in the second "act" of the poem, in which he dramatizes the conquest of Mexico by Hernán Cortés and the infamous *noche triste*. While the Spaniards take possession of this new American territory, the Aztecs capture, sacrifice, and devour eighty Spanish soldiers. By juxtaposing the Spaniards' conquest with the Aztecs' cannibalistic orgy, thereby skewing chronology and historical evidence at once,[4] Heine sets up an ironic equation between these two acts of literal incorporation. Colonial appropriation is answered by the incorporation of the colonizers, and both colonizers and colonized are transformed in the process.[5] Again, Heine places the emphasis on mutuality.

The third part of the poem concludes this mutual incorporation/ transformation by a shift of scenery from Mexico back to Europe. The dethroned Mexican war god Huitzilopochtli is planning a change of career and location: as devilish "Vitzliputzli," he will discover and haunt the Old World, become a sting in the flesh of the colonizers by calling attention to the plight of the colonized. No longer the awe-inspiring idol but a tragicomic literary figure, Vitzliputzli thus embodies the process of colonization and acculturation. Whereas the Aztec culture that granted him his original identity was apparently annihilated by the dominant Spanish culture, he continues to live, under a different guise, within the dominant culture, a permanent reminder of otherness repressed into sameness. Conquest and colonization have therefore transformed not only the social reality in the New World, but reality and consciousness in the Old.

Heine's vision of the process of assimilation—absorption into a dominant culture—is thus pessimistic and optimistic at once: pessimistic, insofar as hegemony is seen as unavoidable because of unequal distribution of strength; optimistic, insofar as his model implies a continuation, a living on in different form, and thus a mutual transformation of cultures.[6] Not surprisingly, Heine establishes the "indecorous" link between cannibalistic orgy and Eucharist;[7] in both, human sacrifice and literal or symbolic incorporation of the flesh produce a transubstantiation, which affects the body of the Spanish as well as the body of the Mexican people, the body of Christ as well as the "body" of the church. Heine goes beyond what has recently been deplored as the "fetishization and relentless celebration of 'difference' and 'otherness' "[8] by proposing—as early as 1851—a model of cultural interaction in which sameness and otherness intertwine. This model proves dynamic and profoundly historical, since object and subject not only exchange positions, but change their nature, over time.

The political implications of Heine's cannibalistic model are clear: colonialism transforms the economic and social structure of both colonizer and colonized. Yet Heine never operates on the political plane alone. As the history of imperialism has shown, imperialism generates not just economic exploitation and dependencies, but attitudes, colonial mentalities, and a whole body of cultural artifacts that support and eventually question the colonial enterprise itself, from within and from without. Heine had anticipated this process in *Die Nordsee* [The North Sea] (1826), where he had established parallels between the subjugation of the Aztecs in Mexico, the expulsion of the Moors in Spain, and the subjugation of peoples in other parts of Europe. Both in Mexico and elsewhere, he had argued, the experience of subjugation had produced national recollections (*Nationalerinnerungen*) that accumulate and ferment in the bosom of a people until they erupt in revolutionary form.[9] The political is thus part of the general "culture of cannibalism," in which sameness and otherness constantly reconstitute and redefine themselves.

As I have argued elsewhere, Heine's model of incorporation applies to the process of literary production as well.[10] In contrast to the *Sturm und Drang* ideology of original creation, propagated by Goethe's disciples throughout the nineteenth century, the concept of "literary cannibalism" suggested in Heine's *Romanze* acknowledges the indebtedness of all authors to past linguistic artifacts that they "devour," contain, and transform.

On this metaphorical level, "cannibalism" can also serve to characterize the act of translation, in which an original text is "killed," incorporated into, and digested by another linguistic-cultural context. As J. Gerald Kennedy has argued, "all translation entails duplication and effacement, a retracing which both mirrors the original and abolishes it in the sense that every translation sacrifices the letter of the original text to reconstitute its spirit in another language."[11] A definition of translation as an act of literary cannibalism shares Kennedy's notion of effacement and sacrifice. Such a definition transcends, however, the somewhat mechanistic implications of Kennedy's terms "mirroring" and "reconstitution" and avoids the disjunction between "letter" and "spirit" that he establishes. A cannibalistic conception of translation "organicizes" and renders dynamic the process of transfer, for literary cannibalism implies that both the original text incorporated into the body of another literature and the body of literature absorbing the text undergo change. Cannibalism thus expresses in a much more drastic manner the "kinship of languages," the "central reciprocal relationship between languages" that, according to Walter Benjamin, is at the heart of, and is represented by, translation.[12]

To use cannibalism as a metaphor for the cultural transfer that takes place between Europe and the New World is not as farfetched and outlandish as it may seem. Within European colonial discourse from Columbus onward, references to cannibalism had served to articulate the colonizers' fear of the unknown and to project their subconscious desire to appropriate and "civilize" this other. When Heine conceived and wrote *Vitzliputzli*, the "liberated" Mexico was becoming again the prey of colonialism, in its new, "imperial" form.[13] The years 1845 to 1848 brought the Mexican-American War, in the course of which Mexico lost about one-third of its territory to its voracious northern neighbor. They are also the years in which European powers prepared to compete for "incorporation" of Latin America, which gradually opened its doors to foreign capital through the establishment of commercial and political bases. In 1845 the *Revue des deux mondes* published Michel Chevalier's articles on Aztec human sacrifice, cannibalism, and the Spanish conquest side by side with Félix Clavé's urgent plea to the French not to leave the economic conquest of Mexico to England and the United States alone, but to grab their share of the pie as well.[14] No wonder, then, that culinary metaphors figured prominently in Heine's mind.

The implications of this kind of cannibalistic theory for reception studies are obvious. If we want to explore a concrete instance of this process of cultural cannibalism I have outlined, we cannot simply concentrate on the translated texts themselves and ask what happened to the originals in the act of transfer, nor should we limit our focus to assessing "influences" on individual poets or schools. We must examine the "body" that devours a foreign text and is transformed by it or, rather, the body of literature into which this new text is incorporated and the body politic, the society, that felt the need, the "hunger" for incorporation.

This investigation is no small task. Not surprisingly, such an approach has been consciously or unconsciously avoided by all those who have so far studied Heine's impact on Latin American authors, with the result that all these studies end up repeating the same general facts: that Heine was immensely popular in nineteenth-century Latin America, that his popularity reached a peak in the 1880s, that his early lyrical poetry was favored over his prose, and that he somehow "influenced" modernist poets.[15] By failing to take the historical moment of the receptor country into consideration and by concentrating exclusively on Heine's impact on poetic forms of expression, these influence studies are unable to suggest answers to questions they themselves raise, albeit indirectly. Namely: What in fact is the significance of Heine's contribution to Latin American *modernismo*, if *modernismo* represents the "first truly Latin American literary movement"[16] *free* from foreign influence? Why did the liberal, anticlerical, bitingly critical Heine gain popularity and prominence in Latin America precisely at a time when the newly founded German *Kaiserreich*—which embodied everything Heine rejected—was rejecting Heine for his subjectivity, frivolity, and antinationalist, pro-French stance? [17] Why was Heine's more openly political, combative prose not "discovered" until the twentieth century, although the *ensayo*, the political *feuilleton*, and other prose forms had been favorite genres in Latin America throughout the nineteenth? And how did Heine's works, through the process of translation, affect their host culture and produce changes of consciousness even in "paradoxically dissimilar" poets? To attribute the ups and downs of Heine's reception to a "changing spiritual and esthetic climate,"[18] as some critics have done, and to leave it at that, is not enough.

I attempt here to provide tentative answers to some of these questions, focusing on Mexico as a concrete case and on very specific historical moments: the mid-1870s and the mid-1880s, both times when Heine's popularity reached a peak. This "case study" can then be "translated" to larger contexts, in terms of both geography and theory.

When we compare the available information on Heine's role in Mexico and on Mexico's historical development, it becomes immediately apparent that the reception of Heine was more than a purely literary affair. It was linked in some way to Mexican domestic and foreign policies and to Mexico's position vis-à-vis England, France, the United States, and Germany.[19]

As long as trade restrictions limited German economic and cultural influence, Heine remained relatively unknown in Mexico. Yet like the contraband that penetrated and undermined official trade barriers in spite of close vigilance, individual texts managed to make their way into the country—in the luggage of travelers, settlers, or diplomats.[20] Heine's works in German could be found in the library of the Club Alemán in Mexico City as early as the 1830s; French translations entered by means of the *Revue des deux mondes* in the 1840s. From 1850 onward, Spanish translations of Heine poems, some by Latin American Heine enthusiasts just back from European tours, began to appear in newspapers in Cuba, Argentina, Venezuela, and Peru, and these papers occasionally circulated in Mexico as well. As economic imports from the German states, notably Hamburg, Bremen, and Prussia, gradually rose and as the German community in Mexico grew in size and status, cultural imports also increased. Spanish collections of Heine poetry from Madrid and New York appeared on the book market,[21] Mexican literary journals and Sunday supplements previewed or reprinted translations of individual poems, and Mexican authors tried their hands at translating and imitating Heine's songs, creating a whole new genre of "imitaciones de Enrique Heine." At the same time, German newspapers in Mexico—the liberal *Vorwärts* (1872–?); the conservative mouthpiece of the Club Alemán, *Deutsche Wacht* (1871? or 1875?); *El Correo Germánico* (1876); *La Familia* (1883–90); *Deutsche Zeitung von Mexiko* (1888–91; 1900–1943); and *Germania* (1886–94?)[22]—proposed to acquaint Mexicans with the "genio germánico en su verdadera expresión" ["German genius in its true expression"],[23] as the editor of *El Correo Germánico* put it. As a consequence, the German presence in Mexico grew notably, not just physically but ideologically[24]—and with it, Heine's presence.

Between 1872 and 1895, when Mexico completely opened its borders to foreign capital, first under Benito Juárez, then under Porfirio Díaz, the economic and political influence of the new German Empire was further strengthened. These years, curiously, constituted the Mexican Heine boom; 1874, for example, witnessed not only the opening of the Mexican Chamber of Commerce, with the German-born Stephan Benecke as its first president, but also the first peak in Heine translations. After a short decline around 1877, translations reached a second peak in 1884, the beginning of Porfirio Díaz's second presidency.[25] As several literary historians have noted, by the mid-1880s Heine had become *the* favorite German poet in Mexico, with approximately twelve new Heine translations annually, almost all of them from his early volumes of poetry.[26]

Heine's popularity, however, lasted only until about 1895 and went into decline when the United States and France eclipsed Germany as economic and cultural models. In early 1896 new Heine translations stopped appearing altogether. There were short-lived revivals in interest—this time in Heine's prose works—around 1918–19, when German imports picked up after the revolution, and again in the 1940s and early 1950s, when immigrants from Hitler Germany and Franco Spain brought with them their favorite texts. But Heine never regained the prominent position he had held in Mexican letters in the nineteenth century. Currently, there are about eleven Heine titles in print, most of them reprints of earlier editions, including Javier Herrero's 1883 translation of the *Book of Songs*. Although credited by the deceased

Mexican author Rosario Castellanos with being "uno de los genios más brillantes, más completos y más valientes del siglo pasado" ["one of the most brilliant, complete, and valiant minds of the past century"],[27] Heine is now one German author of many, ranging far behind Goethe, with whom he had shared the Mexican Olympus in the nineteenth century. A Spanish translation of Heine's complete works does not yet exist.[28]

This somewhat schematic juxtaposition of commerce and culture, which culminated in the 1880s in the "libre comercio," the free commerce of ideas in the Mexican "intellectual marketplace,"[29] as the *modernista* and Heine admirer Manuel Gutiérrez Nájera phrased it, clearly indicates a connection between Heine's reception and other German imports. Yet it leaves the most important questions unresolved: Which Heine texts were appropriated when into Mexican culture? Why was he popular between 1870 and 1896 and not afterward? What did his poetry mean to the generation that lived through the political optimism of the Juárez years and the graveyard silence of the *porfiriato*? And did it have the same meaning under both administrations? I argue that it did not mean the same; that Heine was, in fact, read and appropriated in very different ways and for very different, and not necessarily literary, purposes; and that he was dropped from the canon, so to speak, when his politics were finally understood in their full dimension.

The first Mexican translation of the Heine poem "La Paz" [Peace], from the first North Sea cycle, constitutes also the first instance of Mexican misappropriation of Heine. It appeared in 1855, shortly after the resignation of Santa Anna, the general who had lost large territories to the United States in the "most unjust war in the history of imperialist expansion"[30] and who was forced to step down after he had sold the Mesilla of Arizona to the United States for ten million dollars. The newly founded periodical that printed Heine's poem, *La Cruz*, characterized itself in its masthead as "exclusivamente religioso" ["exclusively religious"], "establecido ex profeso para difundir las doctrinas ortodoxas y vindicarlas de los errores dominantes" ["founded with the expressed aim of divulging orthodox doctrines and vindicating them of dominant errors"].[31] Clearly, Heine's utopian, quasi-religious vision of peace, the "uncommercial dream-world"[32] of the poem, had appealed to its translator, poet and historian José María Roa Bárcena. He was an unlikely Heine admirer, however, for in his 1883 recapitulation of the Mexican-American War, he would blame the territorial sellout on the loss of

Mexico's religious unity, deplore the widespread "sensualist and atheist philosophy," and dream of a rebirth of virility and patriotism under the "banner of Catholicism."[33] Clearly, Roa Bárcena used Heine for his own purposes. His translation constitutes indeed a "cannibalization" of Heine's text: by choosing to translate the mutilated two-stanza version instead of Heine's "blasphemous" three-stanza original, and by taking the poem out of its context and placing it into a proclerical, conservative "body," Roa Bárcena gives the work the stamp of orthodoxy, of political harmlessness—and discloses his own antiliberal agenda.

The depoliticized, "orthodox" reading of Heine that achieves "wholeness" and "harmony" by exclusion became the norm during the first period of Heine's popularity, from 1870 to 1876. They are the years of national reconstruction after the economic and political destruction inflicted on Mexico in a series of violent encounters: the religious civil war (1857–60), foreign intervention (1861–64), and the ill-fated Maximiliano episode (1864–67). Having successfully fought conservative landholders and clergy; French, English and Spanish creditors; and the French occupation army; and having executed the Habsburg emperor imposed on them by Napoleon III, the liberals under Benito Juárez's and Lerdo de Tejada's leadership next attempted to reunify and rebuild the divided, bankrupt nation. Their pronounced economic centralism and their vehement anticlericalism faced constant challenges, however, from regional *caciques* and Catholic conservatives. To neutralize opposition, the liberal leaders opened Mexico's borders to foreign commerce and propagated a nationalist-liberal countermyth or counterreligion, "la religión de la libertad."[34] While their policy of *librecambismo* was designed to accelerate economic reconstruction, their "religion of liberty" was supposed to rally the people behind the liberal banner. Prussia, which had already served as arbiter in the 1848 negotiations between Mexico and the United States, became Mexico's favorite trade and treaty partner, since it was considered politically neutral, seemingly unaffected by the colonial greed of the other industrialized nations.[35] The trade agreement of 1870 between Mexico and Germany (first Prussia, then the German Empire) reflected this new *germanofilia*. Profiting from the friendly feelings that Alexander von Humboldt's sympathetic accounts had generated in Mexico a generation earlier,[36] the treaty, which lasted until 1880, declared Germany the most favored nation and granted it the right to complete economic reciprocity.[37]

Heine's appeal cannot be dissociated from this background of anti-

French, anticolonial, pro-Germanic sentiments. While Germany reaped praise for its victory over Mexico's exenemy France, for its successful unification, and for its traditional colonial restraint, Heine's poetry was hailed for its "typically northern" sensibility. Almost exclusively associated with the German *Lied*, "Heine" stood for moonlit nights and dark forests, foggy valleys and profound philosophy, an imaginary Romantic Germany. Manuel de Olaguíbel described this sensibility as "tierno como el suspiro de una virgen; de corta duración como el placer en esta tierra; dulce como el eco de una melodía de Schubert; así es el *lied* de los alemanes." ["Tender like the moans of a virgin; of short duration like pleasure on this earth; sweet like the echo of a Schubert melody: such is the *Lied* of the Germans."] And Gutiérrez Nájera wrote, "El lied, es Alemania." ["The *Lied* is Germany"].[38] Heine wrote *Lieder*; ergo Heine *is* Germany. Not surprisingly, translators and publishers chose Heine's "simple" lyrical love poems from the *Book of Songs* over his complex political prose.

The amalgam of a longing for a national identity à la Germany based on a reconciliation with a mythic past and a mythic future, of anti-French (defined as anti-Latin) sentiments and reverence for Teutonic "profundity," forms the political unconscious of the first Mexican translation of Heine's *Vitzliputzli* (1873), the ballad with a particular Mexican appeal. Translated by Jorge Hammeken y Mexía and Manuel de Olaguíbel, it appeared in two installments in the literary magazine *El Domingo*.[39] In their introduction the translators, both lyric poets in their own right, praise Heine as "a first-rate poet" who unites in his compositions "German philosophy with French esprit." In a tortured sentence—tortured, because they bow to two sides at once—they complain about Mexico's "deplorable state of ignorance" with respect to "the intellectual world of Europe" ["el lamentable estado de ignorancia en que nos encontramos respecto del mundo intelectual europeo"]. They consider this ignorance proven by the fact that Mexicans did not know, or had forgotten, that in *Vitzliputzli* Heine had "sung their glory anathematizing the foreign invader" ["que hubiese cantado nuestras glorias anatematizando al invasor extranjero"]. To atone for Mexican "ingratitude," Hammeken and Olaguíbel offer their translation:

Costumbre era entre los aztecas celebrar en el presente mes de Agosto la segunda fiesta dedicada á Huitzilopochtli. Los templos se cubrian de flores; el incienso elevaba, con caprichosas y aéreas alas, su perfume hasta la frente del dios; y morenas vírgenes venian á ofrecer ante las gradas de su trono, ovaciones fervorosas para aplacar sus salvajes resentimientos. Nosotros, amantes de las tradicciones [*sic*] y costumbres de nuestros antepasados, venimos hoy á depositar tambien nuestra ofrenda en sus altares,—ofrenda humilde, ofrenda pobre pero sincera y concienzuda.—¡Mucho incienso es necesario para ocultar la sanguinaria mirada de Huitzilopóchtli! ¡Derramamos aquí nuestra parte de copal y liquidambar; suban ahora las nubes olorosas y las espirales fantásticas hasta sepultar en los pliegues de su blanco sudario al dios de la guerra!

[It was a custom among the Aztecs to celebrate in the present month of August the second fiesta dedicated to Huitzilopochtli. The temples were covered with flowers; incense, on its capricious and airy wings, carried its perfume up to the god's face, and dark-skinned virgins came before the steps of his throne to offer their fervent prayers to appease his savage resentment. We who love the traditions and customs of our forebears come today to deposit our offerings on their altars—humble offerings, offerings that are poor but sincere and well-intentioned.— Much incense is necessary to cover up the bloodthirsty expression of Huitzilopochtli! Let us shed our part of *copal* and liquid incense; may the odorous clouds and fantastic spirals ascend until they bury the god of war in the folds of their white shroud!][40]

The vocabulary of the translators, their allusions to "virgins," "incense," and the "shroud" that veils the angry pagan god, clearly refer to the Catholic church. They evoke the Aztec past but literally cover it up with Catholic imagery. Their reference to the gods to whom the translation is offered further reflects the generation of referential ambiguity through "enshrouding": whose wrath at having been ignored has to be placated, the old Aztec gods' or the white gods' of northern Europe? Jorge Hammeken's article on Byron and Castelar, which precedes the second installment of the poem, clarifies the intent of the sacrifice. In this piece Hammeken complains that the Latin peoples only rarely concern themselves "with the products of the north," blindly accepting Bouhours's verdict that Germans do not have esprit. According to Hammeken, Castelar deserves praise for "placing the rich talents of his artistic nature, the prettiest flowers of his poetic sensibility before the altar of a German, a barbarian, an Englishman!" ["deposita las mas ricas dotes de su naturaleza artística, las mas lindas flores de su sensibilidad de poeta ante el altar de un germano, de un bárbaro, de un inglés!"][41] Hammeken and Olaguíbel thus offer their translation as a token of gratitude, a present, a sacrifice on the altars of the foreign gods. Mixing the *copal* of the pre-Columbian past with the incense of Spanish colonialism and the *brumas*, the fog of the German woods, they create a conciliatory smog that will efface any prevailing resentment.

The offering, their translation of *Vitzliputzli*, reflects this unconscious intent to cover up conflict and please foreigners and gods of the past alike. The translators have restored and thus distorted the meaning of the ironic, assimilated title: "Vitzliputzli" reverts to "Huitzilopochtli," to the unadulterated god of Mexican mythology. The somewhat pedantic prose rendition, which relies heavily but not exclusively on the French prose version of 1851,[42] smooths out Heine's irreverent rhymes and anticlerical asides. The *Mehlbreispeis*, a kind of sticky, pasty porridge, is retranslated into *oblea de harina*, flour wafer or wheaten host;[43] the cocky "clerics strutting in their robes of colored feathers" ["im Ornat von bunten Federn spreizt sich heut die Klerisei"] turn into banal "priests dressed in multicolored feathers" ["clero revestido de plumas de todos colores"].[44] While the New World's reality is "upgraded" from "healthy" ["gesund"] to "how strong and healthy" ["cuán robusto y cúan sano"],[45] the degrading diminutive for Vitzliputzli, "liebes Göttchen,"[46] is dropped, although diminutives are germane to Mexican linguistic usage, and "diosito" could easily have been integrated into the rhythm of the prose sentence. The description of Mexico City, finally, reads like an advertisement in a tourist guide. Instead of

> Mexico, die Inselstadt
> Liegt in einem großen See,
> In der Mitte, flutumrauscht:
> Eine stolze Wasserfestung,
>
> Mit dem Uferland verkehrend
> Nur durch Schiffe, Flöße, Brücken,
> Die auf Riesenpfählen ruhen,
> Kleine Inseln bilden Furten.
>
> [Mexico, the island city
> Lies in a big sea
> In the midst of swirling tides:
> A proud water fortress,

> Trafficking with the shore
> Only by boat, float, and bridges,
> That rest on giant posts,
> Small islets forming fords.]⁴⁷

we read:

> México, la ciudad insular, está situada en medio de un inmenso lago
> rodeado [*sic*] de rugientes olas; es una soberbia fortaleza con murallas
> de agua, y sin otra union con las orillas del lago que la que establecian
> los barcos, las balsas ó puentes levantados sobre gigantescos cimien-
> tos; se ven los islotes como otros tantos espías en acecho.

> [Mexico, the island city, is situated in the middle of an immense lake
> surrounded by roaring waves; it is a proud fortress with walls of water
> and has no other connections with the lake shores than those estab-
> lished by boats, floats, or bridges that are erected on gigantic founda-
> tions. Small islands can be seen that are like spies on the watch-out].⁴⁸

Again, we find the tendency to exaggerate the size or sublimity of the
New World's reality: the lake is not just big but immense; the "water
fortress" turns into a "fortress with walls of water," around which the
waves do not plash but "roar." Heine's last line becomes the victim of a
misreading of the French translation in the service of national grandeur:
islets do not "form fords" but help to protect the proud fortress against
foreign invasion.

While everything relating to Mexico is ennobled or aggrandized, the
Spanish invaders are vilified and cut down to size. The cautious assertion in the original that "some of them" are "as ugly as the monkeys" is
translated into *muchos de ellos*, "many of them." And the stanza specu-
lating about monkey tails in the breeches of the conquerors, although
"tactfully" dropped in the French version, is reproduced in all detail.⁴⁹

Hammeken and Olaguíbel's translation not only appropriates Heine
into a patriotic celebration of Mexico's pre-Columbian past shortly after
the premature death of its first Indian president, Benito Juárez. In their
desire to foment the new myth of liberty and national unification, the
translators have obfuscated any anticlerical, demystifying tendency of
the ballad and located the "enemy" outside, with the Spanish *conquis-
tadores*. Heine's half-menacing, half-ridiculous demon who oppresses
first his own people and then haunts the colonizers is thus re-formed

into the Mexican idol Huitzilopochtli, a pompous cultural ambassador who represents Mexican traditions and folklore to Mexico's friends in the north. Because the translation is meant to underscore a new national self-image, it glosses over the subversive quality of Heine's poem. As representative of *germanidad*, Heine becomes a vehicle for the expression of *mexicanidad*.

        A very different Heine image emerged in the 1880s and, with it, a new understanding of *Vitzliputzli*. Heine's popularity reached a second peak around 1884, the beginning of the *porfiriato*, Porfirio Díaz's military dictatorship. It is—in Octavio Paz's words—a "period of historical falseness,"[50] a period in which an economic boom due to large-scale foreign investment only thinly disguises social unrest, brutal repression of any opposition, and extensive censorship; a period that culminates in the 1910 revolution. As before, Heine's reception is intimately linked with, or caught up in, the internal Mexican problematic and Mexico's shifting foreign alliances.

Several factors affected Mexican-German cultural relations between 1884 and 1895. The resurrection of France as the cultural model of the elites, together with the increasing economic importance of the United States, gradually eclipsed Germany and anything "German."[51] The German Empire's unexpected colonial ventures in Africa and in the Pacific (1884–85) raised doubts as to its imperial harmlessness. In the eyes of many Mexicans, German "culture" became anathema to French *civilisation* and *savoir vivre*; the boisterous, beer-drinking, spiked-helmet-wearing Prussian bully supplied the visual image of growing *germanofobia*, particularly in liberal circles.[52] Heine profited from the shift in allegiances precisely because he was identified no longer with Germanicity but with its critique, and because his lyrical poetry, which remained a favorite among Mexican poets, was read as an act of defiance performed "in exile." As political opposition to Díaz's dictatorship was brutally silenced by Mexican authorities—especially in the 1890s, when many liberal journals were closed and journalists were imprisoned in the infamous Belén Penitentiary[53]—many Mexican writers took refuge in lyrical poetry that supposedly provided them with an escape to aesthetic space, an inner exile from politics. Finding their main allies in French symbolists, in Poe, and in Heine, Mexican *modernista* poets decried the crass materialism, the ostentatious bad taste displayed by official *porfiriato* culture, and proposed beauty, rather than utility, as the lofty aim of all art.[54] Heine was seen as an ally, as an advocate of art for art's sake.

Again, the appreciation of Heine seems based on a misreading, or a one-sided reading. Yet while Heine continued to be imitated as the writer of verses of "inimitable beauty" (Francisco Sellén), as poet of nightingales, love, and a perfumed Orient, of a counterworld of pure poetry, a somewhat more politicized Heine made his appearance.[55] The dialectics of poetry and reality, which had been considered an extraneous phenomenon, were now accepted as the internal, integral structure of Heine's work.

This double-tracked Heine perception in Mexico dates back to 1877. In the summer of 1876 a German expatriate, the Baron Otto von Brackel-Welda, founded a German newspaper in Mexico, El *Correo Germánico* (not *Alemán!*), designed to improve German-Mexican relations by providing a "true" picture of Germany's achievements. The language in which he paid tribute to Mexico, this "young nation, the most beautiful of all American virgins," revealed the predatory imperial-mercantile interests behind the cultural project.[56] And indeed, the baron, corresponding member of the Geographic and Statistic Society and the Mexican Mining Association, unabashedly tried to sell a variety of German products, first in his periodical, which folded after only three months, then as free-lance journalist. Brackel-Welda advocated that Mexico, "soberana y centro del comercio espiritual y material del hemisferio occidental" ["queen and center of the spiritual and material commerce of the Occident"], open her arms to Germany, center of the Orient, to receive from it the cultural impulses that will make it strong and enable it to reproduce.[57] Not surprisingly, Heine figures prominently, and negatively, in Brackel-Welda's cultural cross-fertilization project. In fact, "el licencioso Heine" ["the licentious Heine"], is the real enemy.[58] In complete agreement with literary historians of Wilhelminian Germany, the baron praises the sweet visions, the dreamy feelings, the stylistic perfection of Heine's early poetry in order to decry all the more Heine's biting irony, his cynicism and destructiveness. Brackel-Welda warns the impressionable Mexican youth not to be taken in by this Mephistopheles, who will seduce them with his genial madness, lead them astray, causing nothing but disenchantment and death.

Brackel-Welda's warning, directed in an open letter to one of the most promising young Mexican poets, Manuel Gutiérrez Nájera, had an immediate effect: whereas Gutiérrez Nájera, in 1876, had praised Heine's beautiful, melancholy verse, he now condemned the German in scathing terms: "Heine is doubt, skepticism, satire personified. His songs are drops fallen from the ocean of bile churning in his chest. One cannot read Heine without one's injured spirit bursting forth in lament. That chain of sarcasms makes one shudder. That incessant laughter is the hysterical laughter of the castaway. Heine is an abyss."[59]

Despite Gutiérrez Nájera's severe criticism, echoed in Manuel Reina's homage to Heine that same year and institutionalized in Marcelino Menéndez y Pelayo's widely reprinted 1883 introduction to Heine's *Book of Songs*,[60] Heine's relevance for Mexican poets—even Gutiérrez Nájera—did not diminish. The "abysmal" quality, the proximity of death and laughter, the sublime and the ridiculous in his poetry —that is, Heine's profoundly antiauthoritarian, irreverent stance— which Gutiérrez rightly noted but failed to appreciate in 1877, became appealing to a generation faced with official duplicity, brutality, and the ridiculous pomp of public self-representation.

Again, a *Vitzliputzli* translation serves as key to this new, dual, or duplicitous perception of Heine. A new prose rendition, made by the Spanish translator Manuel María Fernández y González, appeared in 1884 under the title "Vitzliputzli" in *La Epoca Ilustrada*, a liberal journal of short duration.[61] The journal's subtitle, "semanario de literatura, humorístico con caricaturas" [humorous weekly literary magazine with cartoons], is a first indication of the new understanding of Heine's aesthetic-political position. It clearly marks Heine's displacement from Germanic bard to exiled satirist. Exclusively based on the French prose version of 1851, the 1884 *Vitzliputzli* translation accepts its satiric interpretation of Heine's poetry, "cette poésie si gracieuse et si désolante, ces frais *lieder* qui distillent du poison, ces satires où une raillerie fantasque semble bouleverser tout, littérature et politique, philosophie et religion, tandis qu'elle ne fait que mettre à nu les ruines morales du pays de Hegel" ["this poetry that is so charming and so depressing at once, these fresh *Lieder* that exude poison, these satires in which whimsical mockery seems to confound everything—literature and politics, philosophy and religion—while it does nothing but expose the moral ruin of the country of Hegel"].[62]

Consequently, Fernández y González restored to *Vitzliputzli* not just its hybrid title, but also its aggressiveness and its ambiguity, which are further highlighted by the changes in the general political context. The first lines of the poem, for example, give Heine's "europeanized" ["europäisieret"] America a new, actualized meaning: "América que se las arregla ya á la europea y se marchita" ["America, which manages its affairs à la Europe and withers away"],[63] is not an America that has gone downhill because of the conquest, but an America that degenerates because it apes European fashions today.[64] Vitzliputzli, the monster, "so putzig, so verschnörkelt und so kindisch" ["tan exornado, tan peripuesto y tan pueril"] ["so quaint, so ornate and so childish"], surrounded by laymen and ostentatious priests ["la clerigalla" que se "pavonea con sus plumas tuticolores"], visually relates to the pompous display of Porfirio Díaz and his "*caballada*," his troop of horses, as the dictator jestingly calls his cabinet.[65] In the new translation Vitzliputzli's devilish European "comrades" become his "cronies": better than "*camaradas*," the Mexican "*compinches*" connotes the complicity, nepotism, and favoritism typical of the *porfiriato*. Even the last lines, the idol's promise to avenge his "idolized Mexico" ["idolatrada México"],[66] acquire an ironic connotation, as Díaz gives away one-fifth of Mexico's territories to foreign speculators and "friends," turning Mexico into "the mother of foreigners and the stepmother of Mexicans," in the words of historian Lesley Byrd Simpson.[67] The poem's abyssal humor and satirical potential directed against both Europe and Mexico are thus more exposed in this translation because new circumstances had created a new awareness. With his seismographic sensibility, Heine had grasped and articulated in 1851 the sense of crisis that would be generated by uninhibited colonial expansion, externally and internally. In the Mexico of 1884 Heine's irony could finally be fully understood and appreciated.

The two images of Heine—the poet of beautiful love songs and the poet of biting satire—could now coexist, even coincide in the mind of Mexican critics, since both images allow for a sense of alienation, of *Zerrissenheit*. Because of their opposition to "the overpowering force of material things," Theodor Adorno observes, Heine's poems provide an aesthetic refuge for "escapist" *modernistas* (such as Gutiérrez Nájera and Amado Nervo).[68] And because of their antiauthoritarian or openly revolutionary stance, many of Heine's poems appealed to the more politically active writers, such as the Cuban José Martí (who was working in Mexico in the late 1870s and translated *Die Weber*) and the editors of the oppositional journal *Diario del Hogar*.[69] Whether critics stressed the beauty of Heine's poems or their sacrilegious sarcasm, the emphasis remained on the poems' resistance to appropriation or, to remain within the cannibalistic metaphor, their "indigestibility." The never-accomplished process of digestion created appetite for Heine's more outspokenly political prose, which began to appear in the 1890s, until Mexico's own brand of revolutionary writing swept aside all foreign models.[70]

Heine's translation from Europe to Mexico thus duplicates Vitzli-putzli's trajectory from Mexico to Europe. Like the Mexican war god Huitzilopochtli, who acquired a new identity of resistance in Europe as the demonic Vitzliputzli, Heine was incorporated into Mexican culture, where he changed from the awe-inspiring Germanic bard to the Mephis-tophelic satirist. Like colonized Aztec mythology, Heine's poetry not only was transformed in this process of assimilation, but effected changes in the body of his host culture, creating a new awareness of conflict, a new "language of suspicion."[71] Once interiorized, his ballad *Vitzliputzli*, appropriated first in 1874 because of its supposed celebra-tion of *mexicanidad* and its antagonism toward the former *conquista-dores*, could expose and denounce the inner American conflict between colonizing *caudillos*, accomplices of foreign imperialists, and colonized peoples, victims of contemporary acts of cannibalism. From the inside, it could contribute toward the fermentation of ideas that would erupt in a revolution—a cannibalistic feast that, as Heine well knew, would end up devouring its own children.

Looking backward to the conquest and forward into the future of his own times, the historian-prophet Heine had thus anticipated Latin American developments of the twentieth century. The image of the "Kannibalencharivari," with which he had described the "cultural ex-change" between Europe and the New World, was adopted by Latin American authors themselves. Between 1896 and the 1930s, *modernis-tas* in various Latin American and Caribbean countries reappropriated the notion of cannibalism to characterize their own cultural practice. In the later writings of Gutiérrez Nájera and Aimé Césaire, for ex-ample, Latin American identity is tied no longer to the nativism that had formed the background of the first translation of *Vitzliputzli*, but to the mutual devouring of Europe and America stressed in the second.[72] To discover the *"antropófago"* within, as Brazil's modernist manifesto of 1928 proposed, implied not a return to pre-Columbian "roots" in search of "difference," but a recognition that Latin American culture is a hybrid, formed and transformed in active and mutual appropriation. "Viramos canibais" ["we became cannibals"], the newly founded *Revista de Antropofagía* states:

Aí descobrimos que nunca havíamos sido outra cousa. A geração actual coçou-se: apareceu o antropófago: nosso pai, principio de tudo. Não o índio. O indianismo é para nós um prato de muita sustáncia. Como qualquer outra escola ou movimento. De ontem, de hoje e de amanhã. Daqui e de fora. O antropófago come o indio e come o chamado civilizado; só éle fica lambendo os dedos. Pronto para engulir os irmãos. Assim a experéncia moderna (antes: contra os outros; depois: contra os outros e contra nós mesmos) acabou despertando em cada conviva o apetite de meter or garfo no vizinho. Já começou a cordeal mastigação.

[It was then that we discovered that we had never been otherwise. The present generation scratched the surface, and the cannibal appeared: our father, the beginning of all. Not the native. Nativism for us is but a substantial dish. Like any other school or movement. Yesterday's or today's or tomorrow's. Local or foreign. The cannibal eats the native and eats the so-called civilized. He is the only one left licking his fingers. Ready to devour his brothers. Thus modern experience (first against the others, then against others and against ourselves) ended up wakening in each guest the appetite to stick his fork into his neighbor. And that's how the happy chewing began.][73]

Remembering and anticipating these barbarous banquets, Heine's *Vitzliputzli* is thus not only a precursor of modernism, but a literary *olla podrida* that joins *conquista* to *reconquista*, the discourse of colonialism to the discourse of imperialism, colonial territorial appropriation to postcolonial cultural appropriation, fears of extinction to fears of retaliation. It contains, indeed, the substance, or rather, the "stock," for a theory of culture that acknowledges the irreversible hybridization, the mutual incorporation of all cultures in our modern world.

ACKNOWLEDGMENTS

This essay was conceived long before I participated in a seminar entitled "Methodologies of Empire" with Edward Said in the summer of 1988. The connection between modernism and empire and its implications for Heine reception studies, however, became clear to me during our discussions of Conrad, Forster, and Gide. I want to thank Professor Said for his many useful, albeit indirect, suggestions, and the John and Eliza Howard Foundation and the Marion and Jasper Whiting Foundation for their generous support of this project.

NOTES

1. Joseph A. Kruse, "Heines Leihpraxis und Lektürebeschaffung," in *Die Leihbibliothek als Institution des literarischen Lebens im 18. und 19. Jahrhundert*, ed. Georg Jäger and Jörg Schönert, Wolfenbüttler Schriften zur Geschichte des Buchwesens (Hamburg: Hauswedell, 1980), 3:197–228. Kruse lists, for example, Sealsfield's, Gerstäcker's, and Dickens's descriptions of North America; Solís's and Xerez's accounts of the conquests of Mexico and Peru; and many travelogues from across the globe.

   All translations from Spanish, French, or German into English in this chapter are the author's, unless otherwise indicated.
2. See Heinrich Heine, *Werke und Briefe*, ed. Hans Kaufmann, 10 vols. (Berlin: Aufbau, 1961), 2:599–600.
3. Actually, "smelled such *spectacles*," yet for the sake of consistency, I decided to use Hal Draper's translation throughout this essay. See his *Complete Poems of Heinrich Heine: A Modern English Version* (Boston: Suhrkamp/Insel, 1982), pp. 599–614; for this particular quotation, see p. 600. All German quotations of *Vitzliputzli* are from Heine, *Werke*, 2:57–78.
4. See Helene Hermann, *Studien zu Heines Romanzero* (Berlin: Weidmannsche Buchhandlung, 1906), pp. 191–192 and 128–133.
5. I disagree with Jürgen Brummack's assertion that this juxtaposition and switching of allegiances implies a relativization of Heine's anticolonial stance. Heine sides with the victim, whether it be the individual or the people, but does not condone the conquest by referring to the Aztecs' cruelty, as Spanish chroniclers used to do. See Jürgen Brummack, *Heinrich Heine: Epoche-Werk-Wirkung* (Munich: Beck, 1980), p. 272.
6. I do not agree with Prawer's interpretation that *Vitzliputzli* is a deeply pessimistic poem. As Prawer's allusion to Yeats indicates, the "inferno" evoked in *Vitzliputzli* does bring forth a "terrible beauty," which refers to an aesthetic as well as political "rebirth." See Siegbert S. Prawer, "Heine's 'Romanzero,'" *Germanic Review* 31 (1956): 293–306.
7. See Peter Hulme, *Colonial Encounters: Europe and the Native Caribbean, 1492–1797* (New York: Methuen, 1986), p. 84.
8. Edward Said, "Representing the Colonised: Anthropology's Interlocutors" (paper delivered at "Methodologies of Empire," New York City, summer 1988), p. 15.

9. Heine, *Werke*, 3:114.

10. Susanne Zantop, "Lateinamerika in Heine—Heine in Lateinamerika: 'das gesamte Kannibalencharivari,'" *Heine-Jahrbuch* 28 (1989): 72–87.

11. J. Gerald Kennedy, "The Horrors of Translation: The Death of a Beautiful Woman," in his *Poe, Death, and the Life of Writing* (New Haven: Yale University Press, 1987), p. 61.

12. Walter Benjamin, "The Task of the Translator," in his *Illuminations*, trans. Harry Zohn (New York: Schocken, 1977), p. 72.

13. I follow here Said's distinction between "colonialism" ("the implementation of settlements on distant territories," before 1800) and nineteenth-century neocolonialism, or "imperialism" ("the practice, theory, and attitude of ruling a distant territory from a dominating metropolitan center"), which he suggested in the "Methodologies of Empire" seminar mentioned in note 8.

14. Michel Chevalier, "De la civilisation mexicaine avant Fernand Cortez," *Revue des deux mondes* 9 (1845): 965–1020; "Du Mexique avant et pendant la conquête," *Revue des deux mondes* 11 (1845): 197–235; and Félix Clavé, "La question du Mexique: Relations du Mexique avec les Etats-Unis, l'Angleterre et la France," *Revue des deux mondes* 12 (1845): 1029–1059.

15. Cf. John E. Englekirk, "Heine and Spanish-American Modernism," *Comparative Literature: Proceedings of the International Comparative Literature Association at the Univ. of North Carolina, Sept. 8–12, 1958* 2 (1959): 488–500; Hanna Geldrich, *Heine und der spanisch-amerikanische Modernismo* (Bern and Frankfurt am Main: Herbert Lang, 1971), pp. 19–22; Marianne O. de Bopp, *Contribución al estudio de la letras alemanas en México* (Mexico City: UNAM, 1961), pp. 125–127; Marianne O. de Bopp, "Heinrich Heine: Bibliografía en México," *Anuario de Letras* 1 (1961): 181–190; Udo Rukser, "Heine in der hispanischen Welt," *Deutsche Vierteljahrschrift für Literaturwissenschaft und Geistesgeschichte* 30 (1956): 454–510; Claude R. Owen, "Dario and Heine," *Susquehannah University Studies* 8 (1970): 329–349; Claude R. Owen, "Ezequiel Martínez Estrada und Heine," *Heine-Jahrbuch* (1971): 52–75; Donald F. Fogelquist, "José Asunción Silva y Heinrich Heine," *Revista Hispánica Moderna* (1954): 282–294; José Zamudio Zamora, *Heinrich Heine en la literatura chilena: Influencia y traducciones* (Santiago: Ed. Andrés Bello, 1958); and others. For further references, consult the bibliographies in Geldrich, *Heine und der spanisch-amerikanische Modernismo*, and in Claude R. Owen, *Heine im spanischen Sprachgebiet* (Münster: Aschendorf, 1968). In her detailed, thorough study Geldrich refers to "practical reasons" that kept her from including political references (p. 11).

16. Englekirk, "Heine and Spanish-American Modernism," p. 490.

17. Cf. Johannes Weber, "Heines 'Frivolität' und 'Subjektivität' in der älteren

deutschen Literaturgeschichtsschreibung," *Text und Kritik* 18/19 [Special Heinrich Heine Issue] (1982, rev. ed. of 1968 issue): 84–116, esp. p.91; and Joachim Bark, "Literaturgeschichtsschreibung über Heine," in *Heinrich Heine: Artistik und Engagement*, ed. W. Kuttenkeuler (Stuttgart: Metzler, 1977), pp. 284–304, esp. p. 290.

18. Quoted from Englekirk, "Heine and Spanish-American Modernism," pp. 499, 498. He discusses this question with reference to two Cuban poets "influenced" by Heine, the "melancholy" Casal and the "militant" Martí.

19. Information is still scarce and imprecise. For the development of German-Mexican cultural and trade relations, see Brígida von Mentz, Verena Radkau, Beatriz Scharrer, and Guillermo Turner R., *Los pioneros del imperialismo alemán en México* (Mexico City: Centro de Investigaciones y Estudios Superiores en Antropología Social, 1982). Unfortunately, this study covers only the time period from 1821 to 1872, from independence until the end of the liberal Juárez period.

20. See ibid., pp. 60–62.

21. E.g., Eulogio Florentino Sanz's *Poesía alemana* (Madrid: 1857); Jaime Clark's *Poesías líricas alemanas* [including poetry by Heine, Uhland, Zedlitz, Rückert, Platen et al.] (Madrid: 1872); Manuel María Fernández y González's *Joyas prusianas* (Madrid: 1873); and Francisco Sellén's translation of the *Lyrisches Intermezzo, Intermezzo lírico* (New York: 1875).

22. The dates given are those of Owen, *Heine im spanischen Sprachgebiet*, p. xxviii. They do not always coincide with those provided by Bopp, *Contribución*, pp. 231–234 and pp. 300–301, or those given by Mentz et al., *Los pioneros*. According to Mentz, the *Deutsche Zeitung* existed from 1883 to 1885 and from 1900 to 1943, and was first Prussian nationalist, later notoriously Nazi in its political affiliation; according to Bopp, it ceased to exist in 1886 and was restarted in 1900. See *Los pioneros*, p. 412, and Bopp, *Contribución*, p. 313.

23. Editor's note in *El Correo Germánico*, rpt. in Boyd G. Carter's *Manuel Gutiérrez Nájera—Estudio y escritos inéditos* (Mexico City: Ed. Andrea, 1956), p. 18.

24. According to Verena Radkau, Germany held fourth place in foreign trade, behind England (65%), France (13%), and the United States (12%) in the years 1856 to 1872. Yet while the total value of European imports decreased in that time span because of the Maximiliano debacle, German commerce with Mexico grew from 9 to 13% (see Mentz et al., *Los pioneros*, pp. 69–84). Another indication of the importance of the German community in Mexico is the fact that as early as 1844, the German Savings Bank and the German Support Association were founded in Mexico City, followed in 1849 by the Casino Alemán.

25. Bopp, "Bibliografía," p. 181, and *Contribución*, p. 126. Since Bopp's numbers

refer indiscriminately to individual poems that appeared in newspapers and to longer selections in print, they have to be used with caution and can serve only to indicate general trends.

26. The Heine boom in the mid-1880s seems to have occurred throughout the Hispanic world. See Rukser, "Heine in der hispanischen Welt," p.510: "Ich glaube nicht zu irren, wenn ich die Behauptung wage, daß an Popularität Heine von allen deutschen Dichtern an erster Stelle in der hispanischen Welt steht" ["I don't think that I am wrong when I maintain that Heine is the most popular German poet in the Hispanic world"].

27. Rosario Castellanos, "La Alemania de Heine," *Novedades* (July 11, 1960), p. 4.

28. I have consulted a 1985 edition of *Libros en venta en Hispanoamérica y España*, a current Mexican list, as well as the 1974 edition of *Libros en Venta*, edited by Bowker in Buenos Aires.

29. "El cruzamiento en literatura," *Revista Azul* (September 9, 1894), rpt. in Manuel Gutiérrez Nájera, *Obras* (Mexico City: UNAM, 1959), 1:102; this particular passage actually dates back to 1890.

30. Octavio Paz, *The Labyrinth of Solitude: Life and Thought in Mexico*, trans. Lysander Kemp (New York: Grove, 1961), p.123.

31. Boyd G. Carter, *Las revistas literarias de Hispanoamérica* (Mexico City: Ed. Andrea, 1959), p.100.

32. Siegbert S. Prawer, *Heine: "Buch der Lieder"* (New York: Barron, 1960), p.19.

33. José Maria Roa Bárcena, *Recuerdos de la invasión norte-americana, 1846–1848, por un jóven de entónces* (Mexico City: Juan Buxó, 1883), pp.640–641. The actual "peace" of 1848 had not brought about the spiritual reunification Roa Bárcena had envisaged. In his words: "La discordia afirmó aquí su imperio en vez de perderle, y la serie de los años posteriores dejó señalada su marcha con ancho reguero de lágrimas y sangre, y nos acercó más y más al abismo de que nos debiéramos haber alejado" (p.635). ["Discord confirmed its rule, instead of relinquishing it, and the years afterward marked their way with a wide stream of tears and blood, bringing us closer and closer to the abyss we should have left behind."]

34. Cf. Hammeken y Mexía's article on Castelar, "Byron y Castelar," in *El Domingo* 4 (1873): 480.

35. Verena Radkau, "Relaciones diplomáticas e ingerencia política," in Los pioneros, p.300.

36. See Carter, *Manuel Gutiérrez Nájera*, 12:14.

37. Radkau, "Relaciones diplomáticas," p.298.

38. Manuel de Olaguíbel, quoted in Gutiérrez Nájera, "Páginas sueltas, de Agapito Silva," *Obras*, 1:117; ibid., p.118.

39. Heinrich Heine, "Huitzilopochtli," trans. Jorge Hammeken y Mexía and

Manuel de Olaguíbel, *El Domingo* 4 (1873): 465–467, 480–482.

40. Ibid., p. 465.

41. Ibid., p. 480.

42. Bopp (Contribución, 161) believes that Hammeken, of German origin, and Olaguíbel based their translation on the German original. Yet they must have also consulted the French version that appeared in the *Revue des deux mondes* in 1851, for although they include the anti-Spanish stanza the French version deleted, they misread and therefore mistranslated a French sentence: Heine's "Kleine Inseln bilden Furten" becomes "des îlots forment des gués" in the French version and "se ven los islotes como otros tantos espías en acecho" ["islands can be seen which look like spies on the watchout"] in the Spanish translation: the authors mistook *gués* (fords) for *guet*, *être au guet* (to be on the watch).

43. See Heine, *Werke*, 5:70, and "Huitzilopochtli," trans. Hammeken and Olaguíbel, p. 481.

44. See Heine, *Werke*, 5:69 and "Huitzilopochtli," trans. Hammeken and Olaguíbel, p. 480.

45. See Heine, *Werke*, 5:57, and "Huitzilopochtli," trans. Hammeken and Olaguíbel, p. 465.

46. Heine, *Werke*, 5:73.

47. Heine, *Werke*, 5:64. The unrhymed translation here is provided by the author to permit close attention to Heine's diction.

48. Heine, "Huitzlipochtli," trans. Hammeken and Olaguíbel, p. 467.

49. See Heine, *Werke*, 5:74, and "Huitzlipochtli," trans. Hammeken and Olaguíbel, p. 482.

50. Paz, *Labyrinth of Solitude*, p. 132.

51. Paz speaks of a "unilateral imitation of France, which has always ignored us." Ibid., p. 134.

52. Gutiérrez Nájera, in *El cronista de México* (Nov. 6, 1880), rpt. in Boyd G. Carter, *En torno a Gutiérrez Nájera y las letras mexicanas del siglo XIX* (Mexico City: Ed. Botas, 1960), p. 222. See also Bopp, *Contribución*, pp. 372–376.

53. The crackdown on the liberal press is described by John Mason Hart, *Revolutionary Mexico: The Coming and Process of the Mexican Revolution* (Berkeley: University of California Press, 1987), pp. 87–90; and by José C. Valadés, *Breve historia del Porfirismo (1876–1911)* (Mexico City: Ed. Mexicanos Unidos, 1971), p. 151. Hart reports that on August 13, 1893, more than fifty newspaper editors were imprisoned in Mexico City's Belén prison. Between 1893 and 1900 all liberal opposition journals were closed, and the other journals were controlled by members of the ruling party, i.e., governors, personal friends of Porfirio, or the treasury.

54. See Gutiérrez Nájera, "El arte y el materialismo" (1876), rpt. in Carter,

Manuel Gutiérrez Nájera, pp. 113–144; Owen, "Dario and Heine," pp. 333–337; Geldrich, *Heine und der spanisch-amerikanische Modernismo*, p. 168; and Englekirk, "Heine and Spanish-American Modernism," p. 498.

55. This parallel perception may explain why Gutiérrez Nájera and Rubén Darío both praise and scorn, imitate and reject Heine as a model.

56. It is perhaps no coincidence that Brackel-Welda was a correspondent for the periodical *El Propagador Industrial*, whose editor was Gutiérrez Nájera's father. The first contacts between Brackel-Welda and Gutiérrez Nájera were established via an article by the former entitled, "Commerce in Songbirds: Proposal to Introduce a New Industry or Export Article into the Mexican Republic. Dedicated to the Mexican Society of Natural History and the Mexican Mining Society"—a remarkable instance of industrial-scientific-aesthetic collaboration.

57. Othon E. de Brackel-Welda, *Epístolas a Manuel Gutiérrez Nájera*, comp. Marianne O. de Bopp (Mexico City: UNAM, 1957), p. 78.

58. Ibid., pp. 49–50.

59. Gutiérrez Nájera, "Los Ensueños de Pedro Castrera," *El Federalista* (March 27, 1877), rpt. in his *Obras*, vol. 1, *Crítica Literaria*, p. 124 n.

60. Manuel Reina, "Astros," printed in *La Libertad* (Jan. 4, 1880):

> Es su canto el sarcasmo y la ironía;
> El pesar que devora las entrañas
> —Y un mundo de clamores y de risas,
> De llantos y ruidosas carcajadas.

> [His song is sarcasm and irony
> sadness that eats up the inside
> —and a world of noise and laughter
> of tears and clamorous cackles.]

Menéndez y Pelayo, however, considers Heine's "audacities as polemicist," his "vindictive and bloody pages," his "choleric screams" of passing importance: they will not obscure his fame and importance as a poet of musical, ethereal verse, of "intensely lyrical poetry . . . which could not have been more removed from the conditions of race and time." Translated from "Prólogo" (1883), rpt. in Enrique Heine, *Libro de los Cantares/Prosa Escogida* (Mexico City: Porrúa, 1984).

61. Heinrich Heine, "Vitzliputzli," trans. Manuel María Fernández y González, *La Epoca Ilustrada* 45 (Aug. 8, 1884): 714–719.

62. Fernández y Gonzáles, Introduction to "Romancero: Poésies inédites," *Revue des deux mondes* 4 (1851): 338.

63. Cf. Heine, *Werke*, 5:57, and "Vitzliputzli," p.714.
64. This is, incidentally, also the meaning given by Hammeken and Olaguíbel: America is not the victim of the invaders, but the victim of its own desire to imitate.
65. Cf. Heine, *Werke*, 5:68, and "Vitzliputzli," trans. Fernández y González, p.715.
66. See Heine, "Vitzliputzli," trans. Fernández y González, p.719.
67. Lesley Byrd Simpson, *Many Mexicos*, 4th rev. ed. (Berkeley: University of California Press, 1967), pp. 290, 293.
68. Theodor W. Adorno, "Lyric Poetry and Society," *Telos* 20 (Summer 1974): 58. See also Max Henriquez Ureña, *Breve historia del modernismo* (Mexico City: Fondo de Cultura Económica, 1954), pp. 467, 474; and Geldrich, *Heine und der spanisch-amerikanische Modernismo*, pp. 212–231. Another, more famous, example of this modernist move is Rubén Darío. See, for example, Owen, "Dario and Heine," in which Owen states the affinities in mood and ironic treatment between Darío's *Abrojos* (1887) and Heine's *Intermezzo* and *Heimkehr* (pp. 336, 339, 344, 349).
69. See Geldrich, *Heine und spanisch-amerikanische Modernismo*, pp. 142, 191–193; and James D. Cockcroft, *Intellectual Precursors of the Mexican Revolution, 1900–1913* (Austin: University of Texas Press, 1968), pp. 81–82.
70. See, for example, Cockcroft, *Intellectual Precursors*, pp. 65–66.
71. This term was coined by Edward Said in his lectures for the seminar "Methodologies of Empire."
72. Gutiérrez Nájera does not yet use the term *cannibalism* but speaks of "*cruzamiento*" [hybridization] (see "El cruzamiento en literatura"), possibly under the influence of Brackel-Welda, who developed a highly suspicious theory of receptivity to foreign influence as the basis of a national grandeur that abounds in allusions to the act of devouring ("proceso digestivo mental"). For Aimé Césaire (*Cahier d'un retour au pays natal*, 1935), cannibalism has become a central metaphor. See *The Collected Poetry of Aimé Césaire*, trans. Clayton Eshleman and Annette Smith (Berkeley: University of California Press, 1983), p.64.
73. Antonio de Alcantara Machado, ed., *Revista de Antropofagia* 1 (1) (São Paolo, May 1928). Facsimile ed., São Paolo, 1975.

WORKS CITED

Adorno, Theodor W. "Lyric Poetry and Society." *Telos* 20 (Summer 1974): 56–71.
Alcantara Machado, Antonio de, ed. *Revista de Antropofagia* 1 (1). São Paolo, May 1928. Facsimile ed., São Paolo, 1975.

Bark, Joachim. "Literaturgeschichtsschreibung über Heine." In *Heinrich Heine: Artistik und Engagement*, ed. W. Kuttenkeuler. Stuttgart: Metzler, 1977.

Benjamin, Walter. *Illuminations*. Trans. Harry Zohn. New York: Schocken, 1977.

Bopp, Marianne O. de. *Contribución al estudio de las letras alemanas en México*. Mexico City: UNAM, 1961.

————. "Heinrich Heine: Bibliografía en México." *Anuario de Letras* 1 (1961): 181–190.

Brackel-Welda, Othon E. de. *Epístolas a Manuel Gutiérrez Nájera*. Comp. Marianne O. de Bopp. Mexico City: UNAM, 1957.

Brummack, Jürgen. *Heinrich Heine: Epoche-Werk-Wirkung*. Munich: Beck, 1980.

Carter, Boyd G. *En torno a Gutiérrez Nájera y las letras mexicanas del siglo XIX*. Mexico City: Ed. Botas, 1960.

————. *Manuel Gutiérrez Nájera—Estudio y escritos inéditos*. Mexico City: Ed. Andrea, 1956.

————. *Las revistas literarias de Hispanoamérica*. Mexico City: Ed. Andrea, 1959.

Castellanos, Rosario. "La Alemania de Heine." *Novedades* (July 11, 1960), p. 4.

Césaire, Aimé. *The Collected Poetry of Aimé Césaire*. Trans. Clayton Eshleman and Annette Smith. Berkeley: University of California Press, 1983.

Chevalier, Michel. "De la civilisation mexicaine avant Fernand Cortez." *Revue des deux mondes* 9 (1845): 965–1020.

————. "Du Mexique avant et pendant la conquête." *Revue des deux mondes* 11 (1845): 197–235.

Clavé, Félix. "La question du Mexique: Relations du Mexique avec les Etats-Unis, l'Angleterre et la France." *Revue des deux mondes* 12 (1845): 1029–1059.

Cockcroft, James D. *Intellectual Precursors of the Mexican Revolution, 1900–1913*. Austin: University of Texas Press, 1968.

Englekirk, John E. "Heine and Spanish-American Modernism." *Comparative Literature: Proceedings of the International Comparative Literature Association at the Univ. of North Carolina, Sept. 8–12, 1958* 2 (1959): 488–500.

Fernández y González, Manuel María, trans. *Joyas prusianas*, by Heinrich Heine. Madrid: 1873.

Fogelquist, Donald F. "José Asunción Silva y Heinrich Heine." *Revista Hispánica Moderna* (1954): 282–294.

Geldrich, Hanna. *Heine und der spanisch-amerikanische Modernismo*. Bern and Frankfurt am Main: Herbert Lang, 1971.

Gutiérrez Nájera, Manuel. *Obras: Crítica literaria*. Mexico City: UNAM, 1959.

Hart, John Mason. *Revolutionary Mexico: The Coming and Process of the Mexican Revolution*. Berkeley: University of California Press, 1987.

Heine, Heinrich. *The Complete Poems of Heinrich Heine: A Modern English Version*. Trans. and ed. Hal Draper. Boston: Suhrkamp/Insel, 1982.

———. "Huitzilpochtli." Trans. Jorge Hammeken y Mexía and Manuel de Olaguíbel. *El Domingo* 4 (1873): 465–467, 480–482.

———. "Vitziliputzli," Trans. Manuel María Fernández y González. *La Epoca Ilustrada* 45 (Aug. 8, 1884): 714–719.

———. *Werke und Briefe*. Ed. Hans Kaufmann. 10 vols. Berlin: Aufbau, 1961.

Henriquez Ureña, Max. *Breve historia del modernismo*. Mexico City: Fondo de Cultura Económica, 1954.

Hermann, Helene. *Studien zu Heines Romanzero*. Berlin: Weidmannsche Buchhandlung, 1906.

Hulme, Peter. *Colonial Encounters: Europe and the Native Caribbean, 1492–1797*. New York: Methuen, 1986.

Kennedy, J. Gerald. "The Horrors of Translation: The Death of a Beautiful Woman." In *Poe, Death, and the Life of Writing*. New Haven: Yale University Press, 1987.

Kruse, Joseph A. "Heines Leihpraxis und Lektürebeschaffung." In *Die Leihbibliothek als Institution des literarischen Lebens im 18. und 19. Jahrhundert*, ed. Georg Jäger and Jörg Schönert, vol. 3. Wolfenbüttler Schriften zur Geschichte des Buchwesens. Hamburg: Hauswedell, 1980.

Menéndez y Pelayo, Marcelino. Introduction to *Libro de los Cantares/Prosa Escogida*, by Enrique Heine. Mexico City: Porrúa, 1984.

Mentz, Brígida von, V. Radkau, B. Scharrer, and G. Turner R. *Los pioneros del imperialismo alemán en México*. Mexico City: Centro de Investigaciones y Estudios Superiores en Antropología Social, 1982.

Owen, Claude R. "Dario and Heine." *Susquehannah University Studies* 8 (1970): 329–349.

———. "Ezequiel Martínez Estrada und Heine." *Heine-Jahrbuch* (1971): 52–75.

———. *Heine im spanischen Sprachgebiet*. Münster: Aschendorf, 1968.

Paz, Octavio. *The Labyrinth of Solitude: Life and Thought in Mexico*. Trans. Lysander Kemp. New York: Grove, 1961.

Prawer, Siegbert S. *Heine: "Buch der Lieder."* New York: Barron, 1960.

———. "Heine's 'Romanzero.'" *Germanic Review* 31 (1956): 293–306.

Roa Bárcena, José Maria. *Recuerdos de la invasión norte-americana, 1846–1848 por un jóven de entónces*. Mexico City: Juan Buxó, 1883.

Rukser, Udo. "Heine in der hispanischen Welt." *Deutsche Vierteljahrschrift für Literaturwissenschaft und Geistesgeschichte* 30 (1956): 454–510.

Sellén, Francisco, trans. *Intermezzo lírico*, by Heinrich Heine. New York: 1875.

Simpson, Lesley Byrd. *Many Mexicos*. 4th rev. ed. Berkeley: University of California Press, 1967.

Valadés, Jose C. *Breve historia del Porfirismo (1876–1911)*. Mexico City: Ed. Mexicanos Unidos, 1971.

Weber, Johannes. "Heines 'Frivolität' und 'Subjektivität' in der älteren deutschen Literaturgeschichtsschreibung." *Text und Kritik* [Special Heinrich Heine Issue] 18/19 (1982, rev. ed. of 1968 issue): 84–116.

Zamora, José Zamudio. *Heinrich Heine en la literatura chilena: Influencia y traducciones*. Santiago: Ed. Andrés Bello, 1958.

Zantop, Susanne. "Lateinamerika in Heine—Heine in Lateinamerika: 'das gesamte Kannibalencharivari.'" *Heine-Jahrbuch* 28 (1989): 72–87.

HARTMUT STEINECKE

"The Lost Cosmopolite":
Heine's Images of Foreign Cultures and Peoples in the Historical Poems of the Late Period

Sterbend spricht zu Salomo
König David: Apropos,
Daß ich Joab dir empfehle,
Einen meiner Generäle.

*[On his deathbed, David told
His son Solomon: "Behold,
You must rid me, in all candor,
Of this Joab, my commander."]*
—Heinrich Heine, König David [King David]

These verses seem almost more reminiscent of Wilhelm Busch (1832–1908) than of Heinrich Heine. The casual treatment of language and of great figures in world history—both essential features of a poetry that often provided a stimulus for humoresque and cabaret—come together here almost programmatically in the rhyme "Salomo / Apropos." The poem continues:

Dieser tapfre General
Ist seit Jahren mir fatal,
Doch ich wagte den Verhaßten
Niemals ernstlich anzutasten.

Du, mein Sohn, bist fromm und klug,
Gottesfürchtig, stark genug,
Und es wird dir leicht gelingen,
Jenen Joab umzubringen.

> [Captain Joab's brave and tough
> But he's irked me long enough;
> Yet, however I detest him,
> I have never dared arrest him.
>
> You, my son, are wise, devout,
> Pious, and your arm is stout;
> You should have no trouble sending
> Joab to a sticky ending.][1]

After proceeding so nonchalantly, the poem concludes with a rather macabre point. Even if it is expressed in a fairly unconcerned and light-hearted manner, the legacy that David bequeaths to his son Solomon is the task of murdering Joab. And anyone familiar with the Old Testament knows just how Solomon carried out this mission. In addition to the inappropriateness of the language for this theme, one must take into account the irritation evoked by the dramatis personae: David is the most esteemed of Jewish kings, and the last stanza repeatedly reminds us of the well-known piety and devoutness of wise Solomon.

The poem speaks for itself; its cynical moral is evident. Heine does not formulate it as a conclusion to be drawn at the end of the story, the way ballads usually do. Instead, he places it at the opening as an introduction:

> Lächelnd scheidet der Despot,
> Denn er weiß, nach seinem Tod
> Wechselt Willkür nur die Hände,
> Und die Knechtschaft hat kein Ende.
>
> [Smiling still a despot dies,
> For he knows, on his demise,
> New hands wield the tyrant's power—
> It is not yet freedom's hour.][2]

With unmistakable clarity a historical law is enunciated here: arbitrariness and abuse of power are the marks of every ruler; therefore, every system of rule is despotism and implies servitude. This law is also true of the most respected Jewish king; hence, how other rulers must think and act requires no further explanation. In the second stanza this assessment is repeated and confirmed in reference to the circumstances of the ruled:

Armes Volk! wie Pferd' und Farrn
Bleibt es angeschirrt am Karrn,
Und der Nacken wird gebrochen,
Der sich nicht bequemt den Jochen.

[Like the horse or ox, poor folk
Still stay harnessed to the yoke,
And that neck is broken faster
That's not bowed before the masters.][3]

This drastic image of brute animals under the yoke—the symbol of despotism and brutal oppression—shows the results of tyranny without any romanticizing. Since these two generalizing stanzas open the poem, it is no longer possible to read the subsequent verses and the—at first glance—rather amusing rhymes à la Wilhelm Busch as my reading first suggested. Indeed, the disparity between the brutally depressing historical maxim and the apparently nonchalant and playful tone makes the abyss between reality and appearance even more clear. It is only a step from the sublime to the ridiculous: these words of Napoleon's are known to have been one of Heine's favorite quotations, and they fittingly describe one of his most important poetic techniques. Heine's historical poetry shows that from the horrible and macabre of world history it is only a short step to the laughable.

The poem *King David* stands somewhere in the middle of the book *Historien* [Tales]. These historical tales comprise the first part of *Romanzero* (1851), which Heine himself saw as the "third pillar" of his "lyrical fame."[4] The opening poem of the *Historien*[5] involves another king, Rhampsenitus of Egypt, who is obviously a far more congenial ruler than David. After his treasure chamber has been burgled, Rhampsenitus places his daughter on guard in the chamber. Yet she cannot resist the thief:

Schätzehütend diese Nacht
Kam ein Schätzlein mir abhanden.
So sprach lachend die Prinzessin

[While I guarded your trove stoutly,
Ah, I lost my own sweet treasure.
So she spoke, the laughing princess.]

Theft and rape are occasions not for anger and thoughts of revenge, but for endless laughter—the word *laugh* recurs seven times in the poem:

> . . . selbst die Krokodile
> Reckten lachend ihre Häupter
> Aus dem schlammig gelben Nile.

> [. . . Even crocodiles were laughing
> From the Nile's mud-yellow waters.] [6]

Just as surprisingly, the king expresses "sympathy" for the thief and searches for him via a proclamation offering him the princess in marriage and the right of succession to the throne:

> So geschehn den dritten Hänner
> Dreizehnhundert zwanzig sechs
> Vor Christi Geburt.—Signieret
> Von Uns: Rhampsenitus Rex.

> [Done this third of January,
> Thirteen twenty-six B.C.,
> Signed and sealed by Rhampsenitus,
> Rex and Imp., his Majesty.]

And indeed, the king keeps his promise, and the thief becomes his successor:

> Er regierte wie die andern,
> Schützte Handel und Talente;
> Wenig, heißt es, ward gestohlen
> Unter seinem Regimente.

> [So he ruled like other rulers,
> Trade was fostered, talent kindled.
> Under his regime, they tell us,
> Theft and depredation dwindled.] [7]

This is a laughing—or should one say laughable? or ridiculous?—prelude to the poems compiled in the *Historien*. Accepted forms of behavior and moral norms are turned topsy-turvy and ridiculed. Historical poetry's assiduous attention to sources is parodied (rather clumsily) in the pedantic meticulousness with which the date is noted (which moreover counts in the wrong direction, since the theft is dated at 1324 B.C. and the proclamation at 1326 B.C.), the specification "B.C.", and the latinized signature. At the same time, the prevailing historical mode is mocked somewhat more subtly through the inclusion of a long excerpt from Herodotus's *Tales*, from which the story is taken. (Strictly speaking, Heine was interested solely in the initial situation. The greatly embellished main section and conclusion are largely his own invention.)

The conclusion of the poem shows that the king's cleverness consists in integrating the thief into the system of domination. From this perspective, the first lines of the last stanza—"So he ruled like other rulers"—become equivocal. The sentence situates Rhampsenitus and the thief alike in the series of rulers and despots whose behavior Heine had portrayed and commented on in other poems. Moreover, the lines point to the interchangeability of king and thief, of high and low. Power here derives quite literally from theft: the criminal is predestined to be sovereign. The fundamental principle of legitimacy upholding all monarchies is thereby put in question, undermined, and ridiculed. Naturally, in 1851 every reader knew that this principle had not been in force just in ancient Egypt, but that it also acted as a mainstay of European power politics during the restoration period. This principle had been severely shaken by the Revolution of 1848–49, yet it was once again being asserted by the political reaction as part of its effort to ground its claims to rule.

King David and *Rhampsenitus* are two examples of the twenty-one historical tales and more than fifty historical poems Heine wrote from his sickbed during the postrevolutionary period. More than half of his later poetry deals with historical material, including the most extensive poems of his final period: "Jehuda ben Halevy," *Vitzliputzli*, and *Bimini*. Although these tales constitute a major part of Heine's late work, they have enjoyed far less attention and esteem than his poems about death or personal suffering or his political poems dealing with issues of the postrevolutionary era.[8] Only a few of the countless interpretations of Heine's poetry offer convincing and detailed treatments of individual historical poems. How is this gap to be explained?

Explicitly or covertly, criticisms of Heine's historical poetry most frequently rely on three basic arguments: escapism, arbitrariness in the treatment of other cultures, and pessimism about history. Significantly, these reproaches are made not so much by Heine's conservative detractors, as is typically the case, but instead primarily by those who think rather highly of his other work. Just how justified and how substantive are these arguments?

First, Heine's poetry before the March Revolution of 1848, and part of his poetry afterward, is in many instances poetry of the times—sharp and insightful analyses and criticisms of political and social conditions, especially those existing in Germany. Historical materials and themes are certainly not rare in his pre-1848 work, but they are never found in the form of historical panoramas. On the contrary, they appear as evidence of the history leading up to the present time. Many critics have understood the abundance of historical poetry in Heine's later work in terms of a flight from the present and its problems. The fact that German history only occasionally supplied the materials for these poems was seen as lending credence to this charge of escapism. For the most part, the historical tales are concerned with themes and materials belonging to the history of foreign peoples and exotic cultures. They range from Egypt and India, to Greece and Spain, to China and America.

As for the second argument, Heine's scenes from foreign countries display an unusual variety of themes and materials. One encounters famous kings and generals, beautiful and shrewd women, murderers, petty swindlers, madmen, fools, and bizarre figures. Droll anecdotes are just as liable to be the subject of the story as historical events; comic and bloody episodes are narrated—stories of deception, betrayal, and revenge with erotic and political overtones. Most interpreters have regarded this variety in subject matter as capriciousness and have discerned a romantically colored showroom of world history in these poems about faraway lands and ages past. Some critics have attempted to make a virtue of this troublesome whimsicalness. The most recent version of this strategy can be found in a 1987 essay by Gerhard Höhn. The historical poems remind him, "in a confused way, of the *Zeitgeist* that holds sway in the mid-80s of our century," that is, of "posthistoire" and "postmodernity."[9] Rescue attempts like this, which ignore Heine's specific historicophilosophical position, reveal the helplessness of even well-intended critics vis-à-vis what continues to be interpreted as eclectic and whimsical historical poetry.

As far as the third argument is concerned, the view that the strong preference for themes obtained from foreign histories is an expression both of escapism and of a political change of heart in the direction of conservatism is buttressed by the model of history one can derive from some of Heine's poems. In the poem *Valkyries* we read:

Und das Heldenblut zerrinnt
Und der schlechtre Mann gewinnt.

[Heroes' lives will bleed away,
And the worst will win the day.] [10]

These lines are cited time and again in the critical literature on Heine as the motto and leading motif of his late historical poetry.[11] The poem *Schlachtfeld bei Hastings* [The Battlefield at Hastings], which follows *Valkyries* in the *Historien*, is read more or less as an illustration of this maxim:

Gefallen ist der beßre Mann,
Es siegte der Bankert, der schlechte,
Gewappnete Diebe verteilen das Land
Und machen den Freiling zum Knechte.

[The best of men has fallen there
By the hands of bastards and knaves,
And thieves in armor rule the land,
And make the free men slaves.] [12]

One encounters the same picture in all times and countries, regardless of whether the despot is called David, or bears another name, or lives in another century. The eternal return of the same in history—the victory procession of the knaves—appears to reflect Heine's postrevolutionary resignation and seems to conflict with his earlier positions as summed up in the fragmentary work from the early 1830s, *Verschiedenartige Geschichtsauffassung* [Diverse Conceptions of History]. In this work Heine denounces the Ranke school's cyclical conception of history as a "fatally fatalistic view" and ridicules its "indifferentism." He sees its counterpoint in teleological thinking, a belief in progress that places its hopes in the future. Heine certainly puts the latter view of history in a more positive light, but in the end he rejects it as one-sided. He opposes both of these positions, which share a certain distance from life, with a third model that insists on "life as a right" and the right to the present.[13] In view of this work, it seemed to many critics that the development of Heine's understanding of history had itself become cyclical and regressive. It was seen as moving from a concern for the present day during the 1830s, toward the optimistic belief in progress expressed in the pre-1848 poems addressing contemporary issues, only to end in the pessimism about history one finds in the late period.[14]

From such a conception of historical pessimism, only more conservative interpreters of Heine are in a position to benefit: they diagnose it as Heine's resignation in old age and regard the cyclical model of history as a rejection of the Young German enthusiasm for the present and of the Communist belief in progress and revolution. In this manner they use Heine to legitimate the actual course of history. On the other hand, for those who value the political Heine of the prerevolutionary period, and who celebrate his democratic and socially minded ideas as flashes of light in the generally benighted era of German restoration, these works with their depiction of history remain something of an embarrassment. These three widespread prejudices—that the thematization of history represents an escapist response to the present, that the concern with foreign cultures indicates a withdrawal from German problems, and that Heine's pessimism about history results from an old man's resignation—form the decisive reasons for the marginalization of the "historical" poem in Heine research.

In the face of these views and biases, a different approach would mean seeking the current in the historical. In his groundbreaking essay " 'Politische Ballade': Zu den *Historien* in Heines *Romanzero*," Hans-Peter Bayersdörfer argues that the stories act for Heine as a Romantic guise for "political statements," as an "alibi in view of the censor," and further as extended "frameworks" for directing invective against contemporary targets.[15] The feasibility of this approach has been confirmed by impressive interpretations of individual poems such as *Karl I* and *Maria Antoinette*, allowing for a better, more profound understanding of some of the historical poems. I believe, however, that it is important not merely to select a few poems and then rescue them from disparaging judgments by demonstrating that they are "political." Rather, it is necessary to employ this approach when one is dealing with the *Historien* poems, which, at first glance, appear to be unrelated to the context within which they were written. As I indicated in my opening remarks about *King David* and *Rhampsenitus*, the tales turn out to possess the greatest relevance to the change in atmosphere of the post-1848 period when they are studied from the perspective of *histoire du mentalité*. As a third and somewhat more comprehensive example of this approach, I discuss here the second poem of the *Historien, Der weiße Elephant*

[The White Elephant], since it is read as a humorous trifle more often than any of Heine's other poems.

The title hero, the "white melancholic," has dreamed of his match in whiteness and bulk, the Lady Bianca of Paris, and has suffered ever since from lovesickness:

> Er ist ein vierfüßiger Werther geworden,
> Und träumt von einer Lotte im Norden.
>
> Geheimnisvolle Sympathie!
> Er sah sie nie und denkt an sie.
> Er trampelt oft im Mondschein umher
> Und seufzt: wenn ich ein Vöglein wär!
>
> [He, once happy and heart-whole,
> Is now a fourfooted Werther betimes
> And dreams of a Lottie in northern climes.
>
> Mysterious sympathy, as it were!
> He saw her never, yet broods on her.
> While tramping through moonlight with hardly a word, he
> Keeps sighing, "If only I were a birdie!"][16]

Moonlight Romanticism, the longing for Paris, exoticism, and sentimentality are all lampooned in the most comical and yet loving way in this delightful piece of humoresque. The passage also introduces an element of intertextual self-irony by incorporating the *Wunderhorn* passage from Heine's "Ich steh' auf des Berges Spitze" [I Stand on the Mountain's Peak] in the *Buch der Lieder*.[17] It cannot come as a surprise that, depending on the temperament and ideological position of the critic, this poem is either praised as a humoresque engaging in purposeless Romantic play or condemned as a "playful story . . . without . . . end . . . or point. . . . For us, it . . . lacks relevance and interest."[18] At best, interpreters could recognize a concrete political reference in the figure of the somewhat dense and perpetually drowsy King Mahavasant of Siam. For this "lord" one finds the impudent rhyme "snored," and his fruitless attempts to think are captured in verses that ridicule royal dignity per se:

> Er dachte hin, er dachte her;
> Das Denken wird den Königen schwer.

[He thought of this—and that—and things:
Thinking is rather hard for kings.][19]

In comparison with these superficial political overtones, a reading of the poem as a virtual historical allegory reveals a profusion of hidden references to matters of topical interest. René Anglade's subtle interpretation has shown the insights that are disclosed to the careful reader and to those who are familiar with Heine's use of metaphor. Anglade points to the elephant's function as a medieval religious symbol and notes the analogy existing between the large white noblewoman and Delacroix's famous image of "Freedom at the Barricades." The curious verse "Oh, this whiteness is implacable" realizes its explosive power only when one has recognized it as a quote from Gautier and thereby understood that "the demand for freedom is implacable, ineluctable, and universal."[20] In the poem the elephant and the white lady do not (yet) come together. This possibility is improbable, absurd, and fabulous. Yet the theme of fairy tale versus reality is addressed in the poem itself:

Hier überflügelt der Wirklichkeit Pracht
Die Märchen von Tausend und eine Nacht.

[Yet his treasure house is so immense,
So vast and full of magnificence,
That its splendors outshine the marvelous sights
Of the most fantastic Arabian Nights.][21]

Heine had used similar figures of speech only a short time before in his comments on the February Revolution in Paris: "Yes, that is unbelievable! That exceeds . . . all the fairy tales of '1001 Nights'!" If Scheherazade had told this one, the sultan would have "exclaimed": "Never again will I allow myself to be taken in by something so unheard of as the February fairy tale about Paris or by stories concocted by malevolent lunatics about impossible, hocus-pocus revolutions that are supposed to have occurred on the shores of the Donau and the Spree!"[22] That Germans would start a revolution is fabulous and unreal; that they would fail is a predictable reality. Yet in the fabulous and absurd world of the poem, why shouldn't the elephant attain his beloved and why shouldn't the yearning for freedom also be able to triumph in Germany?

Although I have briefly indicated only a few aspects of this problem, the example demonstrates that the apparently merely playful, comical, and digressively elaborated poem is replete with references to issues of topical importance. These references are not couched in an exotic guise primarily to serve an orientalizing ornamentation, but instead illustrate in manifold ways that the yearning for freedom possesses a universal character and is not to be strangled by material superabundance or by medieval or religious ties.

No—Heine did not use the history of foreign peoples simply as a Romantic guise and a splendid backdrop. Nor did he want to offer colorful historical tableaux as concessions to the period's need to depict historical scenes. He also did not wish to produce evidence for the fatalistic saying "There is nothing new under the sun"[23] when he drew on other cultures and other historical periods. And least of all is he a predecessor of the new capriciousness that has begun its triumphal march through aesthetic and literary discussions of theory under the rubric of "postmodernity." For Heine, history is always open to the present. His choice of foreign historical material should be described and evaluated not only negatively, but also positively, as a turning to history and alien societies, to historicity in its intercultural dimension.

This new perspective becomes clearer if one replaces the dichotomy German/foreign with the concepts national/supranational. From this point of view Heine's historical poems manifest a turn away from national history in the direction of world history. The expression "turn away," however, in no way signifies an estrangement or flight from the present and from German problems. Instead, world history enters into a discordant relationship with national history. World history, while it takes account of national history's fruitful aspects, also situates national history in a larger field of vision. For Heine, concentrating on Prussian-German history in the long run held the danger of confinement to and obsession with a specific historical situation and problematic. Universal history offered the possibility of broadening his vision, of recognizing analogies and differences, and of comparing disparate processes.

Perhaps this approach will prove more illuminating if we draw a comparison to the relationship between national literature and world literature.[24] A universalistic vision could, of course, be regarded as a rejection of the national heritage during a period in which literary-historical study and historiography in general became increasingly nationalized. This view was the basis of the national enthusiasts' attack against Heine and the Young Germans during the era before the 1848 Revolution: Heine and company courted betrayal, indeed, destruction of the national in favor of a supranational world literature. This same accusation has now been leveled against Heine by well-meaning patriots, democrats who are concerned for the future of Germany. This time, the criticism has been inverted, and Heine is chastised for having paid too little attention to the national *misère*.

To clarify the point: one cannot follow Friedrich Nietzsche in praising Heine as a European or as a citizen of the world and at the same time reproach him for making Europe and the world the setting for his historical poems. It seems to me that Heine's inclusion of foreign nations and world history in his work is related to changes in his understanding of history, that is, to his increasingly pessimistic view of history. To begin with, however, it is important to maintain against reductive interpretations of the work *Verschiedenartige Geschichtsauffassung* that— as recent research has shown[25]—the three models proposed there do not have to be construed as alternatives. For strategic reasons of effect, Heine almost satirically depicts the first two conceptions of history as extreme positions, which he then rejects. But taken together, the three different conceptions he sees as possible in the prerevolutionary era form a dialectical combination that nevertheless clearly gravitates toward the focalization on the present Heine introduces as a synthesis.

This way of relating the various models is confirmed by Heine's literary works, which are in any case markedly more complex than his theoretical ones. Here one encounters, in a form by no means trivialized, images of the "pathetic, eternally repetitious game" of history (for instance, in Heine's remarks on his visit to a portrait gallery in Genoa, in the *Reisebilder* [Pictures of Travel]); or, in an equally serious vein, enthusiastic revolutionary and utopian visions of the future (for instance, in the *Tagebuch aus Helgoland* [Heligoland Diary], composed on hearing the news of the July Revolution).[26] But for all that, the claim on the present predominates time and again: from the reports out of Paris and the poems addressing topical issues, to the *Börne* book and *Deutschland: Ein Wintermärchen* [Germany: A Winter's Tale].

This emphasis also holds true for Heine's late period, which is hardly as uniformly pessimistic as the typical judgments cited above suggest. In this later work as in the earlier, differing but dialectically interrelated conceptions of history are simultaneously present. Although the pessimistic outlook certainly predominates, it by no means completely represses the other viewpoints or renders them obsolete. One may wish to point to an ever-increasing pessimism, but it seems to me more useful to speak of growing skepticism toward faith in progress. At the same time, however, one cannot simply equate this posture with fatalism: fatalism signifies, after all, resignation before a predetermined destiny. But Heine's every poem—and certainly every one of his political and historical poems—is a protest against fatalism.

Over and over again the pessimism about history found in the later works has been attributed to the steadily worsening illness that plagued Heine in the latter part of his life. Unquestionably, a connection exists between the two, but again it seems to me inadequate to overemphasize this causal link and highlight Heine's private life, for it ignores the growth that took place in his thinking at the same time. I believe it is more significant to call attention to the fact that Heine's view of history had a strongly subjective bent from the very beginning. Most of Heine's contemporaries viewed the process of history as an objective force. History enjoyed popularity and respect—both as a science (historiography) and as a form of literature (historical poetry)—because of its objectivity, a characteristic people began to associate intimately with realism.

Heine's position, which he shared with few authors and hardly any historiographers, is remarkable for the degree to which it regards history as a subjective phenomenon. This approach holds true even for the *Weltschmerz* he stylized during the 1820s. Heine writes in the third volume of his *Reisebilder*: "Since the heart of the poet is the center of the world, it follows that it could not help but be miserably broken at the present time. Whoever boasts of his heart that it has remained whole merely admits that he has a prosaic, remote, and shallow heart."[27] The old metaphor of bleeding hearts is taken up again more frequently in the late poems, as in the epigraphic poem of the *Historien* or, particularly impressively, in *Enfant perdu* [Lost Child]:

> Die Wunden klaffen—es verströmt mein Blut.
>
> Ein Posten ist vakant!—Die Wunden klaffen—
> Der eine fällt, die andern rücken nach—
> Doch fall ich unbesiegt, und meine Waffen
> Sind nicht gebrochen—Nur mein Herze brach.
>
> [My wounds are gaping—hot the red blood flows.

My wounds are gaping wide—A post's unmanned!
One sentry falls, another takes his part—
And yet I fall unvanquished, sword in hand—
The only thing that's broken is my heart.][28]

The turn to world history and the turn to the most private sphere—
personal suffering—are not antagonistic extremes. The subjective character of all history and the universal significance of every self (especially
the poet-self) make the transitions between the two realms fluid. Thus
the *Romanzero* can encompass both historical tales and Lazarus poems,
and the historical tales can speak of the poet-self (as in *Apollogott* [God
Apollo]) while the Lazarus works include an *"enfant perdu"* who bleeds
to death in humanity's war of liberation. In many earlier interpretations
such subjectivity was regarded as a vestige of an outmoded, Romantic
view of history. To the contemporary reader, however, it seems to be an
anticipatory view that realizes that history, too, is not objective and can
be only subjectively experienced.

The three principal premises of this chapter—the fruitful tension
between national history and world history, the positive power of the
pessimistic view of history (in its protest against fatalistic resignation),
and the subjective basis of every view of history—are shown well in the
America poems *Vitzliputzli* and *Bimini*. Since the picture of America
offered by both of these poems has already been dealt with exhaustively
elsewhere, I limit myself to exploring the understanding of history
documented in the two works.[29]

Dieses ist Amerika!
Dieses ist die neue Welt!

[This is America indeed!
This is a new world, really new!][30]

So begins the "Prelude" to *Vitzliputzli*, as well as Heine's play with
the idea of the "new"—

Neuer Boden, neue Blumen!
Neue Blumen, neue Düfte!

[New the soil, and new the flowers!
New the flowers, new the perfumes!]

—a play into which the word "healthy" soon enters as a synonym:

> Wie gesund ist diese Welt!
>
> · · · · · · · · ·
>
> Aus gesundem Boden sprossen
> Auch gesunde Bäume.

> [Oh, how healthy is this world!
>
> · · · · · · · · · ·
>
> From a healthy soil spring also
> Healthy trees.]

The concepts "old" and "sick" are placed in opposition to these two terms. If health is linked to the New World, old age and illness are associated with the Old World, Europe, and a series of symbols:

> . . . Kirchhof der Romantik,
> . . . alter Scherbenberg
> Von verschimmelten Symbolen
> Von versteinerten Perücken.

> [. . . Romanticism's graveyard
> . . . ancient junk heap
> Piled with mouldy moss-grown symbols
> And old fossil periwigs.]

Yet what appears clear-cut is already shown in an ambivalent light, as suggested by the concept of "Romanticism" (inserted anachronistically here into the historical period of the Spanish conquest). When the poem alludes to Heine's own illness by remarking that none of the healthy Americans has "consumption of the spinal marrow," the subjective moment of this view of history manifests itself. Indeed, the lyrical "I" makes an appearance as early as the fourteenth stanza of the "Prelude": "I looked the new world over / In this way, with startled eyes," and it remains present throughout the rest of the poem. Initially taken for "a ghost from the old world" by a monkey in the new, the lyrical self responds:

> Affe! fürcht dich nicht, ich bin
> Kein Gespenst, ich bin kein Spuk;

> Leben kocht in meinen Adern,
> Bin des Lebens treuster Sohn.

> [Monkey, calm your fears! I am
> Not a ghost or apparition:
> Life is seething in my body,
> I'm the truest son of life.]

It is simply that through the "years-long commerce / With the dead" he has taken on their "demeanors, ways and manners"; the long period in Kyffhäuser's cavern, "In the Venusberg, or other / catacombs of Romanticism," he says, have had their effect on him.

In the course of the "Prelude" the traditional categories of historical models are put in question, abolished, and even reversed: the new is located in the past, whereas the old and ailing are found in the present; the self is old and sick, but it accepts "life" as a central value. When the main section of the poem depicts atrocities committed by Spaniards and bloody sacrificial rites carried out by Indians, or when the gods, idols, and demons of the Old and New worlds join forces with those of exotic cultures, or again when Vitzliputzli curses the Europeans (perhaps with syphilis) in return for the evil they have done, the pessimism expressed about history is certainly unmistakable. But at the same time, the long procession of savage acts of violence does not nullify the affirmation of life in the "Prelude." According to Heine's *Verschiedenartige Geschichtsauffassung*, the affirmation of life always contains an affirmation of the present.

In the poem *Bimini*, which by virtue of its scale could be called a verse epic, the prologue likewise plays with the opposition between old and new:

> Eine ganze neue Welt—

> Eine neue Welt mit neuen
> Menschensorten, neuen Bestien,
> Neuen Bäumen, Blumen, Vögeln,
> Und mit neuen Weltkrankheiten!

> [. . . a whole new world—

> Yes, a whole new world, and with it
> New varieties of people,

And new beasts and birds and blossoms,
And new world diseases also!][31]

The opposition between old and new is dissolved from the outset
by this last line—which already refers to Vitzliputzli's legacy—and the
same process as seen from the other side takes place in the ensuing
passage:

Unterdessen unsre alte,
Unsre eigne alte Welt,
Umgestaltet, ganz verwandelt
Wunderbarlich wurde sie

Durch Erfindnisse des Geistes

[In the meantime our own world,
That old world we had grown up in,
Was completely metamorphosed,
Marvelously all transfigured.

By inventions of the spirit.]

These changes were wrought by the printing press, the Bible, humanist culture, and not least by the technical innovations that made ocean
travel possible. It was the beginning of wonderful discoveries as well as
of colonialism's savageries, horrible crimes, and an intoxication with
money and gold.

The thoroughgoing dialectic also takes up the concept of "Romanticism," which is alluded to in the opening lines of the poem with the
words "blue flower":

Wunderglaube! blaue Blume,
Die verschollen jetzt, wie prachtvoll
Blühte sie im Menschenherzen
Zu der Zeit, von der wir singen!

[Faith in marvels! Old blue flower,
Now forgotten—how resplendent
Was its blooming in our spirits
In the days of which we sing!]

Romanticism is therefore viewed as belonging to the past, to the era of
America's recent discovery and Ponce de León, and is shown in an en-

tirely positive light. The American past—the new—and the European present—the old—come together under the catchword "Romanticism" in the "yearning" for the paradisical island of Bimini. As the island of eternal youth—the dream wish of both the Spanish conquerors and the mortally ill European poet—Bimini becomes a cipher for Romanticism, longing, the "dead dreams of youth," and utopia.

The key term in this dialectic, involving inversions of old and new, and Romanticism, is the fundamental Romantic power: fantasy. The traditional epic invocation of the Muse asks for the "magic of the noble art of poetry," and the song becomes an "enchanted ship" that is limned in detailed poetic images:

> Aus Trochäen, stark wie Eichen,
> Sind gezimmert Kiel und Planken.
>
> Phantasie sitzt an dem Steuer,
> Gute Laune blüht die Segel,
> Schiffsjung ist der Witz, der flinke.
> Ob Verstand an Bord? Ich weiß nicht!
>
> Meine Rahen sind Metaphern,
> Die Hyperbel ist mein Mastbaum,
> Schwarz-rot-gold ist meine Flagge
>
> [Out of trochees strong as oak beams
> Are its keel and planking fashioned.
>
> Helmsman Fancy holds the rudder,
> Blithe Good Humor swells the canvas,
> Wit's the nimble cabin boy.
> Is Good Sense on board? I know not!
>
> Metaphors are all my yardarms,
> A hyperbole my foremast;
> Black-red-golden is my banner.][32]

At the close of the prologue, the entire magical journey of fantasy is characterized as foolishness:

> . . . mein Narrenschiff . . .
> . . . meine Narrenfahrt
> Nach der Insel Bimini.

[Scoffing at my ship of fools and
At my foolish passengers,
At the folly of my voyage
To the isle of Bimini.]

Heine's frequent characterizations of himself as a fool and his well-known fondness for Shakespearean fools dovetail with his view that the poet is the fool absolute.

The depiction of Ponce de León's expedition often bears traces of such foolishness, of the comical and ridiculous, as well as the infantile, which is connected to the return of youth. In his aged decrepitude, Ponce de León is a portrait of the poet-self, and the characterizations of him (*Fant* [fop], *Geckentracht* [strangely decked apparel]) are similar to the representations of the god Apollo in the *Historien*. Ponce de León's voyage leads to a paradox: the search for youth makes him older day by day; in the quest for the fountain of life he finds the river of death. The poet, too, is a fool. He is driven by longings and dreams; utopia beckons to him. Nevertheless, the poet's ship of fantasy differs from Ponce de León's expedition in one essential respect—the poet is outfitted with "wit," humor, and irony; this difference does not in any way invalidate the poetic utopia, but it certainly plays with and reflects on it.

In the eightieth *Atheneum Fragment* Friedrich Schlegel writes, "The historian is a prophet gazing backwards."[33] In this sense Heine's historical poems make him a historian. The more severely Heine was cut off from the outside world in the later years of his life, the more he opened himself up to literature as a source (especially to travel books and historical works), and the more his mind's world opened up. At the same time, the connections he drew between different historical periods became more free. For Heine, the historical tales may have been fanciful visions, projections, and utopias.

This approach formulates an answer to the question posed at the outset of this essay: why does Heine deal so frequently with foreign countries and their histories in his later poetry? In a paraphrase of Schlegel's words, one might say that he is a cosmopolitan nationalist. Even in the later period Heine's concerns are time and again focused on Germany and its future. But he now views this problem more often as a part of larger contexts. For this reason, images that relate to personal impressions and experiences do not dominate to the same degree as they do in his early works about foreign countries like Poland, Italy, England, and

France. The power of fantasy makes him less dependent on the personal. Although he is just as concerned with the problems of the present and of Germany, he is now aware that the view from outside often shows these problems in a clearer light. In this manner he can portray the problems without having to take domestic considerations into account. At the same time, he also avoids the hatred that the German condition increasingly excited in him and that limited the influence of his poetry among his contemporaries. In the end, he sees the present day as part of the continuum of history and the problems of Germany as embedded in the context of global issues.

Heine referred to himself several times as a "cosmopolite" and even as "cosmopolitanism incarnate."[34] The preoccupation with foreign countries and their histories is one of the signs of such a cosmopolitanism. Heine was, however, not only a German without a fatherland, but also a cosmopolite without a home. In the bitterly sarcastic poem *Jetzt Wohin?* [Now, Where to?] from the *Romanzero*, the voice of the poet rejects the possibility of returning to Germany from France. Yet the poem also rejects departing for England, America, or Russia. It ends with the ironically resigned verses:

> Traurig schau ich in die Höh,
> Wo viel tausend Sterne nicken—
> Aber meinen eignen Stern
> Kann ich nirgends dort erblicken.

> Hat im güldnen Labyrinth
> Sich vielleicht verirrt am Himmel,
> Wie ich selber mich verirrt
> In dem irdischen Getümmel.

> [Sadly gazing to the sky
> I see stars in thousands there—
> But the star that is my own,
> I can't see it anywhere.

> Maybe it has lost its way
> In a maze that's silver-pearled,
> Just as I myself am lost
> In the tumult of the world.][35]

I called Heine a cosmopolite without a home. Perhaps one could better characterize his cosmopolitanism with the adjective "lost," from the closing lines of the poem above. The paradox of an openness to the world created out of a love for Germany might then be grasped with the following formulation: Heine was a "lost cosmopolite."

NOTES

1. Heinrich Heine, *König David*, in *Sämtliche Schriften*, ed. Klaus Briegleb, 12 vols. (Munich and Vienna: Ullstein, 1976), 11:40. The English translations of the poems are taken, with some minor changes, from Hal Draper, trans., *The Complete Poems of Heinrich Heine* (Boston: Suhrkamp/Insel, 1982). This quotation can be found on pp. 586–587.
2. Heine, *Schriften*, 11:39; *Poems*, p. 586.
3. Ibid.
4. Letter to Julius Campe from September 28, 1850; see Heinrich Heine, *Werke-Briefe-Lebenszeugnisse*, 27 vols., Säkularausgabe (Berlin: Akademie; Paris: Editions du Centre National de la Recherche Scientifique, 1970), 23:52.
5. *Rhampsenit*, in Heine, *Schriften*, 11:11–13; *Rhampsenitus*, in Heine, *Poems*, pp. 563–565.
6. Heine, *Schriften*, 11:12; *Poems*, p. 564.
7. Heine, *Schriften*, 11:13; *Poems*, p. 565.
8. The most important works concentrating on the *Historien* are Hella Gebhard, "Interpretation der *Historien* aus Heines *Romanzero*" (Ph.D. dissertation, University of Erlangen, 1956); Hans-Peter Bayersdörfer, " 'Politische Ballade': Zu den *Historien* in Heines *Romanzero*," *Deutsche Vierteljahrsschrift für Literaturwissenschaft und Geistesgeschichte* 46 (1972): 435–468.

The larger works dealing with the *Romanzero* or with Heine's poetry in general contain more or less extensive sections on the historical tales. See in particular Helene Herrmann, *Studien zu Heines Romanzero* (Berlin: Weidmann, 1906); Siegbert S. Prawer, *Heine, The Tragic Satirist: A Study of the Later Poetry, 1827–1856* (Cambridge: Cambridge University Press, 1961); Frauke Bartelt, "Entstehung und zeitgenössische Aufnahme des *Romanzero* von Heinrich Heine: Studien im Zusammenhang einer historisch-kritischen Edition" (Ph.D. dissertation, University of Kiel, 1973); Gerhard Storz, *Heinrich Heines lyrische Dichtung* (Stuttgart: Klett, 1971); Jeffrey L. Sammons, *Heinrich Heine: The Elusive Poet* (New Haven and London: Yale University Press, 1969); Helmut Koopmann, "Heines *Romanzero*: Thematik und Struktur," *Zeitschrift für deutsche Philologie* 97 (1978)

[Sonderheft]: 51–70. The current state of research is summarized in Gerhard Höhn, *Heine-Handbuch: Zeit, Person, Werk* (Stuttgart: J. B. Metzler, 1987). The *Romanzero* is discussed on pp. 112–126.

9. Translated from Höhn, *Heine-Handbuch*, p. 122. (Translations of material other than Heine's poetry—for which Draper's translations are used—are provided by Brian Urquhart.)

10. Heine, *Schriften*, 11:20–21; *Poems*, p. 571.

11. For example, Höhn, *Heine-Handbuch*, p. 117.

12. Heine, *Schriften*, 11:21–22; *Poems*, p. 572.

13. Heine, *Schriften*, 5:21–23.

14. Cf. the following quotation, translated from Höhn, *Heine-Handbuch*, p. 119: "Heine's dialectical understanding of history . . . after 1848 comes strikingly close to the pessimism of the cyclical model that *Diverse Conceptions of History* characterized as 'bleak' and 'fatalistic.'"

15. Translated from Bayersdörfer, "'Politische Ballade,'" pp. 437–439.

16. Heine, *Schriften*, 11:13–18; *Poems*, pp. 565–570.

17. Heine, *Schriften*, 1:97.

18. Translated from Storz, *Heines lyrische Dichtung*, p. 175.

19. Heine, *Schriften*, 11:18; *Poems*, p. 569.

20. Translated from René Anglade, "Eine Begegnung, die nicht stattfand. Heines *Der weiße Elefant*: Eine Interpretation," *Jahrbuch der deutschen Schillergesellschaft* 20 (1976): 483.

21. Heine, *Schriften*, 11:14; *Poems*, p. 565.

22. Translated from "Über die Februarrevolution 1848, Bericht vom 22. März," in Heine, *Schriften*, 9:213–215.

23. This phrase is translated from its citation in the *Verschiedenartige Geschichtsauffassung*, in Heine, *Schriften*, 5:21.

24. For a more extensive discussion, see Hartmut Steinecke, "Weltliteratur: Zur Diskussion der Goetheschen 'Idee' im Jungen Deutschland," in *Das Junge Deutschland*, ed. Joseph A. Kruse and Bernd Kortländer (Hamburg: Hoffmann & Campe, 1987), pp. 155–172.

25. See Helmut Koopmann, "Heines Geschichtsauffassung," *Jahrbuch der deutschen Schillergesellschaft* 16 (1972): 453–476; Susanne Zantop, "Verschiedenartige Geschichtsschreibung: Heine und Ranke," *Heine-Jahrbuch* 23 (1984): 42–68; Gerd Heinemann, "'Variazionen': Heines Geschichtsauffassung nach 1848," in *Rose und Kartoffel: Ein Heinrich Heine-Symposium*, ed. A. A. van den Braembussche and Ph. van Engeldorp Gastelaars (Amsterdam: Rodopi, 1988), pp. 69–84.

26. See Heine, *Schriften*, 3:388 and 7:53–55, for these passages.

27. Translated from Heine, *Schriften*, 3:405.

28. Heine, *Schriften*, 11:121; *Poems*, p. 650.

29. For another discussion of Heine's idea of history in his later work, see Benno

von Wiese's chapter " 'Ich grüße dich, Phöbus Apollo!' Mythos und Historie in Heines später Lyrik," in his *Signaturen: Zu Heinrich Heine und seinem Werk* (Berlin: E. Schmidt, 1976), pp. 167–195.

30. The lines from *Vitzliputzli* are found in Heine, *Schriften*, 11:56–60, and *Poems*, pp. 599–601.

31. The lines from *Bimini* are found in Heine, *Schriften*, 11:241–266, and *Poems*, pp. 745–763. For commentary on *Bimini*'s historical themes, see Wiese, *Signaturen*, and Jürgen Jacobs, "Der späte Heine und die Utopie: Zu 'Bimini,' " *Etudes Germaniques* 22 (1967): 511–516. The problems of the arrangement of the text pointed out by Michael Espagne are less important for the aspects dealt with here; see his "Die fabelhafte Irrfahrt: Heines späte Entwicklung im Spiegel der Handschriften zu 'Bimini,' " *Heine-Jahrbuch* 23 (1984): 69–89.

32. Notice the recurrence here of the national colors in an irreverent context, as with the monkey in *Vitzliputzli* (Heine, *Poems*, p. 601), whose

> hairless leathern backside . . . [displays]
> just the colors that I love.

> Dear old hues! Black-red-gold-yellow!

Such passages should serve to warn against nationalist interpretations.

33. Translated from Friedrich Schlegel, *Kritische Schriften*, ed. Wolfdietrich Rasch (Munich: Hanser, 1964), p. 34.

34. Translated from a letter to a friend in Hamburg, beginning of April, 1833. See Heine, *Werke*, 21:52.

35. Heine, *Schriften*, 11:101–102; *Poems*, p. 634.

WORKS CITED

Anglade, René. "Eine Begegnung, die nicht stattfand. Heines *Der weiße Elefant*: Eine Interpretation." *Jahrbuch der deutschen Schillergesellschaft* 20 (1976): 464–491.

Bartelt, Frauke. "Entstehung und zeitgenössische Aufnahme des *Romanzero* von Heinrich Heine: Studien im Zusammenhang einer historisch-kritischen Edition." Ph.D. dissertation, University of Kiel, 1973.

Bayersdörfer, Hans-Peter. " 'Politische Ballade': Zu den *Historien* in Heines *Romanzero.*" *Deutsche Vierteljahrsschrift für Literaturwissenschaft und Geistesgeschichte* 46 (1972): 435–468.

Espagne, Michael. "Die fabelhafte Irrfahrt: Heines späte Entwicklung im Spiegel der Handschriften zu 'Bimini.' " *Heine-Jahrbuch* 23 (1984): 69–89.

Gebhard, Hella. "Interpretation der *Historien* aus Heines *Romanzero.*" Ph.D. dissertation, University of Erlangen, 1956.

Heine, Heinrich. *The Complete Poems of Heinrich Heine.* Trans. and ed. Hal Draper. Boston: Suhrkamp/Insel, 1982.

————. *Sämtliche Schriften.* Ed. Klaus Briegleb. 12 vols. Munich and Vienna: Ullstein, 1976.

————. *Werke-Briefe-Lebenszeugnisse.* 27 vols. Säkularausgabe. Berlin: Akademie; Paris: Editions du Centre National de la Recherche Scientifique, 1970.

Heinemann, Gerd. " 'Variazionen': Heines Geschichtsauffassung nach 1848." In *Rose und Kartoffel: Ein Heinrich Heine-Symposium,* ed. A. A. van den Braembussche and Ph. van Engeldorp Gastelaars. Amsterdam: Rodopi, 1988.

Herrmann, Helene. *Studien zu Heines Romanzero.* Berlin: Weidmann, 1906.

Höhn, Gerhard. *Heine-Handbuch: Zeit, Person, Werk.* Stuttgart: J. B. Metzler, 1987.

Jacobs, Jürgen. "Der späte Heine und die Utopie: Zu 'Bimini.' " *Etudes Germaniques* 22 (1967): 511–516.

Koopmann, Helmut. "Heines Geschichtsauffassung." *Jahrbuch der deutschen Schillergesellschaft* 16 (1972): 453–476.

————. "Heines *Romanzero*: Thematik und Struktur." *Zeitschrift für deutsche Philologie* 97 (1978) [Sonderheft]: 51–70.

Prawer, Siegbert S. *Heine, The Tragic Satirist: A Study of the Later Poetry, 1827–1856.* Cambridge: Cambridge University Press, 1961.

Sammons, Jeffrey L. *Heinrich Heine: The Elusive Poet.* New Haven and London: Yale University Press, 1969.

Schlegel, Friedrich. *Kritische Schriften.* Ed. Wolfdietrich Rasch. Munich: Hanser, 1964.

Steinecke, Hartmut. "Weltliteratur: Zur Diskussion der Goetheschen 'Idee' im Jungen Deutschland." In *Das Junge Deutschland,* ed. Joseph A. Kruse and Bernd Kortländer. Hamburg: Hoffmann & Campe, 1987.

Storz, Gerhard. *Heinrich Heines lyrische Dichtung.* Stuttgart: Klett, 1971.

Wiese, Benno von. *Signaturen: Zu Heinrich Heine und seinem Werk.* Berlin: E. Schmidt, 1976.

Zantop, Susanne. "Verschiedenartige Geschichtsschreibung: Heine und Ranke." *Heine-Jahrbuch* 23 (1984): 42–68.

T. J. REED

History in Nutshells:
Heine as a Cartoonist

What a mysterious faculty, this queen of faculties,
imagination. She touches all the others, excites them, sends
them into combat. . . . She is analysis, she is synthesis.
—*Baudelaire,* Salon of 1859

The graphic elements in Heine's writings are not news. In particular, his verbal caricatures have been the subject of two substantial studies by Siegbert S. Prawer: *Heine's Jewish Comedy: A Study of His Portraits of Jews and Judaism* and *Frankenstein's Island: England and the English in the Writings of Heinrich Heine.*[1] Prawer's method, as his titles make plain, is to bring together everything of interest that Heine wrote on the two stated themes, to analyze his attitudes and techniques piece by piece, and so to build up a comprehensive picture of each thematic area and its literary treatment.

The approach might be extended to other staple themes of Heine's, but it seems unlikely any essentially new stylistic insights would emerge. That might appear to conclude the matter. Yet there seem to me to be other functions of Heine's visual imagination still left to explore and things still to be said about its realization, effects, and origins. Nor are these peripheral remnants; they are things central to Heine's acts of comprehension and communication of his experience. They concern the relation of intellectual or ideological content to its formal embodiment, of visual means to sociopolitical ends; that is, they concern the eternal triangle of reality, image, and idea at a historical moment. They are also, lest this all sound too solemn, full of Heine's unique humor.

Clues to what I have in mind are scattered through the discussion of the 1970s and 1980s in some of the visual terms critics have used when describing Heine's effects. At the literal end of the scale—literal rather than metaphorical in terminology, and literal in the kind of correspon-

dence assumed between reality and Heine's rendering of it—Jacques
Voisine and others have discussed the historical portraiture contained
in Heine's journalistic writings. Prawer and Sander Gilman have asked
how far Heine was a photographically objective observer, following up
the canard he himself started when he said his articles composed an
"honest daguerreotype" of his times.[2] Moving progressively away from
that extreme, Wolfgang Preisendanz speaks of a "pictorial formula" and
of "picture puzzles" ["Bildformel," "Vexierbilder"], Dolf Sternberger of
a "rapid vision" in which "insight is packaged," and Jeffrey Sammons
of "real observations" being turned into "imaged epiphanies," or "a
momentary experience into a symbolic epiphany."[3] What is at issue in
all these cases, as in so much recent Heine scholarship, is the poet's
understanding and presentation of historical events and the historical
process. And the nonliteral terms I have quoted—formulas, puzzles,
visions, and epiphanies—all carry us well beyond the scope of verbal
caricature.

Not beyond the scope of cartoon, however. Here a distinction, or
rather a bundle of distinctions, is necessary and more easily made in
English than in German, in which the one word *Karikatur* serves for
both. *Caricature* means the representation of an actual person or human
type, with exaggeration and distortion used as a means of satirical attack or ridicule. We sometimes use the term *cartoon* as well for this
meaning, but generally *cartoon* has the much broader sense of the representation of actual or imagined figures or sets of figures, composed
into scenes and actions that convey a message. Caricature concentrates
on an empirical particular; it is centripetal; it cannot stray far from representational realism and can use only such distortions as will leave the
person it portrays still recognizable. Cartoon can freely manipulate empirical particulars and create visual relationships in making the larger
correspondences its message requires; it is centrifugal in that it moves
out from actual persons into the realm of general issues. Caricature
need embody no idea; cartoon is essentially a vehicle for ideas. Caricature may be no more than a joke—it has been psychologically explained
as a temporary, saturnalian release of aggressive feeling;[4] whereas cartoon usually means what it says in full ideological earnest and for good,
however humorous its way of making its point may be. Both of them
aim at recognition, but in different senses. The caricaturist says: "Have
you ever noticed that William Pitt has a long nose? Theodore Roosevelt
looks like a bull moose? Winston Churchill has the features and build

of a bulldog? Look, this is he, a bit exaggerated." The worst that ensues is that the great are treated with a little healthy disrespect, and it may be that we even come to love their familiar caricature images. But the cartoonist says: "Don't you realize how things really are? What's actually happening before your very eyes? The outrageous way these people are getting away with it?"

In other words, the cartoonist has the potentially much more far-reaching effect of revealing something real but intangible; he offers us not an object, but an interpretation. The art historian Sir Ernst Gombrich has shrewdly suggested that the cartoonist is a realist in the medieval sense: he tells us there are general, abstract, categorical truths beyond the things we observe and that they constitute the reality that matters.[5] He uses images to make that reality as concretely visible to us as the everyday things we observe. But the eye of the modern cartoonist is, of course, fixed, as the eye of the medieval philosopher or theologian was not, on society and politics—on the unavowed real motives of human actions, the larger pattern and implications of a policy, or the direction in which, unnoticed by us, history is really moving.

A simple and celebrated example illustrates my distinction and brings us to Heine in Paris in the 1830s. It is commonly known that Louis Philippe's head was pear-shaped and that Charles Philipon (1806–1862) was jailed for showing it to be so in a satirical paper. The image made the king only mildly ridiculous, and the associated slang sense (the French word *poire* = "a sucker") was not wildly defamatory or even politically relevant. The image was simple caricature. It only became politically telling and a *"stehender Volkswitz"* [a standing, popular joke][6] because of the government's overreaction to its first appearance—a familiar process.

But when Heine in *Französische Zustände* [French Affairs] portrays Louis Philippe wearing an unpretentious felt hat and carrying a bourgeois umbrella, but with a crown hidden under the hat and a scepter inside the rolled umbrella, that is a cartoon.[7] It encapsulates fifty years of French history—a revolution, a restoration, a further revolution—and the uneasy compromise of the July Monarchy, which has a subsidiary member of the royal family ruling on new terms: he is not "King of France" but "King of the French"; he calls himself the "citizen King"; he espouses constitutionalism and moderation (the *juste milieu*); and yet he has secret hankerings for absolute power. Heine's image conveys that message immediately as well as amusingly. The interplay of the real hat and umbrella with the emblematic crown and scepter creates no problems, for in cartoons we easily accept the mix of the figurative with the literal. Nothing needs wordy spelling out. It is true that the cartoon has an extensive context, which is Heine's account of the Paris Mardi Gras carnival. But that is not a commentary, but a large cartoon metaphor for the whole *juste milieu* political scene in which everything is false and everyone, typically of carnival time, is playing a role. As the natural center of that scene, Louis Philippe and his pictorial attributes embody his meaning with instant clarity.

That is the mark of the virtuoso artist. As Baudelaire wrote of Honoré Daumier (1808–1879): "The idea stands out at once. You look, and you've got it." All Baudelaire's discussions of nineteenth-century French and European caricaturists return to this essential point of pure *graphic* communication.[8] If a drawing needs caption or commentary, or if objects are made to carry meanings that they do not naturally carry and so have to be labeled to make the message clear, this message has not been realized as graphic form. What should be the viewer's prompt seizing of a point becomes the labored assimilation of a lesson.

This discussion has taken us into our subject in three ways. We have looked at a sample of Heine's verbal cartooning; we have a criterion for graphic quality; and the name of Daumier has provided another lead-in to the Paris of the 1830s—and indeed, the name of Daumier suggests an atmospheric influence that must have been at least as important for Heine as the invention by Louis Daguerre (1787–1851) of a photographic process in 1839. Heine's arrival in Paris coincided with what Baudelaire calls a "fever of cartooning."[9] The first five years of the July Monarchy saw a ferocious campaign against Louis Philippe and his government. The journal *La Caricature* was born in 1830, *Le Charivari* in 1832; Daumier was only the greatest of a group of satirical draftsmen. There were simple caricatures like the Pear, but more (and more effective) cartoons. Daumier went to jail for one of his earliest cartoons, called "Gargantua." It shows Rabelais's omnivorous giant, now pear-headed, being endlessly fed with bags of gold that small figures carry up a ramp to his mouth, while his other end excretes the diplomas and honors the money buys.[10] The *juste milieu* was a money-centered society, which makes Heine's pun on "juste-millionär" much more pungent than the one about Rothschild treating him "ganz famillionär" [completely familiarly].[11]

Censorship was imposed on cartoons in 1835 after Giuseppe Fieschi's attempt on the king. But the politicographic ambience had

had four years to offer Heine something his German environment could not. For there could hardly be political cartoons in a society that, as Heine says, barely had any "räsonnierende politische Journale" ["critically engaged political journals"].[12] Just as aesthetics and theater criticism had to fill the gap left by politics, so too a merely whimsical caricatural humor leading to Wilhelm Busch (1832–1908) had to stand in for the graphic hardstuff. G. W. F. Hegel, characteristically, thought all ridiculing of rulers was wrong, an attitude typical of Biedermeier political prudishness.[13] Yet the need for cartoon, the thrust of the political imagination into the realm of grotesque hyperreality, can occasionally be glimpsed in Germany—again in its verbal form. What sticks in the mind from Georg Büchner's *Hessischer Landbote* [Hessian Country Courier] is not so much the biblical rhetoric aimed at the peasants, nor the use of statistics to document fiscal injustice which looks back to Tom Paine and on to Karl Marx; rather it is the image of the bloodsucking leech that sprawls disgustingly across the body of Hesse-Darmstadt and its people, with the prince its head, his ministers the teeth, and the officials its tail.[14] That is precisely the cartoonist's imagination at work, linking and raising elements of experience into a vision of horrible higher truth.

What we find in Heine is the same impulse toward graphic simplification and coherence, ultimately in a very similar cause. But so far we have had only one instance. Here are some more. Please switch on your own graphic powers and imagine how you, or Daumier, or James Gillray (1757–1815), or some later cartoonist, might realize with a pencil what Heine sketches with his pen. And try to check how far the idea is in each case assimilated into a graphic image so that the meaning is self-evident and needs no clumsy elucidation. For—if I may dispose of a central problem of my thesis in one sentence—although Heine's medium is itself wholly words, it is not hard for us to draw a critical line between the minimum verbalization needed to conjure up a full image, and the baggage train of commentary required by the inadequate image.

Heine's meaning is not always, or at least not always obviously, political. So here are some prima facie purely literary cartoons: Goethe was a massive oak, overshadowing younger, smaller growths, and he was too high to have a red Phrygian bonnet put on his topmost tip; Ludwig Tieck once lived in Berlin in the same house as Friedrich Nicolai (1733–1811), one story higher—the new era trampled on the head of the old; August Wilhelm Schlegel's verse was a polished mahogany surface on which you could easily slip, whereas the verses of Johann Heinrich Voss (1751–1826) were blocks of marble you could stumble over; Goethe, in his pantheistic indifference to both religion and the politics of the day, was attacked from opposite sides, by a black priest with a crucifix and a raging sans-culotte with a pike; similarly, every man's hand was raised against Baruch Spinoza; the phalanx of the French Encyclopedists marched alongside a swarm of black and white monkish cowls; the rabbi of Amsterdam sounded the attack with the shofar of faith while Voltaire played on the piccolo of persiflage; alone of the Romantic writers, E. T. A. Hoffmann was an Antäus with his feet touching the solid earth of reality, while such as Novalis floated free in the blue air of "*Schwärmerei.*" Romanticism was also regressive, and when August Wilhelm Schlegel preached the magic spring of the Middle Ages as an elixir of youth, Tieck drank so much of it that he regressed to total childishness (this cartoon might call for a series of frames . . .); and as a yet more drastic version of the same theme, Tieck, the little boy of the Romantic School, dug his dead ancestors out of the grave and rocked them, in their coffins, to the crazed lullaby: "Schlaf, Großväterchen, schlafe" ["Sleep, little Grandfather, sleep"].[15]

Not that Heine was himself immune to the fascination of things medieval: how could the craggy power and vernacular authenticity of the *Nibelungenlied* be better evoked than by his suggestion that its central figures, with their towering passions, are like the Gothic cathedrals of Europe meeting in love and conflict on an open plain by moonlight? Here, for once, the image of a church carries no negative connotations for Heine, as it does when the younger German generation is pictured queuing up to get back into the spiritual prison of the Catholic church from which their fathers had struggled so hard to escape; or when Heine allows that August Wilhelm Schlegel's lectures on literature have the necessary higher standpoint, but alas it is a Catholic belfry.[16] It may be that Heine exaggerates the number of Catholic conversions in his aetiology of Romanticism, but his real and accurate insight, which he shares with other analysts like Hegel and Eichendorff, is precisely his characterization of the movement's "aesthetic religiosity" and the more-than-aesthetic consequences it had.[17]

As an illustration of this charade we have his picture of a Jesuitized Schelling disguising religion as philosophy and administering the poisoned host to the unsuspecting youth of the University of Munich. This image is merely a grimmer version of the brilliant improvisation Heine, the Italian traveler, offers to a philosophical lizard he encounters in

Lucca: Berlin is a caravan of learning where camels load up with water-skins of Hegelian wisdom, to be carried out into the sandy wastes of the Mark Brandenburg, while in Munich Schelling dispenses from his intellectual fountain, as if it were best beer, the cheap swill of immortality, "Gesöffeder Unsterblichkeit." And to vary the refreshments of philosophy, we later have Madame de Staël arriving politically overheated from France to cool herself off with German philosophy, which comes in many flavors of ice cream: the vanilla sorbet of Immanuel Kant, the pistachio of J. G. Fichte, the Neapolitan tutti-frutti of Schelling.[18]

None of these examples is overtly political, but many are easily convertible, because for Heine all culture has political implications and all politics is ultimately "*Kulturpolitik*" ["cultural politics"]. But there are straight political cartoons, too: with the French Restoration of 1815, the heroic figures of history left the stage and the clowns came on in their place, the fat Bourbons waddling in with their stale old jokes, the ancient nobility emaciated by their years as émigrés and eager to make up for that deprivation, and the inevitable train of monkish figures with their crosses and candles and ecclesiastical banners. The July Monarchy itself still has too many of the old nobility in its Upper Chamber, so for Heine it becomes a hospital for the incurables of the "ancien régime." Meanwhile, the lesser German princes are being steadily swallowed up by Austria and Prussia but remain oblivious, preoccupied as they are with stealing bits of each other's territory—in visual terms, thieves who, even while being driven to the gallows, still pick each other's pockets. At the other end of society the common people whose revolutionary action in 1830 gave Louis Philippe power are by 1831 being put back in their place and trodden down again, like the cobblestones they used as weapons. If this characterization sounds sympathetic to the people, there is the other side of Heine which fears the lower orders and observes the proletariat emerging from the muddy Parisian depths like terrible crocodiles; their German counterparts, the more theoretical Communist egalitarians, have a different subhuman origin: they have been hatched out by Hegel, and the later Heine remembers how in his youth he saw that broody philosophical hen sitting on the fateful eggs of history a-clucking.[19]

Finally, an immense collection of sketches from every phase and genre of Heine's work centers on food—preparing it, eating it, being denied it or cheated of it or corrupted by it. It is an obvious political theme at the literal level, and Heine the political realist necessarily has it always at the back of his mind; but he also rings the changes remarkably on what could easily be a mere cliché and sometimes raises it to an almost visionary level. Food makes political and social supremacy concrete; eating stands are for the enjoyment and even flaunting of power and privilege; hunger and paying the bill for others' consumption mean political powerlessness. The German princes observed on Norderney, being *mediatized,* may no longer wield the scepter, but they can still wield knife and fork, and it is not simple fare they consume and the people pay for. This image is made more intensely graphic by the banquet in post-Restoration Paris at which the narrator of *Das Buch Le Grand* [The Book Le Grand] finds himself passed over and forgotten while all manner of French princes and nobles are fed by armies of lackies; his unoccupied fingers begin to drum on the table, and lo and behold it is the "Guillotinemarsch" he finds himself drumming, learned years ago from Monsieur Le Grand and only now brought back through involuntary memory by the arrogance and fecklessness of the restored ancien régime.[20]

Less visually luxuriant than that grand Hogarthian composition are the later political poems. In the four-frame *Zeitgedicht* "Erleuchtung" [Enlightenment], for example, "der deutsche Michel" has his best dishes stolen from him and is fobbed off with promise of a heaven "wo die Engel kochen / Ohne Fleisch die Seligkeit" ["where the angels stew / pots of bliss—without any meat"] (for Heine a flat contradiction in terms), but then begins to stir and may yet fill his earthly belly and leave the time beyond death for quiet digesting. By contrast, the Germans of "Zur Beruhigung" [Consolation] have eaten themselves into political torpor, unlike the "tyrant-eaters" of ancient Rome—Heine the Shakespearean will not have forgotten the "lean and hungry look" that stamped Cassius a dangerous man in Caesar's eyes. This poem is less strongly visual than others, yet the chorus of self-condemningly complacent burghers is a very real cartoon presence and makes a cartoonist's point.[21] It is a point that Büchner made, too, in something approaching cartoon form, when he wrote to Karl Gutzkow (1811–1878) in 1835 that feeding the peasants would give the Revolution apoplexy: "ein *Huhn* im Topfe jedes Bauern macht den gallischen *Hahn* verenden" ["a chicken in the pot of every peasant will kill the Gallic rooster"].[22] Sparer still in graphic line is Heine's political allegory of the wandering rats which opens with the simplicity of a child's drawing: "Es gibt zwei Sorten Ratten, / Die hungrigen und satten" ["There are two kinds of rat: /

One hungry, one fat"]—then evokes alternately their implacable on-ward movement and grimly alien appearance and customs, until it ends abruptly, adumbrating once again the fundamental reality of food, in comparison with which even political parts of the intellectual *Über-bau* [superstructure], such as the speeches of the moderate revolution-ary Mirabeau, can have no meaning.[23]

There are many other brilliant exploitations of the food image, which I have collected and analyzed elsewhere.[24] Indeed, it is time to stop merely quoting Heine, delightful though it always is to remind our-selves how inventive and comic he can be, and instead to ask some questions. How do his cartoons (if you grant that this is what they are) take effect in themselves and in relation to the surrounding text? How do they fit into Heine's ideological framework and serve his political purposes? Where do they stand in the chronology of his work—are they really a product simply of his experience of the Parisian political cli-mate and its intensive cartooning or did that only confirm an existing inclination? And if so, do they have deeper roots in the history of ideas and forms, within which the history of Heine's ideas and forms is con-tained?

First, the nature of his effects. The effects of individual cartoons, of course, vary—they would soon pall otherwise—and it would take a complete catalogue raisonné to exhaust them, but some principles can be shown to be at work. The verbal cartoonist, like his graphic col-league, practices emblematics and allegory. He can use standard cor-respondences, like the Amsterdam rabbi's "*shofar* of faith," or he can invent his own, like Voltaire's "piccolo of persiflage." Heine largely in-vents his own, and his choice of equivalents can be piquant, startling, impudent, outrageous. His visual effects can also be enriched by typical literary pleasures, like the alliteration in "Pickelflöte der Persiflage."[25] Such enrichment might be seen as compensation for the loss of the ad-vantages that actual drawings have: crucially, the verbal cartoon cannot get the absolutely instantaneous effect of showing everything at a single glance.

Yet this loss can itself be turned into a gain. A disciplined word se-quence not only avoids distracting from the picture by superfluous or inappropriate elements, it can also create a chosen emphasis, build up to a climax, achieve a verbal-cum-visual punchline. Our viewing is not free but directed. We watch the Munich students kneel reverently be-fore Schelling, for a moment we reflect on their illusions, and then we see innocence receiving poison: "Andächtig kniet diese Jugend nieder vor dem Manne, den sie für den Hohepriester der Wahrheit hält, und arglos empfängt sie aus seinen Händen die vergiftete Hostie" ["These young men kneel down reverently before the man whom they consider the high priest of truth and unsuspectingly receive from his hands the poisoned host"].[26] The sequence, with its final switch to a close-up of the hands and the wafer, incidentally brings movement into what would otherwise be static; Heine instinctively applies the principle of Lessing's *Laokoon* that visual description must be converted into action, movement, live process. Hegel as hen is similarly brought to life, in this case by expanding the sense range of what we are shown: "ich sah, wie Hegel mit seinem fast komisch ernsthaften Gesichte als Bruthenne auf den fatalen Eiern saß" ["I saw how Hegel, with his almost comically serious expression, sat like a hen on the fatal eggs"]. At this point, history is still latent, quiescent, an imperceptible process, and not yet a terrible product, a static image. Suddenly, startlingly, the picture moves, the hen gives voice: ". . . und ich hörte sein Gackern" [". . . and I heard his clucking"].[27] We have seen and heard the philosopher prophesy; it is ridiculous and at the same time ominous.

Perhaps Heine's most consummately skillful effort in shaping his material to a point is the banquet scene from *Das Buch Le Grand*, which builds up our sympathetic resentment against the feasting aristocrats and guides our eye through the crowded scene to its center of meaning: the lone neglected guest who stands for all society's neglected guests and whose reaction is an omen of the revolutionary work their idle hands may again take up.[28]

How do Heine's cartoons, then, fit into their textual surroundings? Heine not only builds up to an effect *within* the cartoon by the sequencing of details, he also builds up *to* his cartoon as the simplifying summary of an exposition or a satirical attack. His preceding text may give the reader some familiarity with the issues, which is not at all the same as a commentary that limps along behind the cartoon itself. The text gradually becomes more and more sharply focused, and the cartoon gives the finishing touch. To expand on an example already mentioned: in Article 1 of *Französische Zustände*, Heine deals with Louis Philippe's political power base and prospects in view of the pear-head scandal and the imminence of Charles Philipon's trial, and he argues that regimes can maintain themselves only if they remain faithful to the forces that brought them to power. Louis Philippe owes his power to the Parisian crowd and their cobblestones, but he is now ungratefully betraying them: "Ja, täglich geschehen offenbare Rückschritte" ["Yes, every day obvious backstepping occurs"]—"Schritte" ["steps"] is the first pointer to the political actions of feet, figurative and literal—"und wie man die Pflastersteine, die man in den Juliustagen als Waffen gebrauchte, und die an einigen Orten noch seitdem aufgehäuft lagen, jetzt wieder ruhig einsetzt, damit keine äußere Spur der Revolution übrig bleibe, so wird jetzt das Volk wieder an seine vorige Stelle, wie Pflastersteine, in die Erde zurückgestampft, und, nach wie vor, mit Füßen getreten" ["and just as the cobblestones, which during July were used as weapons and which in certain places had been left lying in piles, are being calmly reset in the streets, so that no outer sign of revolution remains, so too the people are, like cobblestones, being stamped back into their former places in the dirt and, as before, they are being trampled underfoot"].[29] The idiomatic phrase "mit Füßen getreten" ("trampled underfoot"), carefully saved till last, gives the empirical observation a symbolic meaning to make a conclusive image of the betrayal of the people.

Consciously or unconsciously, Heine's reader comes to expect these irresistible illustrations that encapsulate a whole argument or clinch a polemical point. They are the perfect consummation of a mode of writing that is always light but rarely frivolous, always lucid but never superficial. Occasionally, Heine's tone becomes suddenly serious, even a touch *pathetisch,* as when he says apropos of the Romantic poets how much more than poetry was at stake: "die Wirkung, die sie auf die große Menge ausüben konnten, gefährdete die Freiheit und das Glück meines Vaterlandes" ["the influence they were able to exercise on the general public endangered the liberty and happiness of my country"].[30] These rare earnest occasions use his habitual lightness of tone as a foil. But generally, his strategy (or his instinct) is to make the potentially solemn subjects he deals in—literary and philosophical history, political events, cultural criticism—palatable and accessible to an audience that he conceives of as interested and intelligent but not learned, and as in search of entertainment, not just enlightenment. *Exactly* who he thought of as his audience varies. At times he said (rather optimistically) it was the people, the same *große Menge* [great mass] that the Romantics had been trying to reach. He even thought war itself might be ended "wenn wir es dahin bringen, daß die große Menge die Gegenwart versteht" ["if we succeed in making the general public understand the present"].[31] Certainly, if anyone ever had the talent to open the politics of the day to the popular understanding, it was Heine. At other times, however, he seemed to deny the people and shift to the (equally sanguine) belief that he might gain the trust of Europe's reactionary statesmen and bring about the conversion of the most elevated, "die Bekehrung der Hochstgestellten."[32]

Even this shift, however, entailed no change of literary method. Heine remained at heart, and in all his prose practice, a popularizer—indeed, consciously and defiantly so. For example, he defends himself against the real philosophers of Germany who were bound to look down on his *Zur Geschichte der Religion und Philosophie* [On the History of Religion and Philosophy] by pointing out to them "daß das wenige, was ich sage, ganz klar und deutlich ausgedrückt ist, während ihre eignen Werke, zwar sehr gründlich, unermeßbar gründlich, sehr tiefsinnig, stupend tiefsinnig, aber eben so unverständlich sind" ["the little I say is expressed clearly and comprehensibly, while their own works are, to be sure, very thorough, infinitely thorough, very profound, stupendously profound, but equally incomprehensible"]. And even as he defends un-German, Cartesian clarity, he practices it with his usual means, an image, which grows into a minor cartoon: "Was helfen dem Volke die verschlossenen Kornkammern, wozu es keinen Schlüssel hat? Das Volk hungert nach Wissen und dankt mir für das Stückchen Geistesbrot, das ich ehrlich mit ihm teile" ["Of what help to the people are locked granaries for which they have no key? The people are hungry for knowledge and will thank me for the bit of intellectual bread which I will share fairly with them"].[33]

We encounter a similar argument in his pioneering popular account of the way the ancient gods had been demonized by Christianity. Of course, learned men knew all about it before, he says, but it was tucked away in dusty folios; when he rescued it, they followed his lead, without acknowledgment and also, crucially, without any talent for writing:

> sie haben das Thema so zu sagen [and with these words the compulsive visualization starts up again] sie haben es so zu sagen eingesargt in die hölzernen Mumienkasten ihrer konfusen und abstrakten Wissenschaftssprache, die das große Publikum nicht entziffern kann und für ägyptische Hieroglyphen halten dürfte. Aus solchen Grüften und Beinhäusern habe ich den Gedanken wieder zum wirklichen

Leben heraufbeschworen, durch die Zaubermacht des allgemein ver-
ständlichen Wortes, durch die Schwarzkunst eines gesunden, klaren,
volkstümlichen Stiles.

[they have, so to speak, entombed it in the wooden mummy cas-
kets of their confusing and abstract philosophical jargon, which the
general public cannot decipher and must regard as Egyptian hiero-
glyphics. I have called their ideas up out of their crypts and charnel
houses and back into real life through the magic power of the generally understood word, through the black art of a healthy and clear
common style.][34]

With the subtle ambiguity of the word *Schwarzkunst* [black art], Heine
captures the paradox that the clear, straightforward writing he is proud
of is also a profound and rarely mastered art.

I used the phrase "compulsive visualization." That is not my conjec-
ture—Heine declares it himself. An abstract thought, he says, is like a
soul without a body: "Der Gedanke, den wir gedacht, ist eine solche
Seele, und er läßt uns keine Ruhe bis wir ihm seinen Leib gegeben,
bis wir ihn zur sinnlichen Erscheinung gefordert" ["The thought we
have conceived is such a soul, and it leaves us no peace until we have
given it its body, until we have helped it to become a material phenomenon"]. This claim already seems to edge beyond questions of literary
presentation into questions of substantive belief. The next sentence
edges farther: "Der Gedanke will Tat, das Wort will Fleisch werden"
["Thought strives to become action, the word to become flesh"].[35] And
the next paragraph (from the opening of Book Three of *Zur Geschichte
der Religion und der Philosophie*) contains Heine's statement on social
thought and revolutionary action, which makes Robespierre into the
bloody hand drawing from the womb of time the body whose soul had
been created by Rousseau—one more rather grim cartoon, if you like.

More importantly, this incessant visualization exemplifies the deep-
est principle of Heine's system: the interaction or integration of spirit
with matter. In politics, ideas demand to be embodied in action, even
if it is negative, destructive action. In religion, the spirit should har-
monize with a rehabilitated and fulfilled body. And in art, there should
ideally be a balance of spirit and substance, thought and plastic form,
a balance not found in Heine's age of *Zerrissenheit*. The compulsion to
make ideas concrete and visible is thus itself true to the logic of Heine's

system; it is a move toward fulfilling and not just propounding his ideal, and the more so because his choice of images is always so resolutely physical and down to earth.

If Heine's cartooning practice fits into his ideological system in that way, it also—not surprisingly—grows out of specific problems of literary history and his situation in it. The young writer had learned and used the code in which Romanticism understood and represented the world. In the early poetry of the *Buch der Lieder* [Book of Songs] he manipulates its standard emblems with total virtuosity, but with anything but total belief. However enchanting its elements, the code left out too much of experience. As the poem *Wahrhaftig* (Believe Me!) famously puts it:

> Wie sehr das Zeug auch gefällt,
> So macht's doch noch lang keine Welt.
>
> [No matter how much you like such stuff,
> To make a world they're just not enough.][36]

The principal ingredients of reality it omitted were hard economic necessity and a hard-nosed, un-Romantic society.[37] These elements duly peep between the trees and flowers of Heine's poems. So the world the poems show is made up of irreconcilable fragments—some delightful but disbelieved, others distasteful but undeniable. No wonder that another poem says, meeting the problem head on, "Zu fragmentarisch ist Welt und Leben!" ["Life and the world's too fragmented for me!"]. And there is not much serious hope in the plan for solving the difficulty which his next line suggests: "Ich will mich zum deutschen Professor begeben" ["A German professor can give me the key"].[38] So the poet has to make do with his own less heavyweight but more agile intellect. He learns to live and work with fragments and their ironies. Gutzkow later aptly called Heine the "ironic professor."[39]

Heine had just missed a phase of history that had precisely the kind of coherence and purposeful movement that the poetic imagination needs (or believes it needs) to nourish it: the age of Napoleon. By an intriguing use of transferred epithet, Heine talks of Napoleon in literary and epistemological terms as if the emperor himself had achieved poetic form and philosophical coherence. He calls him "the great classicist" and classifies Napoleon's mind as what Kant calls "intuitive"—that is, the kind that human beings don't have, which superhumanly grasps the world as an immediate whole, whereas the normal mind has to build a picture laboriously from the parts.[40] Napoleon's deeds as recorded in contemporary memoirs—such as Philippe-Paul Ségur's (1780–1873) account of the Russian campaign—became an epic of Homeric grandeur; indeed, quips Heine, Napoleon improvised a good epic every day.[41] For the young Heine, these things are brought to life by the eloquent drum of the aptly named Monsieur Le Grand. Thus, even before he went to France, Heine was suffering from a Napoleonic nostalgia that aligns him not with his German but with his French contemporaries—Musset, Vigny, and Stendhal. And behind the figure of Napoleon lay the first French Revolution, which, in addition to beginning a liberation of men from old beliefs and oppressions, itself generated an art of monumental conviction with a powerful sense of history in the making.[42]

As an artist left waiting with almost religious expectation for a further revolution—and after the relative disappointment of 1830, for yet another one (though after the disappointment of 1848, for nothing much anymore)—Heine can in the meantime only work with the fragments available to him. Very early on, it is a settled principle of his that he will read meanings out of, or if necessary into, the objects in God's world.[43] It becomes one of the most basic, teasing techniques of the *Reisebilder:* in a humorous but ultimately serious way, anything the traveler sees can suddenly turn into a sign or omen through the most fleeting of allusions, which the reader is meant to catch but the censor is meant to miss.[44] Even other people's works of art are grist for Heine's mill: he finds political meanings in the pictures of the Paris Salon of 1831— Leopold Robert's *Reapers* and Paul Delaroche's *Cromwell*—as he also does in the cast of a Florentine statue, *The Knife Sharpener*, which he sees in the Tuileries gardens and about which he overhears Parisians making comments ominous of more revolution to come.[45] Though finished works, these are still for Heine fragments in the stream of history, history being for him the long dialectic of spirit and matter which has never achieved balance in modern times, but might yet one day come right.

When a fragment, of his own finding or of someone else's making, comes into focus as significant within that historical framework, or can be manipulated so as to appear significant within the framework, a telling image can be generated: a picture, often a humorous picture—a cartoon. It is a simple, and simplifying, product of a complex process. It is precisely such moments that Wolfgang Preisendanz has argued require an "esoteric reader," that is, an initiate who knows the ideological system implied by each "picture formula" and who can solve every "picture puzzle."[46] But can we not stand that argument on its head and say that Heine's visual effects are on the contrary the *exoteric* means to make his grand argument graspable precisely by the *un*initiated? Cartoon is, and was evolved to be, the most popularly accessible form of communication on great issues. How better, for example—to remind ourselves once again of Heine's skill—how better and more powerfully could the death of the ancient religions and their values be shown than in that image of Christ the pale, bloody-browed Jew, flinging his cross on to the table where Homer's gods and goddesses are feasting?[47] Heine's ability to make complex things graphically simple places him in the tradition of Luther, who said of his own popular works that they were written for the eyes for the sake of the simple.

If there were time, we could watch Heine continuing in that vein through the years of his most active political commitment. The graphic elements perhaps recede a bit in the prose (there seem to me to be fewer of them in *Lutezia* than in the earlier Paris prose writings), but they are all the more prominent in the poems. They are also simpler, more pared down, for an even more direct purpose. *Deutschland* is full of allegorical and emblematic figures—the *Harfenmädchen* [Harp Maiden] at the border, the *Jungfer Europa* [Virgin Europe] in the vision of freedom, the lictor in the nocturnal streets of Cologne, the wolves in the forest, Hammonia in Hamburg. There are caricatures—of Barbarossa, of Ernst August of Hanover. The four stanzas of Caput III, aimed at Heine's most hated target, the Prussians in the Rhineland, are a classic of cartoon, compressing history, character and mores into visual attributes that leap from the page into unpleasant life:

> Noch immer das holzern pedantische Volk,
> Noch immer ein rechter Winkel
> In jeder Bewegung, und im Gesicht
> Der eingefrorne Dünkel.

> Sie stelzen noch immer so steif herum,
> So kerzengrade geschniegelt,
> Als hätten sie verschluckt den Stock,
> Womit man sie einst geprügelt.

Ja, ganz verschwand die Fuchtel nie,
Sie tragen sie jetzt im Innern;
Das trauliche Du wird immer noch
An das alte Er erinnern.

Der lange Schnurrbart ist eigentlich nur
Des Zopftums neuere Phase:
Der Zopf, der ehmals hinten hing,
Der hängt jetzt unter der Nase.

[These people are still the same wooden types,
Spout pedantic commonplaces,
All motions right-angled—and priggishness
Is frozen upon their faces.

They still stalk about as straight as poles,
And stiffly turned out you meet them,
As if they just had swallowed the stick
That once was used to beat them.

The long mustache is but a new form
Of pigtail that time discloses:
The pigtail that used to hang behind
Hangs down now under their noses.][48]

You could swear you had seen them in the pages of *Simplicissimus*. And the inert, overfed Germans of *Zur Beruhigung* [Consolation] in the *Zeitgedichte* [Poems for the Times] are another classic cartoon, maybe needing more than one frame. As for Atta Troll, he is a cartoon series to himself, perhaps even best thought of as a cartoon film.

All this sounds like a happy ending to my argument—a bit too much so. Of course, humor is always a kind of triumph, and we are free to relish the sheer verve and inventiveness of Heine's comic imagination, of which his cartoons are part. That is a profoundly liberal enjoyment, since the valuing of humor has roots in our acceptance of individual viewpoints in all their quirkiness and social nonconformity.[49] But that is *our* freedom. Heine's humor was not an unmitigated triumph for him. His images remain partial and tentative, in the sense that they are skirmishes with an oppressive reality he cannot finally defeat, or gestures toward an ideal that is still a long way off and may never be realized. Perhaps, even, his images were not as sovereignly effortless as we make them seem when we talk as if Heine simply communicated prior insights through deliberately chosen formulations. It may equally well be that his jokes and images and cartoons were first of all his means to his historical experience—a heuristic function before the rhetorical one. Perhaps visual concreteness and clarification sometimes came as he wrote, a kind of "allmähliche Verfertigung der Anschauung beim Zeichnen" ["gradual production of the image while sketching"], analysis and synthesis at the same time. If that were so, it would mean that what Sternberger calls Heine's "rapid vision" and what Sammons calls his "symbolic epiphanies" were glimpses of a pattern that Heine himself had to snatch from the flux of time and events. Far from being the kind of artist he saw in Shakespeare, whose imagination could reconstitute the whole of reality from a given fragment,[50] Heine—if we want an emblem for *him*—is perhaps more like the wanderer on a mountaintop in the famous painting by Caspar David Friedrich (1774–1840): he has achieved a high standpoint—much higher than August Wilhelm Schlegel's Catholic belfry—but he has to peer down through mists to see anything of the landscape.

Heine's vision allows him to live in hope, not certainty; his prophetic gestures spring not from divine inspiration but from tactics. In the later years, uncertainty becomes a growing unease and eventually a certainty of the defeat of what he values. Even a revolution, if it were to come, seems most likely in the long term to be a Communist one—a direction of history that barely half of Heine accepts as just, while the rest of him fears it. That complexity, too, he can still capture in the powerful graphics of *Die Wanderratten* [The Wandering Rats]. And there are graphic touches in the dark lyrics of the *Matratzengruft* [Mattress Grave]: death as the horseman Thanatos, or as a leech gorging itself on what remains of the sick poet; the grim Frau Sorge sitting at the end of his bed with her creaking snuffbox, noisily blowing her nose; and the castle of remembered insults, *Affrontenburg*, with its emblematic weathercock and sphinx, and its cursed garden inhabited by allegorical vipers, rats, and toads.[51]

All this is not the world of photographic accuracy, nor is even Heine's journalism merely that: when he used the daguerreotype simile for his Paris articles, he was being led astray by the growing prestige of photography in the 1850s into claiming what he calls the "solid merits" of an objective record.[52] For we surely do not go to Heine for anything as humdrum as solid merits. We go to him rather for a portrait of the artist as well as the subject, for the feel of the historian who is also a vibrant part of his time and a measure of its complexity. It is in that sense that every sketch he dashes off for us is history in a nutshell.

NOTES

1. S. S. Prawer, *Heine's Jewish Comedy: A Study of His Portraits of Jews and Judaism* (Oxford: Clarendon Press, 1983); and Prawer, *Frankenstein's Island: England and the English in the Writings of Heinrich Heine* (Cambridge: Cambridge University Press, 1986).

2. Heinrich Heine, *Sämtliche Schriften*, ed. Klaus Briegleb, 6 vols. (Munich: Hanser, 1968–76), 5:239. German Heine extracts are quoted from this edition throughout. English translations of poetry are from *The Complete Poems of Heinrich Heine*, trans. and ed. Hal Draper (Boston: Suhrkamp/Insel, 1982), and further pieces are from *The Romantic School and Other Essays*, ed. Jost Hermand and Robert Holub (New York: Continuum, 1985). When no reference to these translations is given in the note, translations into English (from German or French) are provided by the author.

   The critics' comments alluded to appear in Jacques Voisine, "Heine als Porträtist in der *Lutezia*," in *Internationaler Heine-Kongreß 1972* (Hamburg: Hoffmann & Campe, 1973), pp. 219–226; S. S. Prawer, "Heine and the Photographers," *German Life and Letters*, N.S. 34 (1980–81): 64–73; and Sander Gilman, "Heine's Photographs," *Hebrew University Studies in Literature and the Arts* 13 (2) (Jerusalem, 1985): 222–250.

3. Wolfgang Preisendanz, "Der Funktions Übergang von Dichtung und Publizistik" and "Der Sinn der Schreibart in den Berichten aus Paris 1840–1843 *Lutezia*," in his *Heinrich Heine: Werkstrukturen und Epochenbezüge* (Munich: Fink, 1973), pp. 63, 81; Dolf Sternberger, *Heinrich Heine und die Abschaffung der Sünde* (Hamburg: Claassen, 1972), p. 17; Jeffrey Sammons, *Heinrich Heine: A Modern Biography* (Princeton: Princeton University Press, 1979), pp. 172, 179.

4. Ernst Kris and E. H. Gombrich, "The Principles of Caricature," in E. Kris, *Psychoanalytical Explorations in Art* (London: International Universities Press, 1953), p. 202; see also Kris and Gombrich, "Introduction," in *Caricature* (Harmondsworth: Penguin, 1940), p. 26. Both accounts incline to an undue *Verharmlosung* of satire.

5. E. H. Gombrich, "The Cartoonist's Armoury," in his *Meditations on a Hobby-Horse* (London: Phaidon Press, 1963), p. 128; see also the numerous illustrations. M. Dorothy George's *English Political Caricature: A Study of Opinion and Propaganda*, 2 vols. (Oxford: Clarendon Press, 1959), is another work on cartoon as "history, concrete, personal and tendentious" (p. 3).

6. Heine, *Schriften*, 3:158.

7. Ibid., pp.152–153.

8. Translated from Charles Baudelaire, "Quelques caricaturistes français," in *Oeuvres Complètes* (Paris: Gallimard, 1954), pp.741, 749–751. See also p.742 on the pursuit of a (Cartesian) "perception claire et immédiate."

9. Ibid., pp. 734.

10. Reproduced in Loys [*sic*, not "Louis"] Delteil, *Le Peintre-Graveur illustré (XIX.ᵉ et XX.ᵉ siècles)*, vol. 20, no. 34 (Paris, 1925). Daumier was sentenced for "excitation à la haine et au mépris du gouvernement du Roi et d'offenses [*sic*] à la personne du Roi" ["excitation to hatred and mistrust of the government and the king and for offense to the person of the king"].

11. Heine, *Schriften*, 3:151, 2:425.

12. Heine, *Schriften*, 3:423. Baudelaire's account of European caricature includes no Germans, and there is little to show for Germany in Eduard Fuchs, *Die Karikatur der europäischen Völker* (Munich: U. Langen, 1921).

13. Hegel, *Philosophie des Rechts*, § 319: "daß Verletzung der Ehre von Individuen überhaupt, Verläumdung, Schmähung, Verächtlichmachung der Regierung, ihrer Beehrden und Beamten, der Person des Fürsten insbesondere, Verhöhnung der Gesetze, Aufforderung zum Aufruhr u.s.f. Verbrechen, Vergehen mit den mannigfaltigen Abstufungen sind." See Hegel's *Sämtliche Werke*, ed. Hermann Glockner (Stuttgart: Frommann, 1928), 7:429 ["that the wounding of the honor of individuals in general, abuse, inciting disrespect for the government and its officials, and especially for the person of the prince, disregard for laws, incitement to revolt, etc., are crimes and transgressions of various gradations"]. Hegel's failure to discriminate essentially between ridicule and revolt—they are for him merely "gradations" of transgression and crime—is strikingly in tune with his repressive age.

14. Georg Büchner, *Sämtliche Werke und Briefe*, ed. Werner Lehmann (Hamburg: Wegner, 1971), 2:44. In English, see Georg Büchner, *Complete Works and Letters*, trans. Henry Schmidt, ed. Walter Hinderer and Henry Schmidt (New York: Continuum, 1986), pp. 273–274. There are comparable images in earlier criticisms of the German principalities—e.g., in Goethe's picture of the Sachsen-Weimar peasantry as aphids sucked dry by the metaparasitic ants of the Court (letter of April 17, 1782, to Knebel), and the powerful opening of Schiller's *Brief eines reisenden Dänen*, which echoes the grandeur of baroque rhetoric.

15. These characterizations are located as follows: on Goethe, see Heine, *Schriften*, 3:390; Tieck and Nicolai, ibid., p.425; A. W. Schlegel and Voss, ibid., p.384; Goethe attacked, ibid., p.396; Spinoza attacked, ibid., pp.571–572; Hoffmann and Novalis, ibid., p.441; on Schlegel and Tieck, ibid., p.376; on Tieck and grandfathers, ibid., 4:162.

16. On the Nibelungen, see ibid., 3:455–456; on younger Germany, ibid., p.381; on Schlegel's lectures, ibid., p.410.
17. See Sammons, *Heinrich Heine*, p.195; G. W. F. Hegel, *Ästhetik*, ed. Friedrich Bassenge (Frankfurt am Main: Europa, 1965), 1:579ff.; and Joseph von Eichendorff, *Zur Geschichte der neuern romantischen Poesie*, in *Sämtliche Werke*, ed. W. Mauser (Regensburg: Habbel, 1962), 7/1:41.
18. Schelling as Jesuit, found in Heine, *Schriften*, 3:434; caravans in German philosophy, ibid., 2:480; and Kant, Fichte, and Schelling as ice cream, ibid., 6:452.
19. On French Restoration, see ibid., 2:282; on July Monarchy, ibid., p.665; on lesser German princes, ibid., 3:93; common people under Louis Philippe, ibid., p.110; Parisian crocodiles, ibid., 5:239; and Hegel's brood, ibid., 6:471.
20. On German princes, ibid., 2:232; on Le Grand, ibid., p.272.
21. "Erleuchtung," in Heine, *Schriften*, 4:430–431; "Zur Beruhigung," ibid., pp. 428–429; Heine, *Poems*, pp.405, 406.
22. Büchner, *Sämtliche Werke und Briefe*, 2:44. See also Büchner, *Complete Works and Letters*, pp.273–274.
23. Heine, *Schriften*, 6:306; *Poems*, p.783.
24. See Terence James Reed, "Heines Appetit," *Heine-Jahrbuch* (1983): 1–29.
25. Cf., similarly, the passage on the Middle Ages as an elixir of youth: "die armen Dursthälse . . . stürzten nach jenen Wunderquellen, und das soff und schlürfte und schlückerte mit übermäßiger Gier" ["The poor thirsty souls . . . rushed to the miraculous springs to swill and lap and gulp with extravagant greediness"]—an evocative verbal cacophany. Heine, *Schriften*, 3:376; *Romantic School*, p.18.
26. Heine, *Schriften*, 3:434; *Romantic School*, p.71.
27. Heine, *Schriften*, 6:471.
28. Ibid., 2:272.
29. Ibid., 3:110.
30. Ibid., p.494; Heine, *Romantic School*, p.124.
31. Heine, *Schriften*, 3:91.
32. See Heine's letter to Campe, January 23, 1837, in Heinrich Heine, *Werke-Briefwechsel-Lebenszeugnisse*, Säkularausgabe (Berlin: Akademie; Paris: Editions du Centre National de la Recherche Scientifique, 1970), 21:174–177.
33. Heine, *Schriften*, 3:514; *Romantic School*, p.129.
34. Heine, *Schriften*, 6:401.
35. Ibid., 3:593; Heine, *Romantic School*, p.201.
36. Heine, *Schriften*, 1:64; *Poems*, p.45.
37. See Heine's letter to Straube, February 5, 1821, in Heine, *Werke*, 20:38–39.
38. Heine, *Schriften*, 1:135; *Poems*, p.99.

39. Quoted by Manfred Windfuhr, "Heine und Hegel: Rezeption und Pro-
    duktion," in *Internationaler Heine-Kongreß 1972* (Hamburg: Hoffmann &
    Campe, 1973), p. 262.

40. See Heine, *Schriften*, 3:380, 2:234–235.

41. Ibid., 2:238–239, 3:414.

42. For an excellent account of French revolutionary art and its ideological im-
    plications, see Jean Starobinski's *1789: Les emblèmes de la raison* (Paris:
    Flammarion, 1979). Heine himself endorses a laudatory account of David
    (see Heine, *Schriften*, 3:76–78) and later (ibid., 5:375–376, 480), though
    critical of David, is wholly positive about the "republikanische Tugend
    Periode" ["period of republican virtue"] in art.

43. See Heine's letter to Merkl, October 6, 1826, in Heine, *Werke*, 20:260–261.

44. As an example of this sort of travel "description," note the following ex-
    cerpt from the *Reise von München nach Genua* [Journey from Munich to
    Genoa] (in Heine, *Schriften*, 2:333): "Dämmernde Stille, melancholisches
    Glockengebimmel, die Schafe trippelten nach ihren Ställen, die Menschen
    nach den Kirchen" ["Twilit silence, melancholy bell-ringing, the sheep
    stumble toward their stalls, the people toward the churches"]. For the same
    technique in an early poem, see "Zu Halle auf dem Markt," *Heimkehr*
    lxxxiv (Heine, *Schriften*, 1:147–148).

45. Heine's comments on these various works can be found in the following
    passages: Heine, *Schriften*, 3:54–55, 60, 67–68, 111–112. It has been per-
    suasively argued that when Heine says he "heard others" saying things, he
    is presenting his own opinions as if they were an empirical observation,
    so as to ease them past the censor. See Michael Werner, "La dialectique
    de la censure: à propos de l'autocensure dans les articles journalistiques de
    Heine," in *Cahiers de Textologie 1: Exercices de critique génétique* (Paris:
    Minard, 1986), p. 18.

46. Preisendanz, *Heine: Werkstrukturen*, p. 51.

47. Heine, *Schriften*, 2:492.

48. Ibid., 4:581–582; Heine, *Poems*, p. 487.

49. See Wolfgang Preisendanz, "Die umgebuchte Schreibart: Heines literari-
    scher Humor im Spannungsfeld von Begriffs-, Form- und Rezeptionsge-
    schichte," in *Heinrich Heine: Artistik und Engagement*, ed. Wolfgang Kut-
    tenkeuler (Stuttgart: Metzler, 1977), pp. 5–8.

50. Heine, *Schriften*, 6:167.

51. These images can be found on the following pages: Heine, *Schriften*, 5:115;
    ibid., 6:330, 114–115, 199–200.

52. Heine, *Schriften*, 5:239. Evidence of this growing prestige is also provided
    by Baudelaire's need to attack photography and defend the imagination in
    the *Salon de 1859*. See especially the sections "Le public moderne et la

photographie" and "La reine des facultés"—i.e., imagination. (The epigraph
to the present essay comes from this section.)

WORKS CITED

Baudelaire, Charles. *Oeuvres Complètes.* Paris: Gallimard, 1954.
Büchner, Georg. *Complete Works and Letters.* Trans. Henry Schmidt. Ed. Walter
Hinderer and Henry Schmidt. New York: Continuum, 1986.
———. *Sämtliche Werke und Briefe.* Ed. Werner Lehmann. Hamburg: Wegner,
1971.
Delteil, Loys. *Le Peintre-Graveur illustré (XIX.ᵉ et XX.ᵉ siècles).* Vol. 20. Paris:
1925.
Eichendorff, Joseph von. *Sämtliche Werke.* Ed. W. Mauser. Regensburg: Habbel,
1962.
Fuchs, Eduard. *Die Karikatur der europäischen Völker.* Munich: U. Langen,
1921.
George, M. Dorothy. *English Political Caricature: A Study of Opinion and
Propaganda.* 2 vols. Oxford: Clarendon Press, 1959.
Gilman, Sander. "Heine's Photographs." *Hebrew University Studies in Litera-
ture and the Arts* 13 (2) (Jerusalem, 1985): 222–250.
Gombrich, E. H. *Meditations on a Hobby-Horse.* London: Phaidon Press, 1963.
Hegel, G. W. F. *Ästhetik.* Ed. Friedrich Bassenge. Frankfurt am Main: Europa,
1965.
———. *Sämtliche Werke.* Ed. Hermann Glockner. Stuttgart: Frommann, 1928.
Heine, Heinrich. *The Complete Poems of Heinrich Heine.* Trans. and ed. Hal
Draper. Boston: Suhrkamp/Insel, 1982.
———. *The Romantic School and Other Essays.* Ed. Jost Hermand and Robert
Holub. New York: Continuum, 1985.
———. *Sämtliche Schriften.* Ed. Klaus Briegleb. 6 vols. Munich: Hanser, 1968–
76.
———. *Werke-Briefwechsel-Lebenszeugnisse.* Säkularausgabe. Berlin: Akad-
emie; Paris: Editions du Centre National de la Recherche Scientifique, 1970.
Kris, Ernst. *Psychoanalytical Explorations in Art.* London: International Uni-
versities Press, 1953.
Kris, Ernst, and E. H. Gombrich. *Caricature.* Harmondsworth: Penguin, 1940.
Prawer, Siegbert S. *Frankenstein's Island: England and the English in the Writ-
ings of Heinrich Heine.* Cambridge: Cambridge University Press, 1986.
———. "Heine and the Photographers." *German Life and Letters* N.S. 34 (1980–
81): 64–73.
———. *Heine's Jewish Comedy: A Study of His Portraits of Jews and Judaism.*
Oxford: Clarendon Press, 1983.

Preisendanz, Wolfgang. "Die umgebuchte Schreibart: Heines literarischer Humor im Spannungsfeld von Begriffs-, Form- und Rezeptionsgeschichte." In *Heinrich Heine: Artistik und Engagement*, ed. Wolfgang Kuttenkeuler. Stuttgart: Metzler, 1977.

——. *Heinrich Heine: Werkstrukturen und Epochenbezüge*. Munich: Fink, 1973.

Reed, Terence James. "Heines Appetit." *Heine-Jahrbuch* (1983): 1–29.

Sammons, Jeffrey. *Heinrich Heine: A Modern Biography*. Princeton: Princeton University Press, 1979.

Sternberger, Dolf. *Heinrich Heine und die Abschaffung der Sünde*. Hamburg: Claassen, 1972.

Starobinski, Jean. *1789: Les emblèmes de la raison*. Paris: Flammarion, 1979.

Voisine, Jacques. "Heine als Porträtist in der *Lutezia*." In *Internationaler Heine-Kongreß 1972*. Hamburg: Hoffmann & Campe, 1973.

Werner, Michael. "La dialectique de la censure: à propos de l'autocensure dans les articles journalistiques de Heine." In *Cahiers de Textologie 1: Exercices de critique génétique* (Paris: Minard, 1986).

Windfuhr, Manfred. "Heine und Hegel: Rezeption und Produktion." In *Internationaler Heine-Kongreß 1972*. Hamburg: Hoffmann & Campe, 1973.

JOSEPH A. KRUSE

The Diversity of Heine's Reception in Western European and American Art

$\mathcal{E}$ ven during his lifetime Heine's reception was an international phenomenon. His dual German-French strategy no doubt contributed to his reputation and ensured him a lasting function in European literature. Heine's problems with the German censor in no way disturbed the predilection of foreign readers to take up his work. They enlisted Heine as a witness to a broken Romantic poetic tradition, while also seeing him as an exemplar of subjective, critical prose writing. The first complete German-language editions of Heine's work began to appear shortly before his death in the Netherlands and the United States as pirated copies of the individual works; they were finished by 1861. It was not until the same year that the authorized Heine edition, published by Hoffmann and Campe in Hamburg, was finally initiated. (It was completed in 1866, with additional volumes in 1869 and 1884.) Its editor, Adolf Strodtmann, had helped introduce Heine to the United States and went on to establish philological and biographical scholarship on Heine in Germany.

In France, Heine was already regarded as a quasi-French author. He also influenced the form and content of other European literatures through translations and imitations of his work. The Dutch genre of *Heiniaantjes* is a fine example of his widespread importance. The immense number of musical adaptations of Heine's poetry (according to Günter Metzner about eight thousand pieces by around twenty-five hundred composers and musicians) and contemporary performance technology have greatly contributed to Heine's continued influence.[1] Allusions to Heine appear in films from time to time, such as Anatole Litvak's *Decision before Dawn* (United States, 1950), with Silcher's *Lore-Ley* melody; Luchino Visconti's early film *Senso* (Italy, 1954), with a plot consisting of a Heine motif (lyric poetry as a means of seduction); and John Huston's *Freud* (United States, 1961), with references to Heine, Baudelaire, and Rimbaud. Heine, his work, or appropriate textual citations are employed internationally in discussions on censorship and the suppression of free speech. In the novel *The Seven Minutes*, published in 1969 by the best-selling American author, Irwin Wallace, for example, Heine is set in the company of such nonfiction writers as Copernicus, Newton, Paine, Freud, Darwin, and Spengler, as well as such artists as Aristophanes, Rabelais, Voltaire, Whitman, Shaw, and Joyce.[2] Heine was also invoked during the Salman Rushdie debate of 1989 as an authority on the fatal consequences of book burning and murder threats. In the Western media Heine repeatedly plays the role of symbol for international understanding and defender of human rights.

Heine in art as a particular form of reception. Among the many forms of Heine's reception, the artistic treatment of his life and work is a separate and thoroughly respectable variety.[3] Within this form of reception are four different types of artistic expression: first, artists have been preoccupied with Heine's portrait, which by now has its own artistic tradition; second, the unique history of Heine monuments is the most novel aspect of any discussion of Heine's continued importance; third, there are the illustrated editions; and fourth, independent artistic productions constitute further documents of his influence. It is worth noting, however, that the borders between these four types of artistic representations are fluid and the types contain many comparable elements: the monuments often approximate free-associative works or portraits, the portraits may find applications as illustrations, and independent works are often used as illustrations as well.

It is inevitable that most artistic productions of Heine have taken place in Germany. Nevertheless, the wealth of artistic adaptations of Heine in the rest of Western Europe and America is surprising. This related interconnected reception of Heine across political borders can be organized into readily comprehensible fields, all part of the theme *Pictures of Heine.* In the present context a view of West European and American examples of artistic occupation with Heine's work and life emphasizes the particular status of the works that may be described as *Heine productions (Heine-Kunst).*

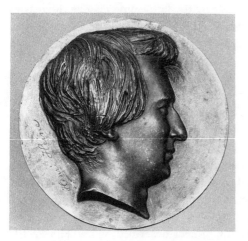

Heinrich Heine. Portrait in
bronze relief from the studio
of David d'Angers, 1834. Photo
by Walter Klein.

*Heine portraits of the French period and the death
mask as the subject of modern art.*   The only record of Heine's actual
appearance is found in the death mask made by Joseph Fontana. In other
words, there exists no direct image of the living author. Heine, as he lay
sick in the *Matratzengruft* [mattress grave], could not bring himself to
let a daguerrotype be made of him. Rather, he left his portrayal in the
hands of a variety of Parisian artists. Of particular expressive force is the
medallion created in 1834, long before Heine's last illness, in the workshop of Pierre-Jean David d'Angers. Thirty-five years later, Adolph von
Menzel remarked that the impression of the medallion's bust was so
irresistible, so exquisitely crafted, that it was impossible not to believe
that one had "the true face of Heine" in hand.[4]

Other early French Heine portraits, whether by Tony Johannot (1837),
Friedrich Pecht (1840), or Samuel Friedrich Dietz (1842), could not con-
vey the same impression. On the other hand, Heine portrayals by Ernst
Benedikt Kietz (1851), Charles Gabriel Gleyre (1852), and Marcelin
Gilbert Desboutin (after 1853) have imparted to readers and admirers
an unforgettable image of the sick Heine. All the portraits of Heine tend
to idealize their subject. The three later portraits by Kietz, Gleyre, and
Desboutin include literary and religious images; the portrayal by Levin
Schücking, a regular visitor to Heine, shows the author as a Christ
figure.[5]

The powerful impression made by the late Heine may be the reason why contemporary artists have been drawn to use his death mask. The 1981 Düsseldorf Heine monument by Bert Gerresheim (born 1935) of Düsseldorf refers to this relic of the personal appearance of the author. The Austrian conceptual artist Arnulf Rainer (born 1929) produced a powerful effect with a 1979 altered photograph that incorporated, among other images, Heine's death mask. Rainer's works must be considered as free adaptations of Heine, for they clearly do not set out to give a realistic posthumous picture of the author. Nonetheless, through its reinterpretation by artists such as Bert Gerresheim, Heine's death expression acquires a magical, as well as irritating, quality.

A creation by Luis Guerrero from Quito, Ecuador (born 1938), achieves a similar effect. Guerrero works in Düsseldorf and participated in a joint German-Dutch Heine project described below. His *Profile H.H.'85* recounts Heine's life and influence through newspaper clippings pasted on a small box containing the author's head. Paper sheafs that approximate Heine's profile and display clearly visible burn marks are set between the gray stone facial pieces of his death mask. The sculptured stone pieces and the burnt paper bundles, which are laid in the stone as if they were set between bookends, produce the image of a head within the wooden box—the very same head that contained the "contraband" searched for by Prussian customs agents in the second volume of *Deutschland: Ein Wintermärchen* [Germany: A Winter's Tale]. At the same time, the association of book burning and Heine's social ostracism is evoked, so that the work of art has the quality of both an emblem and a warning.

French and American monuments as a consequence of the disrupted reception of Heine in Germany. In an age in which Germany was obsessed with constructing monuments, the plan of Austria's Empress Elizabeth in 1887–88 to erect a monument to Heine in his birthplace, Düsseldorf, was violently debated and ultimately defeated. Anti-Semitic and nationalistic arguments carried the day; a critical German author of Jewish descent, who died in exile in Paris, was not considered deserving of a monument. The empress's plan, nevertheless, did result in the making of two different monuments. The first, depicting the old, blind Heine as a melancholy and distinguished seated figure, wearing a dressing gown and holding a quill and paper

Heinrich Heine.
Lithography by
F. Chalupa, 1852,
after a drawing by
Charles Gabriel
Gleyre. Photo by
Landesbildstelle
Rheinland,
Düsseldorf.

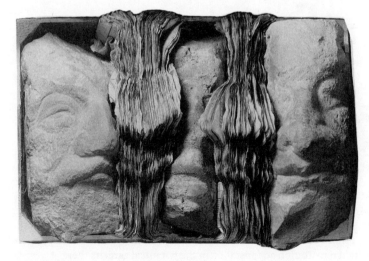

Profile: H. H.'85. Stone carving by Louis Guerrero. Photo by
Walter Klein.

Heinrich Heine Memorial, designed by Louis Hasselriis. It was first displayed in 1879 at an exhibition in Vienna. In 1883, by order of the Empress Elizabeth of Austria, it was transported to the Achilleion in Corfu. From 1910 to 1939 the memorial stood in Hamburg, and in 1939 it was taken to Toulon and installed in the botanical gardens there. Photographed by Dietrich Schubert of Heidelberg and reproduced by Walter Klein.

Heinrich Heine's grave in the Montmartre Cemetery, Paris. The memorial was designed by Louis Hasselriis and erected in 1901. Photo by Walter Klein.

Illustration for Heine's poem "Philistine in Sunday Dress." Photographed by Walter Klein from Raphael Drouart, ed. and illus., *Henri Heine: Intermezzo lyrique* (Paris: Babou, 1931).

Illustration for Heine's poem *Ich weiß nicht, was soll es bedeuten* [I Do Not Know What It Means]. Photographed by Walter Klein from Louis Untermeyer, ed., and Fritz Kredel, illus., *Poems of Heinrich Heine* (New York: Heritage, 1957), p. 76.

Arno Arts's *Heine und Ich: Der Marmor Woraus man Götter macht* [Heine and I: The Marble from which Gods Are Made]. Photographed by Walter Klein from the exhibition catalog *Heinrich Heine* (Düsseldorf: Heine Institute, 1985), p. 24.

Heine Memorial, in the Bronx Park in New York City. It includes a Loreley fountain with daughters of the Rhine by Ernst Herter and a relief portrait of Heine by David d'Angers. Originally proposed for Düsseldorf in 1888, it was installed in New York in 1899. The inscription reads: "To the Memory of their great Poet the Germans in the United States." Photographed by Walter Klein from a photo c. 1905 in "Adopt-A-Monument" (New York: Municipal Art Society, 1987).

Illustration for Heine's poem *Der Schiffbrüchige* [The Shipwrecked], by
G. Pujol-Hermann. Photographed by Walter Klein from Castellana de
José Pablo Rivas, trans., *Poemas de Enrique Heine* (Barcelona: Maucci,
1917), p. 50.

that threatened to slip out of his hand, was created by the Danish sculptor Louis Hasselriis. Initially, it was placed overlooking the sea near the empress's villa, Achilleion, on the island of Corfu. After Empress Elizabeth's death, the statue was acquired by Heine's publishing company, Hoffmann and Campe. It was moved to Hamburg and later to Toulon in France, where it still stands. The bust of Heine on the Toulon monument corresponds closely to Heine's gravestone in the Parisian Montmartre cemetery, which was also sculpted by Hasselriis. The Dane succeeded with both monuments in creating an intimate and meditative memorial to Heine.

The second monument in the empress's plan, the one intended for Düsseldorf, came from the workshop of the Berlin sculptor Ernst Herter and was eventually erected, in 1899, in the Bronx, New York. In contrast to Hasselriis, Herter decided in favor of an allegorical work. His Lore-Ley spring shows a Heine medallion, yet it also glorifies Romanticism and Heine's immortal *Lied*. Nevertheless, that this tribute to Heine's lyric should be standing in the Bronx is not without its ironies: a bitter parody set in the mouth of the Lorelei and published in the satirical journal *Ulk* (in 1897) commented prophetically on the debate over the Heine monument which had resulted in its relocation:

> Nun weiß ich es mir zu deuten.
> Warum ich so traurig bin:
> Man jagt mich zu fremden Leuten.
> Das will mir nicht in den Sinn.
>
> Das Mittelalter dunkelt,
> Doch ruhig fließt der Rhein.
> Er soll jetzt, wie man munkelt,
> auch antisemitisch sein.
>
> Ich glaube, die Wellen verschlingen
> Am Ende noch Cahen und Cohn,
> Mich läßt man ins Ausland bringen
> Wie eine verruf'ne Person.
>
> [Now I know how to explain,
> Why I am so sad:
> I am driven into foreign lands,
> For reasons I can't conceive.

The Middle Ages darken,
Yet the Rhine runs still.
And now it's even rumored
the river's anti-Semitic.

I believe the waves will devour
Cahen and Cohen in the end,
While I am sent abroad
like some notorious criminal.][6]

   Given that the name Cohen in anti-Semitic parlance was flagrantly used as a stigma, the poem combines inseparably the very German figure of the Loreley, which Heine had conjured up in a *Volkslied*, with the German-Jewish fate: the Lorelei's emigration signifies the permanent loss of the Rhineland's Romantic tradition, a culture in which Heine had a significant interest.[7] The parody revealed the eventual consequences of the debate over the Heine memorial. The New York monument, in particular, has been abused, and even the Toulon Heine memorial has not remained undamaged. Their destruction reflects an apparently timeless urge to vandalism that works itself out on defenseless objects of beauty. But although this violence is clearly not directed against the emigrated Heine portrayals as such, it is important to note that both monuments, as unappreciated German witnesses to Heine's importance and fame, ended up in the United States and France out of expedience, rather than as independent artworks or because of a broad-based demand for them. Restoration measures under consideration in New York imply more than just the rescue of impressive literary memorials from the late nineteenth century; in the case of Heine such efforts are directly connected with a consciously modern position in support of Heine's "cause."[8]

         Illustrations as a bibliophilic contribution to the Western European and American reception of Heine.   Art continually applies itself as the servant of the word and creates beautifully illustrated books. In his introduction to an 1837 edition of *Don Quijote*, however, illustrated by Tony Johannot, Heine comments on the dilemma of the relationship between illustration and text: "Are illustrations conducive to true art's interests? I believe not. While they show how the light and ingeniously creative hand of the artist captures and reproduces the author's figures and while they provide an interlude for the tired reader, illustrations are yet another sign of how art, brought down from the pedestal of its own autonomy, becomes the servant of luxury."[9] Publishers and artists did not let themselves be distracted by such considerations. Heinrich Laube's Heine edition with illustrations by various Viennese artists (1884) is a costly and typical example of this trend. The countless German Heine illustrations have been described sufficiently in the secondary literature.[10]

An English edition of *Atta Troll* published 1913 in London with witty sketches by Willy Pogány and vignettes by Horace Taylor, and a 1917 Spanish collection of Heine's poetry with illustrations of individual lyrical scenes by G. Pujol-Hermann, stand out among the Western European illustrated Heine texts. The magically realistic pictures of the Spanish poetry collection seem very similar to defamiliarized photographs and remind one of the mythical-naturalistic saint's images of the period. French illustrators love the decorative: an edition of *Lyrisches Intermezzo* published 1931 in Paris contains twelve etchings by Raphael Drouart which are distinctive for their sense of light and shadow. Likewise, they present authentic visualizations of the poems insofar as they shape an "echo" of the poems' Romantic and ghostly motifs. Half a century later (1988), Sabine Allard has tried to couple the musical reception of Heine with delicate decorations through her visual reinterpretations of Heine poems set to music.

The Dutch Heine tradition's enthusiasm is characterized by simple, robust pictures, particularly in the Dutch pieces made for *Memoiren des Herren von Schnabelewopski* [Herr von Schnabelewopksi's Memoirs], which were published in 1946, 1956, and 1961. Another fine contribution to the tradition of Heine illustrations is the 1947 volume entitled *Poems and Ballads*, published in New York with pictures by Fritz Kredel. The waning of the reading public's interest in Heine during the postwar period as compared to the demand for Heine's work at the turn of the century can be explained partially through changes in the public's political view of Heine, which the illustrations generally resisted. More important, though, are the changes in representational technique within Heine productions. The principal interest in Heine and his work has not changed and actually seems to have moved closer to the author's meaning.

Independent productions as associative approaches to Heine. Until about 1970, Heine productions consisted of monuments whose primary aim was portraiture, allegorization, or memorialization. That is true whether the artworks represented the author in the form of drawings, paintings, reliefs, or complete statues, or whether they illustrated Heine the person, his life, or his works. Since then, the upheavals to which all genres and means of representation have been subject can also be observed in works that have Heine as their theme. These radical changes have left their mark on the most recent Heine memorials in West Germany, as well as on contemporary international works dealing with Heine. It is also apparent that the subject matter and execution of the new independent creations have been determined by the debate surrounding Heine and his statements, life, and influence.

The Dutch-American painter Francis Podulke (1922–1988) provided an eloquent example of how art responds positively to the scholarly discussion of Heine. Podulke was born in Mezeppa, Minnesota, and studied with Max Beckmann and Oskar Kokoschka. For years he lived in Amsterdam as a painter and gallery owner. Then, in 1975, Podulke settled in a northern coastal town near the island of Norderney. During the discussion surrounding the Norderney Heine monument by Arno Breker, Podulke intervened through the use of his magical-realistic paintings and collages to reveal an unlikely historical misrepresentation. A pre-1933 prizewinning plan for a Heine monument in Düsseldorf drawn up by Arno Breker—who had gone on to become the star sculptor for the Third Reich—was constructed and erected on Norderney. While Podulke's collages and pictures criticize the art world and its morals, they are also an homage to Heine as the poet of the North Sea. *Hydra 83* shows Heine's lost death mask lying on the seashore. In the background a snake with many heads is surfacing from the water, disturbing the sea's tranquility.[11]

A similar invocation of the mythic can be observed in the transposition into color of Heine's *Die Götter im Exil* [The Gods in Exile] by the Italian painter Elenora Orioli (born 1925). With a light green-yellow and blue-red land- and seascape, her 1984 painting expresses the sense of ancient divinities banned and dissolved into a secretive Nature that Heine brought to life in his essay.

During 1985 and 1986 an enormous Heine project was undertaken by Dutch and West German artists.[12] The wide interest in Heine's work in the Netherlands was reflected by the participation of almost fifty Dutch painters and sculptors. In light of his political, critical, German-French, Jewish, and poetical existence, Heine served as an inspiration for illustrations, portrayals, and free associative works, as well as a means for the artists to express their own condition. Whether one looks to *Die Kosten meiner Agonie* [The Cost of My Agony], by Kees Salentijn (born 1947), with its mixture of characters and graphic elements in painting; or to the symbolic *Deutschland: Ein Wintermärchen* of Egidius Knops (born 1945), with its cool, distanced relations of metal and plastic; an identification and solidarity with Heine always makes itself obvious. Heine's fate deeply affected some of the artists: Kenne Grégoire (born 1951) brings the desolate *Matratzengrab* [Mattress Grave] onto the canvas as a sign of sympathy and grief, as well as hope in the continued influence of the author.

In his synthetically produced stele *Heine und Ich* [Heine and I], Arno Arts (born 1947) plays ironically with Heine's posthumous fame, as well as with the author himself, by invoking "the marble from which gods are made" ["Marmor, woraus man Götter macht"]. The books that are pressed into the stele, works such as *A Popular History of the Arts*, lend the work a sympathetic humor. Through its ironic play with words, this memorial to Heine and the artists who reproduced him posits a friendly community between the plastic arts and poetry.

We should pay tribute here to a final example of the free transposition of Heine's inspiration: the work of Hanne Darboven (born 1941). The artist, who has lived for a time in the United States and whose prominence is internationally acknowledged, exhibited her 1975 *Atta Troll* in Switzerland. Darboven's piece is an example of modern works of art that treat the world, or rather the Western world, as a coherent unity. Her *Atta Troll* converted Heine's text into its own numerical system. Darboven produced a respectful mechanical transcript of Heine's verse epic by numbers and numerals to count the word units in the text. The poet's words are thereby counted in not too frivolous a manner and are passed on to the art world as a numbers game. The fifth verse of the first volume, about Atta Troll and his wife, Mumma, reads:

> Steif und ernsthaft, mit Grandezza,
> Tanzt der edle Atta Troll,
> Doch der zottgen Ehehälfte
> Fehlt die Würde, fehlt der Anstand.

> [Stiffly, gravely, even grandly,
> Dances noble Atta Troll,

> But his shaggy spouse is lacking
> In good manners and decorum.][13]

Darboven's version of the same verse reads in the following manner:

    5 onetwothreefourfive
    5 onetwothreefourfive
    4 onetwothreefour
    6 onetwothreefourfivesix

Heine productions as pleasant trivialities with a more than symbolic value.   In light of the many works by creative artists on the theme of Heine, it must be pointed out that, in contrast to the musical reception of Heine, the significance of artistic Heine productions has been seriously underestimated and ignored in the research on Heine's reception. The many instances of artists' interest in Heine highlight his importance in cultural and everyday life to such an extent that they deserve our attention. Within the context of the scholarly discussion of Heine, the illustrations and portraits exist only on the margins as pleasant trivialities. The monuments and free creations have more effect in the public realm or at least in artistic circles; they help keep the memory of Heine's genius, his concerns and his message, alive. They do so in a variety of artistic ways, of which the Heine scholars should be jealous, especially since the generally symbolic character of these productions is an essential factor in the continued presence of Heine in a public consciousness that has hardly any literary interests. These artworks complement the line of Heine's musical reception, as well as the political and journalistic discussions described earlier. The contemporary visualization of Heine through artistic creations draws on his most colorful, lively, and (very often) sympathetic qualities. It is hoped that artistic approaches and confrontations with Heine will have a fruitful future, since they enrich everyday culture with a historical awareness of one of its major defenders, someone who from the time of his *Reisebildern* [Pictures of Travel] to his piece on *Lutezia* characterized, ironized, and at the same time extended the experience of daily life.

NOTES

1. The bibliography of musical adaptations of Heine's work was published in *Heine in der Musik*, ed. Günter Metzner (Tutzing: Musikverlag Hans Schneider, 1989).

2. Irwin Wallace, *The Seven Minutes* (New York: Simon & Schuster, 1969), p. 137.

3. The author can cite many holdings of the archive, library, and museum of the Heinrich Heine Institute in Düsseldorf. See also Josef Kruse, *Heinrich Heine: Leben und Werk in Daten und Bildern* (Frankfurt am Main: Insel, 1983).

4. A facsimile of Adolph von Menzel's letter of May 12, 1869, to Hoffmann and Campe was included in the second memorial edition of Heine's *Die Harzreise*, intro. Friedrich Hirth (Hamburg and Berlin: Hoffmann & Campe, 1920).

5. For Levin Schücking's remarks about his visit to Heine on September 20, 1847, see Michael Werner, ed., *Begegnungen mit Heine: Berichte der Zeitgenossen* (Hamburg and Berlin: Hoffmann & Campe, 1973), 2:92.

6. "Abschied der Loreley, die von Professor Herter modellirt, nach New York geschafft werden soll," *Ulk: Illustriertes Wochenblatt für Humor und Satire* 26 (18) (Berlin: April 30, 1897); 5. Bracketed translation provided here and throughout by Daniel Purdy.

7. Dietz Bering, *Der Name als Stigma: Antisemitismus im deutschen Alltag, 1812–1933* (Stuttgart: Kletta Cotta, 1987), p. 396 and the index on p. 552.

8. See the "Adopt-A-Monument" brochure of the Municipal Art Society of New York, 1987, pp. 2–7.

9. Translated from "Einleitung zum Don Quichotte," in Heinrich Heine, *Sämtliche Schriften*, ed. Klaus Briegleb, 6 vols. (Munich: Hanser, 1968–76), 4:151–170.

10. Siegfried Seifert and Albina A. Volgina, eds., *Heine Bibliographie: 1965–1982* (Berlin and Weimar: Aufbau, 1986). See in particular the essays by Horst Bunke and Eberhard Galley.

11. See the exhibition catalog of the Heine Institute, Düsseldorf, 1985: *Heine und die Nordsee: Ölbilder und Collagen. Michael Podulke 1983–1984–1985*.

12. *Heinrich Heine. Een Ontmoeting. Eine Begegnung. Duitse en Nederlandse kunstenaars over Heinrich Heine. Heinrich Heine aus der Sicht niederländischer und deutscher Künstler* (Düsseldorf: Heine Institute, 1985). See in particular pp. 24–26, 86–88, 128–130, 184–186.

13. Heinrich Heine, *Sämtliche Schriften* 4:497; Heinrich Heine, *The Complete Poems of Heinrich Heine: A Modern English Version*, trans. Hal Draper (Cambridge, Mass.: Suhrkamp, 1982).

WORKS CITED

"Abschied der Loreley, die von Professor Herter modellirt, nach New York geschafft werden soll." *Ulk: Illustriertes Wochenblatt für Humor und Satire* 26 (18) (Berlin: April 30, 1897): 5.

Bering, Dietz. *Der Name als Stigma: Antisemitismus im deutschen Alltag, 1812–1933.* Stuttgart: Kletta Cotta, 1987.

Darboven, Hanne. *Atta Troll nach Heinrich Heine in Zahlenworte (abgezählte Worte) wieder aufgeschrieben.* Luzern: Kunst-Museum, 1975.

Heine, Heinrich. *The Complete Poems of Heinrich Heine: A Modern English Version.* Translated by Hal Draper. Cambridge, Mass.: Suhrkamp, 1982.

——. *Die Harzreise.* Hamburg and Berlin: Hoffmann & Campe, 1920.

——. *Sämtliche Schriften.* Ed. Klaus Briegleb. 6 vols. Munich: Hanser, 1968–76.

Heine und die Nordsee: Ölbilder und Collagen. Michael Podulke 1983–1984–1985. Exhibition catalog. Düsseldorf: Heine Institute, 1985.

Heinrich Heine. Een Ontmoeting. Eine Begegnung. Duitse en Nederlandse kunstenaars over Heinrich Heine. Heinrich Heine aus der Sicht niederländischer und deutscher Künstler. Exhibition catalog. Düsseldorf: Heine Institute, 1985.

Kruse, Joseph. *Heinrich Heine: Leben und Werk in Daten und Bildern.* Frankfurt am Main: Insel, 1983.

Metzner, Günter, ed. *Heine in der Musik.* Tutzing: Musikverlag Hans Schneider, 1989.

Seifert, Siegfried, and Albina A. Volgina, eds. *Heine Bibliographie: 1965–1982.* Berlin and Weimar: Aufbau, 1986.

Wallace, Irwin. *The Seven Minutes.* New York: Simon & Schuster, 1969.

Werner, Michael, ed. *Begegnungen mit Heine: Berichte der Zeitgenossen.* Hamburg and Berlin: Hoffmann & Campe, 1973.

Poetry for the Republic:
Heine and Whitman

*I*t was a tricky situation in which Thomas Mann
found himself in October 1922. Addressing a conservative audience hostile to the young Weimar Republic, the renowned
author, whose wartime support for the German Empire against the
Western democracies had won him acclaim in nationalist circles, now
undertook the onerous task of convincing his listeners of the worthi-
ness of democracy. Avoiding the easy path of pragmatic realism—
democracy as the result of the military defeat of the empire in 1918
or as an ideological demand of the emergent American hegemony—
he attempted instead to demonstrate the compatibility of democratic
principles with fundamental aspects of German culture in order to
defend the counterintuitive proposition that the notion of a German
republic was not itself a contradiction in terms.

The literary formula that Mann selected to make his case was Novalis plus Walt Whitman, that is, the presumed affinity of the cipher of
German aesthetic culture with the representative poet of American
democracy. With a series of quotations he suggests that German culture at its most Romantic—and for the public, that meant at its most
German moment—was not at all hostile to the political thought of enlightened modernity. Thus, glossing a Novalis citation on international
law, Mann comments, "That is political enlightenment; it is indisputably democracy—from the mouth of a knight of the blue flower, who
was moreover a born Junker from whom one would expect a medieval
sense of battle or a love of honor in a suit of mail rather than these mod-
ernisms."[1] The clincher then follows with the link to Whitman. For if
Junker and Yankee are at one in their enthusiasm for democracy, the
conservative *Bildungsbürgertum* would do best to follow Novalis's lead
by rallying around the new republic, German to its core, and not—as the

antirepublican right claimed—a foreign form dictated by the victors at Versailles and imposed on an essentially undemocratic German *Volk*.

So far, so good, at least as far as Mann's intentions go, and this speech, "Von deutscher Republik" [The German Republic], can be treated as a literary counterpart to the Weimar constitution, two of the founding documents of republican culture in Germany. That is, however, a very ambivalent praise, implying that Mann's speech and its formula, Novalis plus Whitman, may have been as flawed as the republic and its constitution. For scrutinizing the text, one cannot but wonder if Mann has not conceded too much to his opponents or if the attempt to make the republic palatable has not already eviscerated it. In fact, it seems as if Mann's efforts to assert the identity of a German republic keep running aground on the resilience of the oxymoron he is trying to repress. Does the text, then, in current parlance, subvert itself?

One might note, for example, that the very project of a German republic—Mann stresses the adjective—is not without a nationalist ring, for it is distinguished emphatically from alternative, more radical versions: the individualism of what he calls nefariously "a certain West," and the "political mysticism" of, even more ominously, *Slawentum*, the slavic East; hence a sort of two-front war in the competition of political forms.[2] In addition, the articulation of the republic as a Romantic (and therefore acceptable) possibility is achieved only at the price of adopting the Romantic critique of the Enlightenment state, that is, Novalis's attack on Frederician Prussia. Yet that critique is directed not at all against the authoritarian substance of enlightened despotism but only at its putatively mechanical character, which, according to Novalis, might be overcome with more religion, more enthusiasm, and, particularly trenchant, more uniforms.

Mann's rhetorical strategy may be working backward: instead of persuading conservatives to support the republic, the author may be transforming democracy into a program acceptable to conservatives because it has been robbed of its radical substance, a democracy without a democratic revolution, so to speak. This reading of "The German Republic" as a covertly antidemocratic program despite the author's intentions might be confirmed by an examination of the introduction, a *laudatio* to Gerhart Hauptmann on his sixtieth birthday. Assiduously avoiding any of the likely images of republicanism—popular sovereignty or civic virtue or heroic rebellion—Mann opts instead for a prescription that could hardly offend his recalcitrant public: royal legitimacy and patriarchal authority, whereby it is now the playwright Hauptmann who plays the role of a glorious *Volkskönig*, while the *Reichspräsident* is endearingly invoked as an irresistible Mr. Niceguy, good old *Vater Ebert*. The cast of characters chosen by Mann clearly suggests a political orientation toward a centrist support for the new regime; Hauptmann's social dramas of the 1890s are invoked piously, and in any case Mann affirms his loyalty to the Social Democratic head of state. Nevertheless, the organization of this state of affairs is one in which traditional structures of authority have been retained with only a minor shuffling of the players. Royalty and paternity are the terms that pervade the opening passages of the speech; the logic of power has clearly not been interrupted, the state has not been refashioned by a revolutionary process, and it is therefore only consistent for Mann, the self-described conservative, to suggest that conservatives would do themselves a better service by participating in the political processes of the Weimar Republic rather than opposing it from without.

If the really-existing Weimar Republic was indeed represented by the pair Hauptmann plus Friedrich Ebert (1871–1925), themselves representing the rather unrepublican constellation of king plus father, then something is evidently amiss with the democratic claims of "The German Republic," and the error may well lie in Mann's formula for democracy. Is Novalis plus Whitman a literary Article 48 of the cultural constitution of the Weimar Republic? Should Whitmanesque democracy ever threaten to go too far, conservatives might count on Novalis for a Romantic tradition to preserve law and order—faith and love instead of parliament and popular suffrage.

My point here is to suggest not that Romantic political philosophy is necessarily conservative but that Mann, for obviously tactical reasons, makes this equation to mount the following argument: Novalis is a conservative; Novalis is a democrat; therefore, conservatives may be democrats, and democracy may be conservative. The weakness of that model—a weakness congenital to the Weimar Republic—is that it could quickly transmute Hauptmann and Ebert into Ebert and Noske, and this derives from Mann's definition of the republic as thoroughly inoffensive to the antirepublican right. The response of right-wing political theory, such as that of Carl Schmitt, would be to claim that "the crisis of parliamentary democracy" is inescapable, that mass democracies are always logically impossible, and that, to the extent that a state asserts its sovereignty, it will eventually take the form of a dictatorship, despite the illusions of a bourgeois liberalism ignorant of the exigencies of power. Less cynically and with an eye to the possibility of a democratic culture, one must ask if the problem is inherent not in the emancipation project but rather in its specific formulation and historical manifestation, that is, the inadequacy of the German Republic at its inception. If Novalis plus Whitman was not enough, was an alternative definition imaginable?

One can answer this question without unrolling the political history of the early twenties. It suffices to ravel the speech, because an alternative formula to Novalis plus Whitman is inscribed in this founding text of the republic itself. While Mann's liberal undertaking undermines itself the more it attempts to sublate the self-marginalization of the conservatives by incorporating them into the republican body politic, the text is simultaneously marked by a second vector that locates an outside to the same conservatism Mann is attempting to recuperate. To exhort his audience to participate in the democratic process, he must also scare them by suggesting the consequences of their continued boycott, that is, a more radical republic. Thus the republic may well remain substantively German, a vessel for all the blue-flowered values represented by the reassuring figure of Novalis, but only if the Romantic conservatives take hold of it and do not surrender it to threatening antagonists, whose generic name is revealed in Mann's anxious plea: "I beseech you again: don't be shy. There is no reason in the world to regard the republic as a matter for smart Jewboys [scharfe Judenjungen]. Don't leave it to them! As the popular political phrase goes, take 'the wind out of their sails'—the republican wind!"[3]

That is surely a difficult passage. For the moment, Mann is evidently adopting the anti-Semitic rhetoric of the conservative right: in the semantic value of the pejorative designation *Judenjunge*, in the adjective, and in the exclusionary politics of the exhortation. Yet later in the speech, when the same *Judenjungen* make a second cameo appearance, Mann suggests that they too are an integral part of the German tradition. Nevertheless, even that moderating gloss, bordering on apologetics, pales when one grasps that the phrase presumably refers to Foreign Minister Walter Rathenau (1867–1922), victim of a recent right-wing assassination. Mann in this same speech notes bitterly that the assassins, despite their opposition to the republic, have de facto recognized the actuality of republican culture: As he puts it, "shooting ministers is a superbly republican mode of action,"[4] for it implies the priority of public and political virtue over a solely private sphere of aesthetic culture.

Of course, Mann's intention is neither to advocate political violence nor to foster anti-Semitism, but that initial imperative, the plea to seize the republic from the smart Jewboys, is a crucial moment in the text and ought not be dissolved too quickly into the dialectic of the full argument or the vicissitudes of Mann's subsequent career. My concern here is, after all, not Thomas Mann's intentions, and my goal is even less a harmonious reconciliation of the material in a conservative hermeneutic circle. The point is rather that the cultural formula for the republic that would fail—Novalis plus Whitman—is itself hopelessly flawed because of a repression that comes to the fore in the exclusionary admonition. Yet the very articulation of that repression leaves symptomatic traces of the alternative, the road not taken, a more radical republic not dependent on the marginalization of the Jewboys, smart or otherwise. Translated into literary-historical terms, that would have implied a revision of the cultural formula: instead of Novalis, might Mann have proposed Heine plus Whitman? What more appropriate symbol of a German democratic tradition than Heine? Still, one might object that this imaginary proposal is absurd, and not only because of the irrelevance of retrospective wishful thinking. For a century, Heine's reception had been marked by vitriolic opposition from conservatives—from the initial persecution and censorship of the pre-1848 period through the battles regarding a monument at the turn of the century. Heine was an overdetermined figure, representing all that the right wing rejected: political radical, Left Hegelian, Jew, Parisian exile, sensualist, materialist, internationalist, and so on—hardly a figure to inspire confidence among conservatives in the desirability of the republic, obviously an impossible choice. That, however, is precisely the point. Opting for Novalis, Mann opted for a conservative constitution of the republic: Heine's absence in "The German Republic" is ultimately another chapter in his repression, a negative reception history. Heine appears only as the unnamed object of negation, and it is that exclusion built into the 1922 formula of the republic which cripples the enterprise from the start. Even Mann must have come to a similar recognition less than a decade later when he recast the political project with a more radical formula—Friedrich Hölderlin and Karl Marx—but by then his topic was, instead of a German republic, itself considerably more radical: culture and Socialism.

To identify the smart Jewboy as Heine is an intentional misreading that flushes out the limits of liberal culture at the outset of the Weimar Republic by measuring it against its repressed doppelgänger, the democratic potential of a forgotten nineteenth-century legacy. Now I want to direct some closer consideration to the odd couple Mann could not name, Heine and Whitman, and their significance for a poetry for a republic. At stake is not a positivistic documentation of literary influences or borrowings. The first edition of *Leaves of Grass* appeared in 1855, the year before Heine's death, and it is not likely that Heine's verse contributed significantly to the formulation of Whitman's lyric project. The closest intellectual-historical connection that might be argued is the shared indebtedness to German idealist philosophy of the two Hegelian cousins: Heine's relationship to Hegel is rich and well-known, whereas Whitman's familiarity was presumably only second-hand, part of the extensive midcentury American reception of idealism. The connection is interesting but ultimately somewhat beside the point, since Heine's work—like that of Marx—is better understood as a critical break with G. W. F. Hegel than as a continuation, and for Whitman, in any case, other experiences and endeavors had a considerably more formative impact than the watered-down philosophical lineage. So although a comparison of Heine and Whitman as post-Hegelian poets would not be without some historicist value, the connection would be a strained one. Moreover, it would miss the much more profound similarity, of which the shared idealism was no doubt a noteworthy characteristic, namely, the pivotal role of the two poets in their respective literary traditions. Both were deeply engaged in the construction of a democratic culture, and both were committed to the transformation of the prevailing institution of lyric verse in such a way so as to explore the possibility of a genuine poetry for the republic. Not that their solutions look very much alike on paper: nothing in Heine resembles Whitman's long lines, and little in Whitman approaches Heine's irony. Perhaps, however, Whitman's expansive verse and Heine's ironic demolition of Romanticism represent homologous innovations in the tentative construction of a new culture. The success of their experiments and the failures that they encounter at their limits can tell us something about the social-historical substance embedded in nineteenth-century verse as well as the utopian challenge of a democratic literature. I want to pursue these matters through parallel readings of Heine and Whitman review Tocqueville's account of the corruption of language in democracy as an adequate sociology of Whitman's faulted diction. Whitman's introduction of journalistic experience into literary language is consequently, in Matthiessen's eyes, implicitly a falling off from the intellectual heights of Emerson's "cold intellectuality," to which the mere journalist, carpenter, and country schoolteacher could never be adequate:

> In its curious amalgamation of homely and simple usage with half-remembered terms he read once somewhere, and with casual inventions of the moment, he often gives the impression of using a language not quite his own. In his determination to strike up for a new world, he deliberately rid himself of foreign models. But, so far as his speech was concerned, this was only very partially possible, and consequently Whitman reveals the peculiarly American combination of a childish freshness with a mechanical and desiccated repetition of book terms that had significance for the more complex civilization in which they had had their roots and growth. The freshness has come, as it did to Huck Finn, through instinctive rejection of the authority of those terms, in Whitman's reaction against what he called Emerson's cold intellectuality: "Suppose his books becoming absorb'd, the permanent chyle of American general and particular character—what a well-wash'd and grammatical, but bloodless and helpless race we should turn out!"[6]

Hearing Matthiessen's judgment on the plebeian journalist Whitman, one cannot help but recall similarly derogatory accounts of Heine. Indeed, Karl Kraus (1874–1936) plays out Heine against Goethe in an identical manner to Matthiessen's measuring of Whitman against Emerson and, more broadly, American democracy against "more complex civilizations." Moreover, Theodor Adorno, drawing on Kraus, accounts for the inadequacy of Heine's language by suggesting that he came from a background not quite at home in German—"Heines Mutter, die er liebte, war des Deutschen nicht ganz mächtig"[7] ["His mother, whom Heine loved, did not have a firm grasp of German"]—not far from Matthiessen's "impression of [Whitman's] using a language not quite his own." Yet this cultural conservatism (in the case of Adorno, certainly, a conservatism of the canon that stands at odds with his negative dialectics) mistakes for a failure the social practice of the texts, the effort to articulate a public language less exclusionary than Emer-

with regard to three issues in particular: (1) the public voice of p
(2) tradition and revolution, and (3) the critique of modernity.

To speak of the "pivotal role" of Heine and
man is somewhat of an overstatement, since it suggests the succ
establishment of a literary legacy that their respective poetic trad
in fact withheld (although certainly more for Heine than for Whit
Nevertheless, the pivoting each undertook amounted to the same
to transform the institutionalized character of lyric verse and to r
it with a language adequate to a democratic modernity. Both atte
to dismantle aspects of what can be coarsely labeled as a bou:
aristocratic culture, characterized by aesthetic autonomy, soci
ism, and a strictly vertical hierarchy of cultural organization. For
man, this approach necessitated a painful critique of Emerson, to
he was in fact deeply indebted, and for Heine a parallel distancin
Goethe. In both cases a new literary language had to be construct
would incorporate aspects of everyday life and politics, public co
mediated, again in both cases, by influential experiences in jourr
Despite the surfeit of landscape imagery in Whitman's verse
constant self-identification with the American topography, his
diction is," as F. O. Matthiessen noted in *American Renai*
"clearly not that of a countryman but of what he called him
jour printer,'" that is, a journalist. This point is crucial for M:
sen, since he has to counteract a simplistic reception, common
the first generations of Whitman's admirers, to accept the poe
equation with the geography of the New World. "His speech
spring primarily from contact with the soil, for though his fat!
a descendant of Long Island farmers, he was also a citizen of th
reason, an acquaintance and admirer of Tom Paine. . . . [Whitm
attracted by the wider sweep of the city, and though his langu
natural product, it is the natural product of a Brooklyn journalis
eighteen-forties who had previously been a country schooltea
a carpenter's helper, and who had finally felt an irresistible im:
be a poet."[5]
Yet Matthiessen's insistence on the journalistic and not :
derivation of Whitman's language is more than a reaction again
ralistic reductions of the poet. This emphasis on the journalis
man is hardly a matter of praise. On the contrary, the critic pro

son's or Goethe's, a democratic alternative to the bourgeois-aristocratic culture of criticism and literature in the early nineteenth century. Whitman's distance from Emerson is a direct corollary to the sentiment expressed in Heine's poem *An einen ehemaligen Goetheaner* [To a Former Goethe Disciple]:

> Hast du wirklich dich erhoben
> Aus dem müßig kalten Dunstkreis,
> Womit einst der kluge Kunstgreis
> Dich von Weimar aus umwoben?

> [Have you really gotten free
> From the chilly, vapory cage
> In which once the Weimar sage
> Had you cooped unwittingly?][8]

The rejection of Goethean classicism and Emerson's "cold intellectuality" might have plausibly led to versions of Romantic irony, a hypostatization of the impossibility of any communicative language as a superficially radical critique of the established language of the cultural elite. Heine definitively closes off that option with his judgment on *Die romantische Schule* [The Romantic School]; for the younger Whitman, it was never quite as strong a temptation. His poetic attitude stood, as Matthiessen put it, "in strong contrast to much European romanticism, to the pattern of qualities that Madame de Staël had seen in the emerging new literatures, 'the sorrowful sentiment of the incompleteness of human destiny, melancholy, reverie, mysticism, the sense of the enigma of life.' "[9] This distance from the Romantic option is evident especially in his evaluation of Edgar Allan Poe, whom Whitman ultimately found "almost without the first sign of moral principle, or of the concrete or its heroisms, or the simpler affections of the heart." Despite his appreciation for Poe's "intense faculty for technical and abstract beauty," Whitman concludes by ranking him "among the electric lights of imaginative literature, brilliant and dazzling but with no heat."[10] Poe's brilliance with no heat, Emerson's cold intellectuality, the "kalter Dunstkreis" of the "kluger Kunstgreis," the Romantics with all their magic warts—the counterprograms of Heine and Whitman are parallel in their efforts to expand the participation in cultural life, to give away the esoteric secrets (*ausplaudern*), to strip away the restrictive aura of established art and to develop a secular and nonauthoritarian literary language. Emerson viewed *Leaves of Grass* as a mixture of the *Bhagavad Gita* and the *New York Tribune*.[11]

That secularization was certainly never complete or thoroughly consistent; Whitman could write that "the priest departs, the divine literatus comes."[12] Yet the tendency remains one of deauraticization, the social-historical substance that links the two poetic projects in the search for a public voice. The subsequent reaction against this 'loss of aura, be it in *l'art pour l'art* or Stefan George's symbolism or some of the early Anglo-American modernism, indicates the resistance the modernization of culture encountered. In *Democratic Vistas* Whitman describes this resistance and its social base—he calls it feudalism:

> with the priceless value of our political institutions, general suffrage, . . . I say that, far deeper than these, what finally and only is to make our Western world a nationality superior to any hither known, and outtopping the past, must be vigorous, yet unsuspected Literatures, perfect personalities and sociologies, original, transcendental, and expressing (what, in the highest sense, are not yet expressed at all) democracy and the modern. . . . For feudalism, caste, the ecclesiastic traditions, though palpably retreating from political institutions, still hold essentially, by their spirit, even in this country, entire possession of the more important fields, indeed the very subsoil, of education, and of social standards and literature.[13]

For Whitman, the cultural revolution was still in the making; beyond the rejection of the models represented by Emerson and Poe, it demanded the positive development of new literary forms. As with Heine, this literary project was grounded in the struggle against "feudalism, caste, the ecclesiastic tradition," and it unfolds within a structural feature of the *longue durée* of modernity: the unresolved tension between cultural elitism and what might be termed an emancipation project of a vernacular liberalism. At important points in the oeuvre of the two writers, each explores the problematic of a public language in an exemplary poem: *Beat! Beat! Drums!* from the *Drum-Taps* section of *Leaves of Grass* of 1861, and *Doktrin* [Doctrine], the first of the *Zeitgedichte* [Poems for the Times] in the *Neue Gedichte* [New Poems] of 1844. Despite the seventeen years that separate them, the poems are in a substantive sense contemporary, since each is deeply imbued with the political urgency of the moment: the outbreak of the

American Civil War and the rapid radicalization on the eve of the 1848 Revolution. That shared political urgency explains why these two programmatic poems both commence with nearly identical imperatives of military and acoustic force: "Beat! Beat! Drums!—blow! bugles! blow!" and "Schlage die Trommel und fürchte dich nicht" ["Beat on the drum and don't be afraid"].[14]

In each case the text grounds the possibility of a new poetic language by insisting on the demise of an earlier social order. All established relationships break down and are swept into a whirlwind of radical reorganization:

> ... burst like a ruthless force
> Into the solemn church, and scatter the congregation,
> Into the school where the scholar is studying;
> Leave not the bridegroom quiet—no happiness must
> he have now with his bride,
>
> Nor the peaceful farmer any peace, ploughing his
> field or gathering his grain

Heine's account is tighter but fundamentally compatible: "Trommle die Leute aus dem Schlaf" ["Go drum the people up from sleep"].[15] A new poetry is imagined that can participate in the dismantling of an enervated past, sleepy, private, and above all quiet. The new poetry, in contrast, is loud and decidedly public, a vehicle of mass mobilization. Yet the programmatic exhortation is, despite the sense of emergency, never linked to a particular political crisis. Whitman eschews any reference to slavery or secession, and Heine, who otherwise delights in the inclusion of contextual allusions, mentions no new abuse in Berlin or Munich. These are, therefore, not political poems or protest poems in the manner of a *Tendenzgedicht* [tendentious poem]. On the contrary, they are explorations of the possibility of an innovative poetic language geared to a democratic public sphere, a new literary institution described as an acoustic realm of collective activity and counterposed to the muffled interiorities of Whitman's "school" and "solemn church" and to the indolence of Heine's sleepy readers.

Whitman suggests that this new public sphere will undermine established notions of acquisitive individualism and the market economy: "No bargainers' bargains by day—no brokers or speculators—would they continue?" Moreover, if established social structures and business as usual have grown obsolete, so have established forms of speech and culture:

> Would the talkers be talking? would the singer
>   attempt to sing?
> Would the lawyer rise in the court to state his
>   case before the judge?
> Then rattle quicker, heavier drums—you bugles
>   wilder blow.[16]

In this new public organization of sound, even the familiar figure of the singer, the traditional poet, becomes an anachronism. In the high speed of modernity, where all that is solid melts into air, hegemonic culture is stripped of its aura, and a new postauratic culture presumably becomes possible.

Heine provides the corollary to the end of Whitman's singer, insofar as *Doktrin* asserts that the new activism is the consequence and genuine content and therefore the conclusion of idealist philosophy, which has only interpreted the world.

> Das ist die Hegelsche Philosophie,
> Das ist der Bücher tiefster Sinn.
>
> [That's Hegel's philosophy in short,
> That's the deepest wisdom books bestow!][17]

These lines are not merely a left-wing interpretation of Hegel; they clearly also indicate a supersession, since the dimension of books and scholarship is displaced, as much as is Whitman's singer, by the fearless beating of the drum. That is, both Whitman and Heine indicate the termination of a worn-out organization of culture, in the place of which a postauratic culture model, still unnamed, is taking shape.

Yet when Whitman silences his singer, one cannot but hear a deep sense of anxiety and ambivalence. He is not yet the new poet—if he were, the imperatives would be out of place; has he discovered the possibility of his own demise? Both poems modify their programmatic exuberance with some considerable doubts and fears regarding the possible consequences of the democratic poetry that they nevertheless invoke. At the end of the first stanza Whitman's drums are fierce and the bugles shrill, but the third stanza concludes the poem on an ominous note. This work is not an unbroken paean to cultural modernization:

> Mind not the old man beseeching the young man,
> Let not the child's voice be heard, nor the
>   mother's entreaties,
> Make even the trestles to shake the dead where
>   they lie awaiting the hearses,
> So strong you thump O terrible drums—so loud
>   you bugles blow.[18]

This is the violence of modernity: what begins with the obliteration of moribund cultural forms, the "solemn church" as a cipher of "feudalism," ends with the uncanny silencing of all human relations. The dialectic of enlightenment entails a dialectic of political poetry, in which the galvanizing acoustics of the *levée en masse* turns into the cacophany of "terrible drums," breaking all social bonds. It is the same ambiguity with which *Doktrin* concludes, although Heine expresses it in the less overwhelming register of his characteristic irony:

> Das ist die Hegelsche Philosophie
> Das ist der Bücher tiefster Sinn!
> Ich hab sie begriffen, weil ich gescheit
> Und weil ich ein guter Tambour bin.
>
> [That's Hegel's philosophy in short,
> That's the deepest wisdom books bestow!
> I understand it, because I'm smart,
> I'm a good drummer boy myself; I know.][19]

It was Ludwig Börne (1786–1837) who labeled Heine the drum major of liberalism, and Heine himself elsewhere seems to feel comfortable with such political-military self-identification: he liked to say that he was a brave soldier in liberation wars of humanity. Nevertheless, the concluding point of *Doktrin* indicates a dissatisfaction with a potential reduction of poetry to a mere instrument of political tendency. That sort of reduction might be labeled, in the language of critical theory, a false sublation of life and art, the bad outcome of the process of deauraticization. Heine is as aware of it as Whitman. The two programmatic poems for a democratic literature understand that, after "feudalism," the vicis-

situdes of cultural modernity are by no means certain—hence the ambivalence inscribed in the text, symptomatic of the liminal status of
the modern poet, poised between auratic seclusiveness and public discourse.

If that liminality is a consequence of the historical
setting of the poetic projects—both poets stand, so to speak, with one
foot still in the past of the ancien régime, and both, moreover, understand the foreboding future of aesthetic modernization—historicity is
not only a matter of external contexts. On the contrary, inscribed in the
poetic projects themselves is an imagined past that traps the necessarily
belated writing in a present of neurotic repetition. In other words, the
melancholic recollection of a traumatic event located at some distance
in the past but to which the writer has not yet achieved full critical distance both determines the possibility of writing and sets a limit to the
potential innovation. Poetic secularization cannot proceed untroubled
along a linear path of progressive optimism. The tests are haunted by an
unmastered past; their content is an incomplete *Durcharbeiten* [work-
ing through].

My point now is not to psychoanalyze Heine and Whitman but to
explore the internal temporality of their verse with the help of psycho-
analysis properly understood as a theory of history. For in their two
perhaps best-known poems the original deed that casts its shadow on
subsequent writing is recognized as a death, the texts betray a distorted
experience of guilt, and the prominent ambivalence turns out to be a
matter of remorse. If "O Captain! My Captain!" records the death of
Lincoln, it also locates the poet in a complicitous proximity to the oedi-
pal murder, catching him red-handed. Privy to the knowledge of death,
he is consequently set apart from "the swaying mass, their eager faces
turning," awaiting the victorious leader. While public life goes on elsewhere, the isolated poet is condemned to a repetitive cadence, serving
the same sentence he is writing:

> Exult O shores and ring O bells!
> But I with mournful tread,
> Walk the deck my Captain lies,
> Fallen cold and dead.[20]

Passing over water toward the erotic object on shore, the Captain
is killed; the same primal scene structures the *Lore-Ley*, and the poet

flaunts or feigns his mourning for the anonymous sailor early: "daß ich so traurig bin" ["that / I am so sadly inclined"]. Yet if the accusation in the final finger-pointing lines—"Und das hat mit ihrem Singen / Die Lorelei getan" ["And this is the fate that follows / The song of the Lorelei"]—is supposed to solve the crime and answer the initial question of signification—"was soll es bedeuten" ["I do not know what it means"]—the text is equally a hopelessly incriminating confession. For if it was singing that killed cock robin, the poet stands condemned. As long as blame is projected onto the imaginary figure, that is, as long as the poet does not come to grips with his past, his past grips him, progressive history is prohibited, and an adequate cognition of the present is prevented by permanent ideology: "Ein Märchen aus alten Zeiten / Das kommt mir nicht aus dem Sinn" ["There is an old tale and its scenes that / Will not depart from my mind"].[21]

The parricide in the wake of which poetry takes place is the radical revolution that necessarily entails the murder of the leader. It is not an empirical revolution that matters here—certainly not the American Revolution or the absent German revolution—but the imagined revolutions, the violent breaks with a prior order in which Heine and Whitman both take part vicariously. Yet no matter how fictional, the affective valence of the murderous wish is as great as that of any fantasized trauma of imaginary seduction, "die wahre Gewalt" [true violence]. The identification with the revolution implies a complicity in death:

> Did we think victory great?
> So it is—but now it seems to me, when it cannot
>   be help'd, that defeat is great,
> And that death and dismay are great.[22]

Thus Whitman closes the 1856 *To a Foil'd European Revolutionaire;* within less than a decade the experience of death takes on an American character: the Civil War and Lincoln's assassination. Whitman's representative mourning for Lincoln is homologous to Heine's commemorations of Napoleon and his fantasies of revolution and regicide in *Karl I, Maria Antoinette,* or the guillotine passage in the *Wintermärchen* [Winter's Tale]. The primal murder liberates and burdens simultaneously: the king is dead, long live the king.

If this poetry is always in the wake of a revolution or, better, of a revolutionary wish, the theme of death, even in its most Romantic guises, is always the trace of political violence for which the guilty poet does

penance. In both cases an anterior act of violence is a condition of possibility of verse. Yet here a crucial distinction must be made that may
account for the alternative institutionalizations of poetry in the two
cultures. In the seventh section of the *Wintermärchen* the poet walks
with death, his writing is a bloody scrawl, and it is the gesture of the
poet that unleashes the regicidal force:

> Da sah ich furchtbar blinken
> Des stummen Begleiters furchtbares Beil—
> Und er verstand mein Winken.

> [The fearsome ax shining brightly I saw
> In my mute companion's fearsome hands—
> And he read my signals rightly.][23]

Yet the death of the king is, so the text implies, also the poet's
death—"Blutströme schossen aus meiner Brust" ["And spurts of blood
shot from my breast"]. The revolutionary poet is still deeply implicated
in the old order, and presumably, revolutionary poetry has not broken
cleanly with the categories of hegemonic culture. Whitman, too, sets
death at the origin of poetry in the crucial *When Lilacs Last in the Door-
yard Bloom'd.* Yet whereas Heine stages the struggle within the oppressive and lugubrious confines of a feudal-ecclesiastic interior, Whitman
has Lincoln's coffin pass through the expanse of the American landscape, replete with imagery of vibrant nature and vigorous society. The
poet can survive the murdered leader without an onerous legacy or an
internalized guilt, and an effective public voice is achieved, as the deceased is lain to rest:

> Passing I leave thee lilac with heart-shaped leaves,
> I leave thee there in the door-yard, blooming,
>   returning with the spring.[24]

Heine never reaches a similar reconciliation, and a similarly consol-
ing leave-taking is withheld. For the melancholic Heine, the dead are
not yet buried; Whitman can mourn and describe the funeral procession. In the terms of literary history, Whitman takes leave of the literary
past more effectively than Heine; the desire for the death of the leader,
as both a political and a literary revolution, induces a guilt that impedes
the secularization of German poetry. After Heine, and despite Heine,
the power of tradition and autonomy aesthetics remains considerably

greater than was the case in the wake of Whitman—hence the *Sonder-weg* of German lyric verse in which a subversive countertradition, say from Heine to Brecht, has always remained secondary to the authoritative canon from Goethe to George.

If the death of the father, in literature and politics, burdens the two writers, they can equally appropriate it as part of their project for a public poetry by redirecting it into a vehicle for public criticism. The remorse for the radical rupture makes the poetry all the more sensitive to the failures of the revolution and a bad modernity: was the break with tradition in vain? was all the violence for nought? The vision of death marching arrogantly through their poetry constitutes a radical critique of a developing bourgeois society that denies identity only a split second after promising its fulfillment: everyday life is capital punishment. This vision is not the aestheticist cult of death that Mann ascribed to a Whitman read beside Novalis, death as some weird source of creativity. On the contrary, it is a precise naming of the fatal character of the modern social condition, a night of the living dead, and it simultaneously expresses a challenge and a utopian hope: better dead than reduced to this reality. Hence the death wish at the end of the third of the *Heimkehr* [Homecoming] poems:

> Mein Herz, mein Herz ist traurig,
> Doch lustig leuchtet der Mai;
> Ich stehe, gelehnt an der Linde,
> Hoch auf der alten Bastei.
>
> Da drunten fließt der blaue
> Stadtgraben in stiller Ruh;
> Ein Knabe fährt im Kahne
> Und angelt und pfeift dazu.
>
> Jenseits erheben sich freundlich,
> In winziger, bunter Gestalt,
> Lusthäuser und Gärten und Menschen,
> Und Ochsen und Wiesen und Wald.
>
> Die Mägde bleichen Wäsche
> Und springen im Gras herum:
> Das Mählrad stäubt Diamanten,
> Ich höre sein fernes Gesumm.

Am alten grauen Turme
Ein Schilderhäuschen steht;
Ein rotgeröckter Bursche
Dort auf und nieder geht.

Er spielt mit seiner Flinte,
Die Funkelt im Sonnenrot,
Er präsentiert und schultert—
Ich wollt, er schösse mich tot.

[My heart, my heart is heavy,
Though May shines bright on all;
I stand and lean on the linden
High on the bastion wall.

Below me the moat is flowing
In the still afternoon;
A boy is rowing a boat and
Fishing and whistling a tune.

Beyond in colored patches
So tiny below, one sees
Villas and gardens and people
And oxen and meadows and trees.

The girls bleach clothes on the meadow
And merrily go and come;
The mill wheel scatters diamonds—
I hear its distant hum.

On top of the old grey tower
A sentry looks over the town;
A young red-coated lad there
Is marching up and down.

He handles his shining rifle,
It gleams in the sunlight's red;
He shoulders arms, presents arms—
I wish he would shoot me dead.][25]

"Ich wollt, er schösse mich tot" ["I wish he would shoot me dead"].
The pastoral idyll of a cheerful springtime, the fisherboy, the healthy

servant girls, and the glistening mill wheel—a postcard picture of Old Germany that turns out to be a nightmare, always about to flip over into the brutality that lurks in the heart of *Gemütlichkeit*. The poet invokes the catastrophe; he calls for the shooting to begin, to unmask the structural horror and, as victim, to escape. Heine's contemporary Eichendorff could also invoke violence and destruction in his verse, but it appeared as a Romantic sublime counterposed to a beautiful bourgeois order, therefore presenting a conservative apologetics for the order. Heine's text indicates that it is the order itself that is always the site of catastrophe: there's no place like home.

This concern, early in the *Buch der Lieder* [Book of Songs], antedates by two decades the *Zeitgedichte*; for Whitman, the insistence on the presence of death as a critique of a bad life can be traced in the *Calamus* poems, before the Civil War. That is to say that for both, the social-critical substance of the theme is established before any explicit politicization of the verse. Nevertheless, it is again in *Lilacs* that Whitman comes closest to Heine in articulating the morbidity of the social order:

> Then with the knowledge of death as walking one side of me,
> And the thought of death close-walking the other side of me,
> And I in the middle with companions, and as holding
>   the hands of companions,
> I fled forth to the hiding receiving night that talks not.

There he discovers the possibility of an appropriate incantation, "the carol of the bird," and then "with my comrades there in the night," he has an apocalyptic battlefield vision of the war:

> I saw battle-corpses, myriads of them,
> And the white skeletons of young men, I saw them,
> I saw the debris and debris of all the slain soldiers of the war.[26]

Yet even more poignant than the discovery of poetry or the recognition of the carnage of the war is the very constitution of the seeing subject through "the knowledge of death": a universal negativity that is the substance of the social contract among *soi-disant* "companions." The poet can comprehend the sorrow and bereavement dictated by history only by understanding that bereavement has become the principle of social organization of the failed community. The pseudoidentity of the most intimate relations is susceptible to destruction in the context of total reification; unproblematic self-identity is relegated to a distant and mythic past: Whitman's *Manhatta* or Heine's *Hammonia*. For the present, however, not even the radical poem can achieve that sovereign freedom: Heine's free thought rarely approaches free verse, and Whitman's open lines are condemned to a syntactic eternal return and a repetitive periodic structure. The limits of social emancipation are enfigured in the limits of formal innovation; the emancipation of poetry is blocked by the failure of the revolution that has engendered a failed modernity.

What links Heine and Whitman, then, is the attempt to secularize poetry and to transform it into a public medium; the insight into the dialectics of engaged literature; the exploration of the revolution against tradition and its consequences for democratic culture; the critique of modernity inherent in the thematics of death. It is a shared project, deeply interwoven with the democratic culture of the nineteenth century and presumably too radical for Mann in his 1922 address. The failure of the German republic is a measure of the repression of Heine and of a Whitman understood differently.

The name of the failure of the republic was fascism. Heine and Whitman play an important role in the formation of fascist aesthetics, as objects of negation. The two poets are not merely repressed and marginalized; rather, their insistence on the publicity of poetry is simultaneously denounced and appropriated from the standpoint of a self-described superior poetics: the aestheticization of politics. Adolph Bartels (1862–1945) rants and raves against Heine the political radical to formulate the program for a reactionary literature, devoted to the extremely political project of an illusory national regeneration. Knut Hamsun's early denunciation of Whitman's crudity is still an aestheticist gesture, colored by his lifelong hostility to democracy. Ezra Pound's reception of Whitman is more to the point: Pound is eager to take on the mantle of the great American poet but insists on subjecting Whitman's backwoods boorishness to the imperatives of modernist rigor.[27] The democratic public, Whitman's subject, turns into the national community, subject to imperatives. The acoustic revolution of the beating drums, addressed by Whitman, gives way to the authorial counterrevolution of Pound, addressing American troops on Italian radio: the poetic history of the structural transformation of the public sphere.

I have only briefly outlined an inquiry into the negativity of Heine and Whitman within the construction of a fascist aesthetics. A project of more immediate concern, however, is a consideration, from the standpoint of republican poetry, of the repercussions of fascism in the 1980s and 1990s, and the relevance of a poetry suppressed by fascism to our most self-assuredly postfascist criticism. In this context what is most germane is the discourse on fascism and literary criticism which has developed in the wake of the discovery of the early writings of Paul de Man. There is little reason to spend time demonstrating the self-evident incompatibility of the democratic lyric project of Heine and Whitman with the texts de Man published in the collaborationist press of occupied Belgium. Those texts, usually confused and often egregious, do not provide a conclusive answer to the *Gretchenfrage* of deconstructive criticism: Wie steht es mit der Politik? [Where do things stand politically?]. The answer can be sought instead, ironically enough, in the prose that has been mobilized in de Man's defense, a vigorously political prose that simultaneously denounces his critics for pursuing a political agenda:

> Ich weiß, sie tranken heimlich Wein
> Und predigten öffentlich Wasser.
>
> [I know how in secret they guzzle wine
> and in public preach water-drinking.][28]

This sort of paradox and the corollary contempt for a public culture indicate the continuity of a hierarchical structure of institutionalized culture which Whitman lambasted in *Democratic Vistas*:

> Literature, strictly considered, has never recognized the People, and whatever may be said, does not today. . . . It seems as if, so far, there were some natural repugnance between a literary and professional life, and the rude rank spirit of the democracies. . . . I know nothing more rare, even in this country, than a fit scientific estimation and reverent appreciation of the People, . . . their entire reliability in emergencies, and a certain breadth of historic grandeur, of peace or war, far surpassing all the vaunted samples of book-heroes, or any *haut ton* coteries, in all the records of the world.[29]

Precisely this conflict between the *haut ton* and a "rude rank spirit" is the backdrop to the effort of Heine and Whitman to develop a democratic literature in which belletristic and journalistic languages are mixed to construct a postauratic public voice. This conflict is also the backdrop for de Man's apologists, who denounce the rude journalistic intervention into a sphere of high literary theory allegedly inappropriate for public scrutiny, according to the coterie's motto: close the border, stop the gap. Thus in a letter published in a prestigious literary journal in April 1988, one could read the following comment from a well-respected critic: "When [de Man] resumed writing about literature [after the war], as a graduate student at Harvard, it was to initiate the critique of organicist and narrative figures through which he had sought to master literature for journalistic purposes."[30] Note that according to this account the young de Man had no political and certainly no fascist purposes, but only journalistic ones, as if the error of the 1940s was only a generic peccadillo, his willingness to engage in journalism at all, and not the substance or the location of that particular journalism. How fortunate then—this is the apparent suggestion of the letter's author, a professor of literature—that de Man renounced journalism and chose to pursue a graduate study of literature, at Harvard no less. Whether de Man himself shared this contempt for public discourse, including journalism, is, to say the least, doubtful, and one may eventually be forced to defend de Man against his defenders, at least on this score.

The public voice of literature was, for Heine and Whitman, a key aspect in the demolition of tradition, the radical break with inherited forms in art and politics. In other words, the project of republican poetry and the democratization of culture is not thinkable without a revolutionary gesture, even when, as I have tried to show, the authors are well aware of the dangerous risks inherent in the project. Despite these risks, the project retains a plausibility because of the utopian hopes it awakens, and its failure is not treated as an inescapable fate—because political action is deemed not only urgent, it is also imaginably successful.

How different, then, how much more responsible and sober, is the argument that atones for de Man's political juvenalia by lauding the mature de Man's putative admonition against all politics? Whether this sort of reading of de Man's trajectory is adequate can remain open; more important is the intervention of another critic, writing in the *New Republic*, in order to teach the lesson that politics slides into messianic revolutions that are always likely to end in fascism: "The political culture he championed in the *Le Soir* articles, a culture that claimed to be modern and revolutionary, was based on such a hope," that is, a "messianic" hope in the possibility of "new beginnings." Revolutions of the left, like those of the right, democratic or antidemocratic, are, by implication, always totalitarian. The dialectic of enlightenment, inscribed in the ambiguity of republican poetry, turns out to be no dialectic at all but rather blind fate heading necessarily to catastrophe. For this good citizen, then, "the only activity that escapes the immediate ideological pressure is art itself,"[31] an analysis that clearly falls behind the level of *Doktrin* and *Drums*. Art, already superior to journalism, is now declared superior to bad politics or, rather, to politics, which is always bad.

But if politics is always bad, so is the public voice of a postauratic poetry, and so is any radical critique of modernity. Not in de Man's own texts but in the anxious prose of his defenders one finds the sophisticated version of the hegemonic cultural conservatism of the 1980s and 1990s lodged in a solely ad hoc theory of fascism. It is a conservatism that has as little room for the terms of republican poetry and democratic culture as did Thomas Mann's formula of 1922. In the light of this double repression in the course of the century, Heine, Whitman, and the cultural alternative they represent might seem to fade into the recesses of an irretrievable past, thoroughly irrelevant to contemporary criticism. Yet it is exactly the shrillness of that repression that indicates the continued viability of the emancipation project, in politics and literature and in their potential congruence. Heine and Whitman investigate this potential and chart a terrain that is ours to rediscover or ours to repress. Their challenge stands in either case: to replace the hegemonic culture of conservative criticism with a culture that is critical of the conservative hegemony.

NOTES

1. Translated from Thomas Mann, *Gesammelte Werke* (Oldenburg: Fischer, 1960), 10:843. Unless otherwise noted, translations are the author's.
2. Ibid., p. 835.
3. Ibid., p. 839.
4. Ibid., p. 824.
5. F. O. Matthiessen, *American Renaissance* (New York: Oxford University Press, 1941), pp. 531–532.
6. Ibid.
7. Theodor W. Adorno, *Noten zur Literatur I* (Frankfurt am Main: Suhrkamp, 1971), p. 151.
8. Heinrich Heine, *Sämtliche Schriften*, ed. Klaus Briegleb, 6 vols. (Munich:

Hanser, 1968–76), 4:414. For English, see *The Complete Poems of Heinrich Heine*, trans. Hal Draper (Boston: Suhrkamp/Insel, 1982), p. 393.

9. Matthiessen, *American Renaissance*, p. 540.

10. Cited in ibid., pp. 540–541.

11. Cited in Paul Zweig, *Walt Whitman: The Making of the Poet* (New York: Basic Books, 1984), p. 8.

12. Walt Whitman, *Prose Works 1892*, ed. Floyd Stovall (New York: New York University Press, 1964), 2:365.

13. Ibid., pp. 364–365.

14. Walt Whitman, *Leaves of Grass*, ed. Harold W. Blodgett and Sculley Bradley (New York: New York University Press, 1965), pp. 283–284; Heine, *Schriften*, 4:412; and Heine, *Poems*, p. 392.

15. Ibid.

16. Whitman, *Leaves of Grass*, p. 284.

17. Heine, *Schriften*, 4:412; *Poems*, p. 392.

18. Whitman, *Leaves of Grass*, p. 284.

19. Heine, *Schriften*, 4:412; *Poems*, p. 392.

20. Whitman, *Leaves of Grass*, pp. 337–338.

21. Heine, *Schriften*, 1:107; *Poems*, p. 76.

22. Whitman, *Leaves of Grass*, p. 371.

23. Heine, *Schriften*, 4:595; *Poems*, p. 498.

24. Whitman, *Leaves of Grass*, p. 337.

25. Heine, *Schriften*, 1:108; *Poems*, p. 77.

26. Whitman, *Leaves of Grass*, pp. 334, 336.

27. See Knut Hamsun, "Walt Whitman," *Die Gesellschaft* 26 (1900), I: 24–35; Ezra Pound, "What I Feel about Walt Whitman," in *Selected Prose, 1909–1965*, ed. William Cookson (New York: New Directions, 1973), pp. 145–146.

28. Heine, *Schriften*, 4:578; *Poems*, p. 484.

29. Whitman, *Prose Works 1892*, 2:376–377.

30. Jonathan Culler, letter to the editor, *London Review of Books* (April 21, 1988), p. 4.

31. Geoffrey Hartman, "Blindness and Insight," *New Republic* (March 7, 1988), p. 31.

WORKS CITED

Adorno, Theodor W. *Noten zur Literatur I*. Frankfurt am Main: Suhrkamp, 1971.

Culler, Jonathan. "Letter to the Editor." *London Review of Books*, April 21, 1988.

Hamsun, Knut. "Walt Whitman." *Die Gesellschaft* 26 (1900), I: 24–35.

Hartman, Geoffrey. "Blindness and Insight." *New Republic*, March 7, 1988.

Heine, Heinrich. *The Complete Poems of Heinrich Heine*. Trans. and ed. Hal Draper. Boston: Suhrkamp/Insel, 1982.

———. *Sämtliche Schriften*. Ed. Klaus Briegleb. 6 vols. Munich: Hanser, 1968–76.

Mann, Thomas. *Gesammelte Werke*. Oldenburg: Fischer, 1960.

Matthiessen, F. O. *American Renaissance*. New York: Oxford, 1941.

Pound, Ezra. *Selected Prose, 1909–1965*. Ed. William Cookson. New York: New Directions, 1973.

Whitman, Walt. *Leaves of Grass*. Ed. Harold W. Blodgett and Sculley Bradley. New York: New York University Press, 1965.

———. *Prose Works 1892*. Ed. Floyd Stovall. New York: New York University Press, 1964.

Zweig, Paul. *Walt Whitman: The Making of the Poet*. New York: Basic Books, 1984.

CONTRIBUTORS

RUSSELL A. BERMAN has taught at Stanford University since 1979. Since 1985 he has served as cochairman of the Program on Modern Thought and Literature. His special interests are modern German literature and culture, especially film, and literary theory. His latest monograph is *The Rise of the Modern German Novel: Crisis and Charisma* (1986).

SANDER L. GILMAN has taught at Cornell University since 1969. In 1987 he was appointed to the Goldwin Smith Chair of Human Studies. He has published widely in the areas of modern German literature, cultural history, and the history of psychiatry. Among his recent books in this field are *Difference and Pathology* (1985) and *Jewish Self-Hatred* (1986).

JOST HERMAND has taught at the University of Wisconsin at Madison since 1958. In 1967 he was appointed to the Vilas Research Chair of German. His main areas of research are German literature in the nineteenth and twentieth centuries, cultural history, history of art, and literary theory. He has written books on Heine, on problems of art history and literary history, and on cultural life in postwar Germany.

PETER UWE HOHENDAHL has taught at Cornell University since 1977. In 1985 he was appointed to the Jacob Gould Schurman Chair of German and Comparative Literature. His main areas of research are European literature from the eighteenth to the twentieth centuries and problems of literary criticism, history, and theory. He has published books on expressionist drama, German literary criticism, the sentimental novel, and the German literary system in the age of liberalism.

JOSEPH A. KRUSE has been the director of the Heinrich Heine Institute in Düsseldorf since 1975. He is also a professor of German at the University of Düsseldorf. His publication of four books on Heine attests to his reputation as an outstanding Heine scholar.

T. J. REED has taught as Fellow and Tutor in Modern Languages and as Faculty Lecturer in German at St. John's College, Oxford, since 1963. His main area of research is German literature of the eighteenth and twentieth centuries, especially the history of ideas. He has written a study of Thomas Mann and books on Goethe and Weimar.

EGON SCHWARZ has taught at Washington University in St. Louis since 1961. In 1975 he was appointed to the Rose Mary Distinguished Professor in the Humanities Chair. His main areas of research are German and Spanish literature of the nineteenth and twentieth centuries, and he has published books on Hofmannsthal, Rilke, and Eichendorff.

HARTMUT STEINECKE has served as a professor of German at the University of Paderborn since 1974. He is an internationally acknowledged authority on the European pre-1848 period, especially on the novel. He has written books and articles on the Young Germany and has published numerous essays on Heine.

MICHAEL WERNER has been the director of research at the Centre National de la Recherche Scientifique in Paris since 1984. He has published three books and many essays on Heine and is the leading authority on Heine in France.

LUCIANO ZAGARI is a professor at the University of Pisa and has been the editor of the *Annali Studi Tedeschi* since 1979. He has published books on Büchner, Brentano, Heine, and the history of German Romanticism.

SUSANNE ZANTOP has taught at Dartmouth College since 1984. Her research interests include German women writers of the early nineteenth century and the nineteenth-century cultural relations of Latin America and Germany. She is the editor of *Paintings on the Move: Heinrich Heine and the Visual Arts* (1989) and the editor, with Jeannine Blackwell, of *Bitter Healing: German Women Writers from 1700 to 1830* (1990).

INDEX